Charlie Parker

The Michigan American Music Series

Richard Crawford, Series General Editor

The Michigan American Music Series focuses on leading figures of American jazz and popular music, assessing both the uniqueness of their work and its place in the context of American musical tradition.

Charlie Parker

His Music and Life

Carl Woideck

Ann Arbor

THE UNIVERSITY OF MICHIGAN PRESS

Copyright © by the University of Michigan 1996
Musical examples copyright © by Carl Woideck 1996
All rights reserved
Published in the United States of America by
The University of Michigan Press
Manufactured in the United States of America
♾ Printed on acid-free paper

1999   1998   1997   1996   4 3 2 1

A CIP catalog record for this book is available from the British Library.

Library of Congress Cataloging-in-Publication Data

Woideck, Carl.
    Charlie Parker : his music and life / Carl Woideck.
        p.   cm. — (The Michigan American music series)
    Includes discography, bibliographical references, and index.
    ISBN 0-472-10370-9 (alk. paper)
    1. Parker, Charlie, 1920–1955—Criticism and interpretation.
    2. Jazz—History and criticism. I. Title. II. Series.
    ML419.P4W65   1996
    788.7'165'092—dc20
    [B]   96-30211
                                                                CIP
                                                                MN

Contents

Preface

Music is your own experience, your thoughts, your wisdom. If you don't live it, it won't come out of your horn.

They teach you there's a boundary line to music, but, man, there's no boundary line to art.

I lit my fire, I greased my skillet, and I cooked.

—Charlie Parker

Charlie Parker (1920–55) was one of the most innovative and influential of all jazz musicians, regardless of era. His position in jazz is analogous to Louis Armstrong's in that both musicians advanced the music that they had inherited with regard to melody, rhythm, and harmony, inviting all jazz instrumentalists and composers of any era to reevaluate every aspect of their arts.

Charlie Parker had an artistic brilliance that can never be adequately explained. The overused term *genius* truly describes his gift. He was capable of making remarkable leaps of understanding, conception and execution. Brilliance of the magnitude possessed by Charlie Parker is rare in any art. For him, much like for Wolfgang Amadeus Mozart, there was seemingly no separation between conception and execution. Parker also possessed a remarkable ability to communicate with listeners and to move them emotionally, whether in person or on recordings. Forty years after Parker's death, his music continues to have an immediate and meaningful impact upon listeners.

How did Parker experience the creative act of improvisation? In an interview with a nonmusician, Parker offered a general statement to the effect that an artist can be inspired by "The way you feel, the beauty of the weather, the nice look of a mountain, maybe a nice fresh cool breath of air."[1] Probably more candid were his responses to musicians' queries as to his state of mind while improvising. Although Parker may have been affecting a certain modesty about his gifts, these examples suggest a certain unconsciousness or detachment while in the creative act, like an athlete in "the zone." Violinist Aaron Chaifetz, part of Parker's touring string ensemble of the 1950s recalled,

> . . . I can remember sitting there, and him playing "Laura," and in the middle of "Laura" hearing parts of the *Firebird Suite* of Stravinsky. And, when it was all over, say to him something like, "Charlie, do you know what you did?" And he had no—wasn't even aware of it. It just came extemporaneously."[2]

Guitarist Jimmy Raney reported a particularly candid exchange with Parker.

> Up at the Prescott Hotel, I asked him, "What do you think about when you're playing?" He got serious for a moment; he said he felt like everything disappeared when he put the horn to his mouth; he forgot the outside world, the girls. He said, "Sometimes I look at my fingers and I'm surprised that it's me playing. I get an idea, and I try it til it comes out right."[3]

As one of the architects of modern jazz (often called "bebop"), Charlie Parker has had a profound effect on American music. His music reached such a high level of melodic, rhythmic, and harmonic sophistication that saxophonists and other instrumentalists continue to study it as both a technical challenge and as aesthetic inspiration. The music of Parker and his peers, once considered to be merely the artistic expression of a revolutionary minority within an African-American musical minority, continues to influence American music more than fifty years after bebop's inception. Not strictly the iconoclastic movement that some critics, listeners and musicians believed it to be, modern jazz was based in earlier jazz styles and actually codified the "common practice" techniques of jazz, going on to become the lingua franca of jazz.

Charlie Parker was a heroin addict for most of his life, and he was certainly an alcoholic in the 1950s. So strong was his will and so great was his genius, that, for much of the time Parker's intoxication did not outwardly affect his playing. Closer listening, of course, reveals that an addiction-dominated life-style took a toll on his art, especially in the 1950s. Given his often stated new artistic goals of the 1950s, many have wondered what further artistic heights he might have attained if he had found a way to consistently create in a lucid state of consciousness. This of course is an unanswerable question; he *did* attain lasting artistic heights, and we are fortunate to be able to experience them through his transcendent recordings.

His transcendent talent aside, what artistic values led him to explore melodic, rhythmic, and harmonic sophistication in jazz? In the 1930s, many "journeyman" jazz players still got through their solos with a minimum of harmonic knowledge and with inconsistent technical execution. Some of Parker's values regarding the *clean* execution of musical ideas may be seen in his own statements. Describing one of his early influences, saxophonist Lester Young, Parker said, "He played so clean and beautiful."[4] Continuing that theme, Parker later told saxophonist Paul Desmond, "But, I mean, ever since I've ever heard music, I thought it should be very clean, very precise, as clean as possible anyway, you know?"[5] Parker described bebop, saying "It's just music. It's trying to play clean and looking for the pretty notes."[6] In order to create music cleanly, one needs superior instrumental technique. Parker advised a novice saxophonist: "The thing to do, is to know that horn. Control that horn. . . . Because, if you can control the horn you can get anything you want (to)."[7] Charlie Parker was a living example of that philosophy; through knowing his horn, he attained that rare state of oneness with his instrument that allowed him to "get anything you want."

How did Charlie Parker develop his virtuoso technique? Fellow saxophonist Paul Desmond asked Parker just that.

> PD: Another thing that's been a major factor in your playing is this fantastic technique that nobody's quite equaled. I always wondered about *that*, too; whether there was—whether that came behind practicing or whether that was just from—from playing, whether it evolved gradually.
>
> CP: Well, you make it so hard for me to answer, you know, because I can't see where there's anything fantastic about it at all.[8]

Parker goes on to say that he had practiced long and hard as a youth in Kansas City. Although he was being modest about his ability, Parker must have noticed that virtuoso technique on the level of his was not possessed by most of his fellow musicians. Unlike most instrumentalists, he only had to practice concertedly for a few years. After his major artistic breakthrough of 1937 (see chapter 1), his pursuit of technique took leaps forward in a way that only the most gifted individuals can experience. To the extent that technique came easily to Parker, he certainly could have sincerely seen "nothing fantastic about it."

Parker, whose musical education largely took place through the "oral process," spoke of his respect of study:

> Study is absolutely necessary in all forms. It's just like any talent that's born within somebody, it's just like a good pair of shoes when you put a shine on it, you know? It's like, schooling brings out the polish, you know, of any talent that happens anywhere in the world. Einstein had schooling, but he has a definite genius, you know, within himself. Schooling's one of the most wonderful things there has ever been, you know.[9]

Our knowledge of Parker's study of saxophone technique is sketchy. His formal instrumental instruction seems to have been limited to what he learned in his high school band, and the majority of his study of the saxophone and of music in general was undertaken through self-guided practice. In Kansas City, Parker was able to learn firsthand from local musicians, and studying recorded solos via the phonograph record also played an important part in Charlie Parker's jazz education. Parker found inspiration in the playing of the previous generation, and their ideas provided raw materials for his own developments.

Although he practiced saxophone and studied music with great concentration for a few years in Kansas City, after that he seems to have done so only occasionally (such as during his first years with Dizzy Gillespie). In important ways, Parker often grew artistically by studying and absorbing the harmonic, melodic, and rhythmic concepts of those around him and then making leaps of understanding that often put him in a position to execute those concepts more brilliantly than the musicians who had originally inspired him. He grasped and assimilated with extraordinary quickness the musical ideas he was exposed to, and he moved on to the next level of accomplishment much faster than the average musician.

Around the time Charlie Parker returned to New York for good in 1947, his practice and study habits waned, and from then on he advanced largely through the act of performing. From the late 1940s to the end of his life, Parker did not put much effort into the independent study of music the way that Dizzy Gillespie, Miles Davis, and Coleman Hawkins did, and this ebbing of his earlier study habits adversely affected his ability to act on his later desires to grow and change artistically.

The path of artistic discovery is always a highly personal one. During Parker's years of development, formal college-based study of jazz was not readily available (unlike, for example, Western music, painting, dance, drama, or writing). Despite Parker's limited opportunities for formal instruction, we should in no way minimize the depth of musical knowledge that he attained. He was in many ways a product of a jazz culture that no longer exists, one rich with both older master musicians to serve as role models and a network of countless jam sessions and jobs for experience. In a miraculous and undefinable process, Charlie Parker's brilliant talent, insightful study and many hours of playing music came together to form the artist whose work this book celebrates.

This book begins with a chapter of biography that endeavors to sketch the main events and currents of Charlie Parker's life. There are many unclear, vague, and contradictory aspects to his life story, and I have made every effort to present the clearest and most accurate picture when possible and to note uncertainties and contradictions when necessary. A chapter of introduction to his music then sets out some of the facets upon which discussion of Parker's music is to be based.

A guided tour of the music of Charlie Parker focusing on his improvisational art follows. It is not the purpose of this book to examine every recording that Charlie Parker ever made; rather, a selective approach has been taken with the goal of introducing the reader to a sampling of Charlie Parker's most illustrative works, much like a guided tour through a retrospective exhibition of a particular artist's work.

Readers are urged to purchase and listen to the most important Parker recordings discussed in this book. The transcribed musical examples are keyed to compact disc timings for easy location, and the CD sources for the examples are found in Appendix A. Once the readers have listened to Parker's works while following the verbal descriptions and discussion of musical examples in the book, they will have acquired a significant basis for the appreciation of Parker's musical world. Much like going back, alone, to visit that art exhibition, repeated listenings to the musical examples in this book will yield new discoveries unique to the listener. In addition, it is hoped that the appreciation gained through this guided musical tour will help to illuminate the many other brilliant and moving works in Charlie Parker's recorded legacy that the listener may encounter.

No technical knowledge of music is needed to enjoy the music of Charlie Parker, and readers of this book with no training in music will gain an understanding of Parker's music through discussion of qualities vital to his improvisational art including his facility and virtuosity; intensity of swing feeling; inventiveness and spontaneity; playfulness and sense of humor; and bluesiness and poetic qualities. Many of the musical passages discussed are keyed to compact disc timings and will be easy for the reader to locate and play on Parker CDs. More technical in nature but still accessible to most readers will be descriptions of Parker's music in terms of repertoire; compositional style; rhythmic properties; accents and syncopation; vibrato and timbre; melodic line; and harmonic vocabulary. Readers with a technical knowledge of music will of course glean even more appreciation from these descriptions and will be especially interested in the book's transcribed excerpts of Parker's improvised solos and the accompanying analysis of them. It is hoped that all readers will gain greater appreciation of the depth of the art of one of the most brilliant musical artists of any era or any genre, Charlie Parker.

Acknowledgments

In 1990, my friend and colleague Lewis Porter of Rutgers University gave a copy of my master's thesis on the early music of Charlie Parker to Joyce Harrison, who was then an editor at the University of Michigan Press. She passed the manuscript on to Richard Crawford, musicologist at the University of Michigan. Richard suggested how I might enlarge my thesis into a book-length study of Parker and helped me through the process of shaping my prospectus and getting it approved. Susan B. Whitlock, who became my editor at the University of Michigan Press, helped me as the book developed. Thank you all for your roles in bringing this book to fruition.

Important parts of this book were made possible through research grants. In 1991, I was awarded a National Endowment for the Humanities Travel to Collections grant to research at the Ross Russell Archive at the Harry Ransom Humanities Research Center at the University of Texas at Austin. At the Ransom Center, I was helped by George Leake, Dave Oliphant, and Dell Hollingworth. In addition, Ross Russell gave me permission to quote from his materials. In 1992, I received a Morroe Berger-Benny Carter Jazz Research Fund from the Institute of Jazz Studies at Rutgers University. Thanks go to Ed Berger for his support in my being chosen for the grant, and to Dan Morgenstern (director), Ed Luck, and Vince Pelote, for all their help in my research at the Institute of Jazz Studies. Finally, a 1993 National Endowment for the Humanities Summer Stipend grant gave me valuable uninterrupted time to research and write the last chapter of my book.

I am indebted to the many individuals who knew Charlie Parker and took the time to speak to me. Thanks go to Rebecca Parker, Doris

Parker, Chan Parker, Biddy Fleet, Jimmy Heath, Nat Hentoff, Lee Konitz, Gerry Mulligan, Max Roach, Red Rodney, and Charles White.

Several colleagues and friends read my manuscript and gave insightful comments that helped to improve this book. Mark Gridley of Heidelberg College and Thomas Owens of El Camino College carefully went over the text and provided many observations that gave it greater clarity and focus. Aimee Sullivan and Tim Willcox proofread the musical examples and offered important suggestions for improving their accuracy. Others who provided insight into the music and life of Charlie Parker include Bill Anderson, Lawrence Koch, and Francis Paudras. Thanks also go to Jerry Gleason of the University of Oregon for his expertise in the digital treatment of a faded photograph of Charlie Parker.

Many individuals provided important audio tapes, some of which contain rare or unreleased Parker material. Thank you to Stanley Crouch, John R. T. Davies, J. B. Dickey, John (McLellan) Fitch, Gary Giddins, Don Manning, Lewis Porter, Phil Schaap, Norman Saks, Jay Trachtenberg, and Steve Guattery. Bob Bregman, Jeffrey Ogburn, and Jim Olsen helped with information on current Parker CD issues. Thanks also go to Polygram Records, which helped me obtain CD reissues of the Norman Granz material that is discussed in chapter 5.

Parts of chapters 1 and 2 derive from my 1989 master's thesis ("The First Style-Period [1940–43] and Early Life of Saxophonist Charlie Parker"). Thanks again to Steve Owen, Edwin Coleman, Jr., and Steve Meier for their roles in that earlier work.

My deepest gratitude goes to my wife, Marian Smith, who encouraged me to develop this book project and offered essential support during all its stages. Marian's expertise as musicologist at the University of Oregon came into play in her careful consideration of my manuscript; she is my best reader and editor. Marian's insightful suggestions have improved this book's content and presentation immeasurably.

Part 1.
The Life of Charlie Parker

Chapter 1

A Biographical Sketch

Youth in Kansas City

Charlie Parker was born Charles Parker, Jr., on August 29, 1920, in Kansas City, Kansas.[1] His mother, Adelaide ("Addie") Bailey[2] Parker, was of African-American-Choctaw descent and lived in Oklahoma before moving to Kansas City. His father, Charles Parker, Sr., was an African American from Mississippi and Tennessee who came to Kansas City as an entertainer and settled there for a time.

Little is known about Parker senior. By a previous "wife," he had another son (John), whom he brought with him when he married Addie. Charles senior evidently had an alcohol problem, and when Charlie was still young, his father and mother separated (approximately eight years before Parker senior's death). His dad moved away, possibly with John, and ceased to be an important factor in Charlie's life. Charlie was impressed enough with his father to later say, "He sure was a well-tutored guy. He spoke two, three languages."[3] In his later years, Parker senior worked as a waiter or chef on the railroads, and Charlie saw him infrequently. He reportedly died in a drunken quarrel in late 1939 or early 1940.

It is not clear when the Parkers moved across the state line to Kansas City, Missouri (often called simply Kansas City or K.C.). Charlie Parker was paraphrased as saying that the family moved when he was seven (1927 or 1928),[4] although Charlie's first wife, Rebecca, suggests that the date may have been 1931.[5] Whether Charlie's half brother and father also made the move at either date is unknown. Addie Parker stated that Charlie then attended Crispus Attucks Elementary School in Missouri;[6]

3

however, Rebecca recalled seeing a diploma from Charles Sumner Elementary School in Kansas.[7] In 1931 or 1932, Charlie entered Lincoln High School in Kansas City, Missouri, where he was given an alto horn to play in the school band, directed by Alonzo Lewis. He soon switched to the baritone horn, and continued to play in one or more of the official school bands. (The alto and baritone *horns* are valved brass instruments, and are not to be confused with the alto and baritone *saxophones,* which are keyed reed instruments.)

Addie Parker doted on her son and formed an idealized view of Charlie's success at high school:

> In Lincoln High School he was the pride of his teachers. . . . School was too easy for him in a way. . . . He was the most affectionate child you ever saw. . . . He was not spoiled through [though?], because I think a spoiled child never leaves his parents.[8]

In reality, Parker's academic interest and performance in high school were poor. Lawrence Keyes, a fellow student who would soon become Parker's first band leader, first met Parker at Lincoln High: "If he had been as conscientious about his school work as he was about music, he would have become a professor, but he was a terrible truant . . . he was doomed to be a perpetual freshman."[9] Parker looked up to the older Keyes and asked him for information about piano chords. Around 1933, Parker asked his mother for an alto saxophone of his own, and she obliged by buying a used sax for forty-five dollars. Parker later stated that the recordings of Rudy Vallee inspired him to get a sax.[10] Parker's mother had the sax overhauled, and Charlie played it for a little while before losing interest in it: "A friend of mine was playing saxophone at the time. He had a band, so he borrowed the horn. He kept it over two years, too."[11] During this period, Parker took advantage of Kansas City's active jazz scene by listening to the professional musicians in the bars and nightclubs. Sometimes he could gain admittance, but most of the time he would have to eavesdrop from outside. He was thus exposed to a wide array of talented players, several of whom would become seminal influences upon his own playing.

Parker developed a habit of cutting classes at school, and he was treading water both academically and musically. A pivotal event was when he met Rebecca Ruffin in 1934.[12] Rebecca was fourteen when she, her recently divorced mother, and her siblings moved into the home of

Addie Parker at 1516 Olive Street in Kansas City, Missouri. They were to be boarders at the Parker house. Addie later said that Rebecca was four years older than Charlie; Rebecca stated, however, that she was born February 23, 1920, and thus was only about six months his senior, although this is contradicted by her marriage license, which lists her as being "over the age of eighteen years" on July 25, 1936.[13] They were both students at Lincoln High, and they soon began keeping steady company. Rebecca later said that Charlie would have dropped out of school except for her; indeed, when she graduated in 1935, Charlie dropped out, still a freshman.

Charlie Parker's chronology at this point (1934–35) is again uncertain. At some point, Parker became interested in the saxophone again and got it back from his friend: "He kept it maybe a year after I got out of high school. I got out of high school in 'thirty-five."[14] Lawrence Keyes, however, states that Parker played saxophone with him in a band made up of students while they were at Lincoln.[15] It's possible that Parker was playing on a school saxophone, not the one from his mother.

Other than his school band experience, Parker had no formal music instruction per se, but in the tried-and-true "oral tradition," the many more-experienced older musicians he encountered were potential informal teachers. Parker took what he gleaned from them, plus ideas he heard in live and recorded music, and embarked on a period of self-study in the "woodshed."

While he and Rebecca continued to court, Parker tried to sit in with Jimmy Keith's band at a nightclub called the High Hat. Parker told the story to jazz scholars Marshall Stearns and John Maher:

> I knew how to play—I'd figured—I'd learned the scale and (could)—I'd learned to play two tunes in, in a certain key, in key of D for your [alto] saxophone, F concert? . . . I'd learned how to play the first eight bars of ["Up A] Lazy River," and I knew the complete tune to "Honeysuckle Rose." I didn't never stop to think about there was other keys or nothin' like that . . . so I took my horn out to this joint where the guys—a bunch of guys I had seen around were—and the first thing they started playin' was "Body and Soul," long beat [implied double-time] you know, like this . . . so I go to playin' my "Honeysuckle Rose" and [unintelligible], I mean, ain't no form of conglomeration [unintelligible]. They laughed me right off the bandstand. They laughed so hard [unintelligible].[16]

In another account of the incident, Parker said, "I was doing all right until I tried doing double tempo on 'Body and Soul.' Everybody fell out laughing. I went home and cried and didn't play again for three months."[17]

Parker's above reference to "a bunch of fellows I had seen around" may suggest that he had not played with them before and that this incident took place before he joined the Deans of Swing, the student band led by pianist Lawrence Keyes. (Parker named trumpeter James Ross as being in the Jimmy Keith band that day, and Keith would play in the Deans of Swing with Parker.) Bassist Gene Ramey heard the Deans at this time:

> It was the first band Bird ever worked in, and he seemed to me then just like a happy-go-lucky kid. In fact, the whole outfit was a school band, and Bird was hardly fully grown at the time—he was barely fourteen years old! Bird wasn't doing anything, musically speaking, at that period. He was the saddest thing in the band, and the other members gave him something of a hard time.[18]

It seems that Parker was used to being criticized and humiliated for his playing, experiences that made him emotionally thick-skinned and also motivated him to practice long and hard:

> I put quite a bit of study into the horn, that's true. In fact, the neighbors threatened to ask my mother to move once, you know. When I was living out west, I mean, they said I was driving them crazy with the horn. I used to put in eleven, eleven to fifteen hours a day . . . I did that for over a period of three or four years.[19]

Even if Parker did not literally practice an average of eleven hours a day for three or four years, he certainly practiced concertedly during that period and made important advances. Peer pressure is a strong force; this sheltered and spoiled teenager was not used to the public embarrassment he had experienced, and he was partially motivated by the desire to gain the respect of the older and more experienced musicians he was beginning to hang out with. In the process, Parker found his calling. Parker would soon quit school and begin trying to succeed as a professional musician, initially with the Deans of Swing.

Rebecca Ruffin's high school commencement was June 7, 1935;

Parker played in the Lincoln High School Orchestra during the cere-mony. This was evidently his last association with high school. Parker didn't graduate; he merely "got out." He later recalled, "Oh, a gang of things happened that year. I got the horn. Got married."[20] "A gang of things" was an understatement. During the next *three* years, in fact, Parker would not only have his share of frustration, but he would also see the first bearing of fruit of those long hours in the "woodshed."

As Charlie Parker turned fifteen, in August of 1935, he endeavored to enter the world of the professional Kansas City jazz musician, a world he had been skirting for some time. Corrupt Kansas City alderman and political boss Tom Pendergast set the tone for a "wide-open town" where money and power ruled, and where the effects of the Depression were not as strongly felt as in other parts of the country. Pianist and composer Mary Lou Williams described the atmosphere:

> Now, at this time, which was still Prohibition, Kansas City was under Tom Pendergast's control. Most of the night spots were run by politicians and hoodlums, and the town was wide open for drink-ing, gambling, and pretty much every form of vice. Naturally, work was plentiful for musicians, though some of the employers were tough people.[21]

Prostitution and drugs (both illegal and legal; marijuana was legal until 1937) were plentiful, and the already plentiful supply of liquor was not significantly altered by the eventual repeal of Prohibition in Decem-ber 1933. Bustling Kansas City understandably attracted many enter-tainers, and it became the center of jazz for the Southwest. Just a few of the excellent jazz bands that at one time made Kansas City their home were those led by Bennie Moten, Andy Kirk, Count Basie, Jay McShann, and Harlan Leonard. Significantly, all had to leave town to try to reach a national audience.

Drugs, especially heroin, were to play an increasingly prominent role in the adult life of Charlie Parker. The availability of and tolerance toward marijuana and heroin in Kansas City may have played a part in his initial experimentation with them. Parker told the story (with varia-tions) of his early involvement with drugs to numerous friends and inter-viewers. "It all came from being introduced too early to night life. . . . When you're not mature enough to know what's happening—well, you goof."[22] Leonard Feather paraphrased Parker as saying that the saxophonist experimented with "alcohol, pills and other stimulants . . . as early as 1932. Then late one night in 1935 an actor friend introduced him to heroin."[23] Parker, often vague and inexact about dates, was consistent regarding his exposure to hard drugs at that age; he had a strong reason to remember the year during which his life changed forever. According to Charlie's third wife, Doris: "At fifteen [1935], thanks to some character in Kansas City, he became a drug addict."[24] In 1947, Chan Richardson (soon to be Charlie's fourth wife) wrote: "He's had a habit since he was fifteen."[25] Parker recounted his first hard drug experience to bassist William "Buddy" Jones, who met Parker in Kansas City around 1942: "Getting high for the first time at fifteen, Bird told me what he felt. He pulled out $1.30, which was all he had and was worth more in those days and he said, 'Do you mean there's something like this in this world? How much of it will this buy?' "[26]

Parker played with the Deans of Swing for about a year and a half, until they broke up.[27] In the group, he made close friends with the slightly older trombonist, Robert Simpson. Lawrence Keyes recalled: "To say that Charlie admired him [Simpson] is perhaps too mild, Charlie worshipped him and was in his company a great deal. Suddenly at twenty-one [after the Deans broke up] Robert Simpson died. . . . Charlie was a complete wreck after that."[28] Years later, Parker told Ahmed Basheer: "Basheer, I don't let anyone get too close to me, even you. . . . Once in Kansas City I had a friend who I liked very much, and a sorrowful thing happened. . . . He died."[29] Clearly, the death of Simpson had a profound effect on Parker, and this already defensive teenager who was beginning to escape into drugs added another layer to his emotional armor.

Parker continued to test his skills with older, more experienced players, and he continued to come away frustrated. He and Gene Ramey regularly went to early-morning jam sessions at the Reno Club, where Count Basie was leading his early nine-piece group (ca. 1936). As Ramey recalled, the fledgling Parker took his share of criticism:

> Usually it was one man who became the goat. He might then come in for some kidding. Charlie would shoot back to his teasers' and censors' remarks like "Play you own horn" or "Stick to your script." I remember one night in particular when we were to jam with Basie, and Charlie made no answer. Jo Jones [Basie's drummer] waited until Bird started to play and, suddenly, in order to show how he felt

about Bird, he threw a cymbal across the dance floor. It fell with a deafening sound, and Bird, in humiliation, packed up his instrument and left. Major Bowes was popular then, and Jo Jones had given contestant Parker the gong, like The Amateur Hour maestro used to do.[30]

This was during the days of Major Bowes. You know, if somebody got up to sing, and if they—if it didn't go over too good, the man would hit the gong on them, you know. . . . Well, this thing happened—now, Basie was tellin' Jo Jones "Hit the cymbal on him!" which is a gong, you know. Bird was still playing. Basie, uh, Jo hit the cymbal: "gank!" and still Bird kept on playing. Actually, I think that Bird was tangled up and couldn't get out! [laughs] So, all of a sudden, Jo—they had a small cymbal, I guess it was about, you know, six inches, one of real small cymbals that they have now—most of the Dixieland musicians use now, you know. Well, Jo just took that off and just dropped that on the floor right beside Bird. Naturally, it frightened Bird, and he snatched the horn out of his mouth, and he came over where I was, he says "I'll get 'em! I'll get 'em!" He says, "They rung that bell on me; I'll get 'em!"[31]

In the spring of 1936, Rebecca Ruffin's mother became alarmed at the progress of Charlie's courtship of her daughter and moved the family out of the Parker household. The teenagers continued to see each other surreptitiously and in July decided to marry. Rebecca moved back into the house, and the marriage was official on July 25. Parker's love of music, however, didn't leave much time for a relationship; Parker had no "day job" and spent most of his days playing saxophone and occasionally piano. He spent most of his nights hanging around Kansas City nightclubs, sometimes all night long. Rebecca Parker stoically accepted Charlie's behavior.

In November of 1936, Parker was on his way to a Thanksgiving job in the Ozark Mountains when the car in which he and two other band members were riding had a serious accident: "I broke three ribs. I had a spine fracture . . . I mean, everybody was so afraid that I wouldn't—I wouldn't walk erect no more, but everything was all right."[32] One passenger died in the crash, another was hospitalized. A newspaper account with the headline "Auto Mishap is Fatal to G. W. Wilkerson" incorrectly gives Parker's name as "Jas. Parker, 1516 Olive St."[33] The only good outcome of the accident was an insurance settlement that enabled Parker to buy a new alto sax, which would soon be pawned to raise cash. Parker's recuperation continued into the new year.

That year, 1937, would prove to be transitional for Parker; his instrumental technique would markedly develop, and so would his involvement with drugs. Rebecca Parker was about three months pregnant when she was awakened to the reality of her husband's hard-drug usage:

> 'Bout July of Thirty-Seven, he called me upstairs, and he says "go sit around that side of the bed." I thought he had something for me. I looked in the mirror, and I saw him stick this needle in his arm. And I screamed, and I got up and I said "Why?" And he just smiled, and he took the—his tie was the tourniquet. And I was watching, then it came into my mind that on the dresser, I'd seen so many of the ties in small ties [knots]. But that was all; he didn't said anything, he just wiped his arm and put his tie 'round his—under his—collar, put his jacket on, and come over and kissed me on the forehead and he says, "See you in the mornin'."[34]

When Rebecca was pregnant again, in 1940, their doctor told Rebecca that Charlie's heroin usage began as a way of dealing with the pain from his spinal and rib injuries:

> But he saw the doctor in the third month [of recuperation], in Kansas, and he told him—well, this was after, he didn't but I learned it afterwards—he had to take the heroin to ease the pain of his spine and his ribs. That's what he had to take. So, he didn't use it until July, 1937. . . . He [the doctor] said, "I told Charlie," well, he— "I don't know if you can understand it or not," he said to me, "but Charlie has to take heroin to kill the pain from his ribs and his spine." . . . and this is when I learned from the doctor about the medication, how long he [Charlie] would live. Eighteen to twenty years the most. And he died on the eighteenth year.[35]

Charlie later stated that he had first tried heroin when he was fifteen, so Rebecca clearly was not fully aware of his activities. But it is possible that the prescription painkillers he took for his injuries may have accelerated his evolution from being an occasional heroin user into being a full-blown addict.

Tutty (also spelled Tootie) Clarkin ran a nightclub where Parker worked "in 1937 for $2 a night when he showed."[36] Clarkin reconstructed Parker's drug usage as follows: "When I first knew Charlie, he was getting high on nutmeg . . . From nutmeg Bird went to Benzedrine inhalers. He'd break them open and soak them in wine. Then he smoked tea and finally got hooked on heroin."[37]

Parker continued to absorb all he could about music from older players. Years later, Parker reminisced about a veteran musician who had summed up the essence of music in a way that Parker found striking: "Music is three things: melody, harmony and rhythm. That's true. . . . And the cat who told me that, he used to be trombone player on the Ringling Brothers, Barnum and Bailey Circus [unintelligible], you know? And he said that, he was teaching me, you know . . ."[38]

Breakthrough in the Ozarks

Parker had continued to take jobs at resorts in the Ozarks, often with the group led by saxophonist and clarinetist Tommy Douglas, who evidently helped develop Parker's woodwind technique and knowledge of "passing chords," as did the guitarist Efferge Ware. Gene Ramey said that Efferge Ware "coached a whole group of us, teaching us cycles, chords, and progressions."[39] One member of the Douglas band, trumpeter Clarence Davis, would later use an amateur disc recorder to make the first recordings of Parker (see chapter 2). During that summer, Parker was away from K.C. for an extended time, and he practiced concertedly. According to Gene Ramey:

> In the summer of 1937, Bird underwent a radical change musically. He got a job with a little band led by a singer, George E. Lee. They played at country resorts in the mountains. Charlie took with him all the Count Basie records with Lester Young solos on them and learned Lester cold, note for note. When he came home, he was the most popular musician in K.C. He had gone up in the mountains; and when he came back, only two or three months later, the difference was unbelievable.[40]

At the very least, Parker took with him one of the two 1936 78s of a Count Basie quintet (labeled Jones-Smith Incorporated for contractual reasons). As Ramey remembers:

> Well, that Jones-Smith record come out, and Prez [Lester Young, or "Pres"] had made that "Lady Be Good." And Bird came back and he startled everybody. He hit "Lady Be Good," and all the other saxophone players played, and the cats said, yeah, here come this guy, he's a drag. He gets up and plays Lester Young's solo note for note. ... Couldn't believe that. Six months before that, he was, like, a crying saxophone player.[41]

It's unknown whether Parker took other Basie-Young records with him. Possibly some of the actual "Count Basie and His Orchestra" sessions of January and March, 1937 (recorded in New York), were available by that summer. It has been suggested (but never firmly established) that Charlie Parker heard Lester Young play in person in Kansas City (Young was based there much of the time from some time in 1933 through late 1936, and he played there in Basie's band during 1936). In any case, being able to play repeatedly and study methodically Young's improvised solos *on record* made an important difference for Parker. This 1937 breakthrough marked the beginning of Parker's period of most rapid musical growth.

Apprenticeship

It was after Parker's return from the Ozark Mountains in 1937 that he first met a newcomer to the Kansas City scene, pianist Jay McShann. McShann heard Parker at a nightclub and inquired "Where you been? 'Oh I've been down in the Ozarks workin' with George Lee's band and I just got back. I wanted to go there and woodshed.'"[42] Parker and McShann would soon find themselves working together.

In the fall of 1937, alto saxophonist Henry "Buster" Smith formed a twelve-piece band (sometimes it was reduced to fewer pieces) and chose the fast-improving Parker to join. Jay McShann was the group's original pianist. Parker looked up to the older Smith: "He used to call me his dad, and I called him my boy."[43] Smith helped Parker work on his sound (which was considered by many listeners to be thin) and his improvisation. Parker was an apt pupil and learned his lessons well, as Smith remembered:

> In my band, we'd split solos. If I took two, he'd take two; if I took three, he'd take three; and so forth. He always wanted me to take the

first solo. I guess he thought he'd learn something that way. He did play like me quite a bit, I guess. But after a while, anything I could make on the horn, he could make too—and make something better of it.[44]

As 1937 drew to a close, Parker's addiction to heroin was making his life more erratic and fragmented. He had had a major musical breakthrough, and yet, because of his addiction, was not always able to develop it. Evidently, Parker had no steady employment. He worked for a while with an early Jay McShann group but had to leave because of his drug use. Parker pawned household objects for drug money and asked his wife to abort her pregnancy.[45] He also had an extramarital affair, and he held a gun to Rebecca's head when trying to recover love letters from the other woman.[46]

Charlie and Rebecca arrived at some kind of truce before she gave birth. Their son, born January 10, 1938, was named Francis Leon Parker, the middle name after Leon "Chu" Berry, a well-known tenor saxophonist Parker had admired. Times continued to be tough for Parker; McShann was out of town, and Buster Smith had gone to New York to look for work, having promised to send for his K.C. band. Parker reportedly worked at Tutty Clarkin's Mayfair Club in early 1938, but he showed up erratically. Tutty bought him a better saxophone: "Bird cried and said 'Man, I'll never be late again.' He didn't show for two days. . . . his new sax was in hock . . . He hocked it every week."[47] Rebecca became pregnant again but miscarried in June or July, 1938 (as noted earlier, it was at the time of her miscarriage that their doctor told Rebecca his view of how Charlie became addicted).

Around this time, Parker had a brush with the law. According to his mother,

> Charles got into serious trouble one night when he kept a taxi for six or seven hours and ran up a $10 bill which he couldn't pay. The taxi driver tried to snatch his horn, and Charles stabbed him with a dagger. They took him off to the farm. I told the Police, "how dare you treat my son like that. Bring him back!" He came home the next day.[48]

Later, Parker claimed that his mother wouldn't help him out of his jam, and he was held for twenty-two days, not overnight.[49]

First Trip to New York

Charlie Parker's chronology from late 1938 to early 1940 is also rather sketchy. It is known that his mentor, Buster Smith, left Kansas City for New York in 1938, and that Parker eventually followed suit. By early 1940, Parker definitely was back in Kansas City working with McShann. It is not known exactly when Parker left K.C. or when he returned. On several occasions, Smith estimated that he had been in New York for five or seven months before Parker joined him,[50] and that Parker "hoboed up there" in 1938.[51] More likely, Parker left Kansas City in early 1939. Harlan Leonard not only recalled that Parker worked with him for a few weeks around January, 1939, but, much more specifically, Leonard also stated in one interview that he had a check for two dollars endorsed on the back by Parker and dated January 10, 1939.[52] Harlan Leonard's canceled check firmly places Parker in Kansas City at the beginning of that year. An unpublished radio interview with Gene Ramey defines more specifically the time frame of Parker's 1939 departure for New York via Chicago. Ramey speaks of his and McShann's being given "two weeks in Chicago at the Off-Beat Room [Off-Beat Club]. And when we left to go to Chicago, Charlie Parker picked up and went to New York. . . . So, now, this is in '39, you're speakin' of there."[53] The January, 1939, issue of *Down Beat* magazine gives the opening of the Off-Beat Club as January 18. The March, 1939, issue mentions that McShann's trio "is clicking at the Off-Beat Club." Subsequent issues refer to this Off-Beat engagement as finally lasting six weeks. The statement made by Ramey, who was a generally reliable source, and the references in *Down Beat*, then, confirm Parker's early 1939 departure for New York.

En route, Parker passed through Chicago, where he happened on the 65 Club and its band. Singer Billy Eckstine (who would later be Parker's big band leader) was at the club:

> Let me tell you about Bird and how I first came to hear him play. . . We were standing around one morning when a guy comes up that looks like he just got off a freight car, the raggedest guy you'd want to see at this moment. And he asks Goon [Gardner, saxophonist], "Say, man, can I come up and blow your horn?" And this gets up there, and I'm telling you he blew the hell off that thing![54]

Gardner was so impressed that he took Parker home, gave him clothes, and lent him a clarinet to play musical jobs with. It is not clear how long

Parker stayed in Chicago; he may have briefly worked with the band of King Kolax. Parker soon disappeared with the clarinet and next appeared at Buster Smith's doorstep in New York City.

It's not clear exactly how Parker got to New York, but he was in sad shape when he arrived: "He sure did look awful when he got in. He'd worn his shoes so long that his legs were all swollen up."[55] Despite his wife's protests, Smith let Parker stay at their apartment. Parker would sleep there during the day while Smith's wife worked. At night, Parker would roam around, looking for places to play. A rare necessity, Parker had to resort to several nonmusical jobs. According to Smith, Parker "got a job on the corner, a little old club at 136th St. and 7th Ave., he cleans up when they close at night. He did that for about two weeks . . ."[56] Parker also took a job washing dishes for three months at the Harlem nightclub Jimmy's Chicken Shack.[57] Accounts have generally said that pianist Art Tatum was working a steady job there, although musician Bill "Biddy" Fleet has said that Tatum merely "sat in" often at Jimmy's.[58] Much has been made of Tatum's influence upon Parker, although the effect has been seemingly inferred by critics due to Parker's presence at the nightclub. Because Parker did not make any direct statements about this influence, one must be slightly tentative in adding Tatum to the list of the young Parker's musical influences. Tatum and the post-1940 Parker definitely shared several advanced musical techniques. One was the superimposition or implication of new key centers during performance. This technique was sometimes called "playing out of key" and is now often called "side-slipping." Another related technique was the superimposition of substitute chord progressions that elaborated upon or departed from a song's given harmonies. Tatum also liked to insert quotations of different songs while improvising, a practice that Parker exhibited throughout his career. Certainly, Tatum was already a master of these techniques and thus was a prime potential influence upon the student Parker. Given Parker's presence at Jimmy's, and Parker's acute listening and retention skills, Art Tatum is a very likely direct influence upon the young Charlie Parker (see discussion of "Sly Mongoose" in chapter 5).

It was probably around this time that Charlie Parker took a playing job at a New York dime-a-dance hall. Trumpeter Jerry Lloyd (born Jerry Hurwitz) later recalled, "I got Bird one of his first jobs in New York. . . . I got him a job in a joint called the Parisian [some sources say Parisien] Dance Hall."[59] An account by Ross Russell of the "Parisien" gig puts forth the idea that Parker learned his vast repertoire of American popular song on this job, and that his later practice of creatively quoting one song during the performance of another is directly indebted to his experience at the dance hall. This maximizing of the job's effect on Parker seems oversimplified at best. Parker had a keen aural memory; he would soak up pop songs (and later all sorts of music) from many sources.

It is known that Parker sat in or "jammed" at many Harlem nightclubs. The best-known club in his circuit was Clark Monroe's Uptown House, where he would receive a share of the meager pay. Parker would also sit in informally in the back room at Dan Wall's Chili House, also in Harlem. The center of the activity was the guitarist Biddy Fleet. He has been quoted as saying that he had a four-piece group working there,[60] although he has also said that there was no paying job per se, and that he and the other musicians just had jam sessions in the back room.[61] Fleet was perhaps not a harmonically advanced musician, but he prided himself on his chord voicings. He liked to invert a given chord on every beat, and use "passing chords" to go from one important chord to another. According to Fleet, Parker's knowledge of individual chords was good, but he didn't yet know how to creatively connect them. Fleet also stated that they used to play popular songs in unfamiliar keys to discourage less-talented sitters-in, and that Parker had no trouble in the lesser-used keys.[62] Parker recalled:

> We used to sit in the back room at Dan Wall's chili joint and other spots uptown, and Biddy would run new chords. For instance, we'd find that you could play a relative major, using the right inversions, against a seventh chord, and we played around with flatted fifths.[63]

Breakthrough in New York

Parker's most famous musical breakthrough occurred one night at Wall's with Biddy Fleet, as related by Michael Levin and John S. Wilson in a 1949 article:

> Charlie's horn first came alive in a chili house on Seventh avenue between 139th street and 140th street in December, 1939. He was jamming there with a guitarist named Biddy Fleet. At the time, Charlie says, he was bored with the stereotyped changes being used then. "I kept thinking there's bound to be something else," he recalls. I

could hear it sometimes but I couldn't play it." Working over "Cherokee" with Fleet, Charlie suddenly found that by using higher intervals of a chord as a melody line and backing them with appropriately related [chord] changes, he could play this thing he'd been "hearing."[64]

Most jazz fans and scholars know the version of this story from the 1955 book *Hear Me Talkin' to Ya,* edited by Nat Shapiro and Nat Hentoff. This later version clearly derives from the above article, but the sections in which Parker had been paraphrased are now given as verbatim quotations. The effect is to make the account more vital than the original:

> I remember one night before Monroe's I was jamming in a chili house on Seventh Avenue between 139th and 140th. It was December 1939. Now I'd been getting bored with the stereotyped changes that were being used at the time, and I kept thinking there's bound to be something else. I could hear it sometimes but I couldn't play it. Well, that night I was working over "Cherokee," and as I did I found that by using the higher intervals of a chord as a melody line and backing them with appropriately related changes, I could play the thing I'd been hearing. I came alive.[65]

It is unknown whether the latter version is based on more complete notes obtained from Levin or Wilson, or whether Shapiro and Hentoff fleshed out the already published material on their own. Unfortunately, the surviving editor, Nat Hentoff, cannot reconstruct how the second version came to be written in such a way.[66]

Coming only about two years after Parker's first breakthrough in the Ozark Mountains, this second breakthrough seemed to put in place the technical and creative factors necessary for the next five years of Parker's journey to artistic maturity.

Considering that Parker was based in New York for most of 1939, surprisingly little more is known about his activities. According to Biddy Fleet, Parker would disappear for weeks at a time.[67] Parker said that he bummed around, sleeping where he could. How much of Parker's behavior was related to his drug use is also unclear, but certainly he had less money to spend on drugs and may have moderated his use out of necessity. In 1940, upon his return to Kansas City, he would tell Jay McShann he was off hard drugs.

Return to Kansas City: Jay McShann

At the end of 1939, Fleet and Parker were part of a band led by the entertainer Banjo Burney, which was working in Annapolis, Maryland.
Around that time, Parker received word that his father had died, and that
his mother wanted him to return for the funeral.[68] Sources have dis-
agreed about the year of Parker senior's death. Addie Parker stated that
Charlie was seventeen at the time (therefore 1937 or 1938), and that he
was contacted in Chicago. Rebecca Parker remembered the year as being
1940, and estimated May or June as the month.[69] Charlie Parker himself
merely stated that his father died after Charlie took the Annapolis job.[70]
A note in the February 12, 1940, issue of *Down Beat* mentions that
"McShann is also adding a new alto," possibly but not certainly a reference to Charlie Parker.[71] If Parker was indeed the "new alto," then he
arrived in Kansas City for the funeral at the very beginning of 1940. At
least initially, Parker resumed living at his mother's house. He was about
to establish a surrogate family in another setting.

In two separate accounts, the generally reliable Jay McShann tells of
Parker returning from New York and working briefly with bandleader
Harlan Leonard before reestablishing ties with McShann.[72] Leonard's
band was working in Kansas City until it left for a job at New York City
that began on February 4, 1940,[73] so Parker may have had a brief second
stint with Leonard after the January, 1939, stint established above.
McShann recalled that Parker gave Leonard just two weeks' notice
before joining McShann's band,[74] and that Parker "didn't start blowing
with us till late 1939 or 1940."[75] Since Leonard only reported Parker
working with him once, it's possible that Parker went to New York *twice*
around this time. Weaving together some of the confusing and contradictory stories, this chronology would have Parker going to New York
first in later 1938 (source: Buster Smith), returning to K.C. and working
with Leonard in January, 1939 (source: Harlan Leonard), leaving
Leonard for McShann (source: Jay McShann), returning to New York
when McShann and Ramey gigged in Chicago (source: Gene Ramey),
and staying on the East Coast until his father died (source: Charlie
Parker). It should be emphasized that Parker never mentioned taking *two*
trips to New York before he traveled there with McShann in 1942, and
that these inconsistencies may simply be due to the limits of memory after
many years.

When Charlie Parker returned to Kansas City around the beginning of 1940 at the age of nineteen, he returned as an adult. He did not come back in defeat but with valuable experience gained in New York. Kansas City offered him a nurturing atmosphere far different from the hardships of New York, one that allowed him to recharge his batteries. It was in K.C. that Parker reestablished ties with Jay McShann and joined the band with which he would make his first commercial (as opposed to amateur) recordings and which would send him back to New York with new status. Jay McShann was leading a small group (probably eight pieces) and was in the process of expanding it into a larger band (by the time that Parker left, it was up to fourteen pieces). Parker's old friend, bassist Gene Ramey, was already in the group, which was a plus for Parker. When Parker joined, there is a possibility that he was put on tenor sax at first before playing his usual alto.[76] McShann's group soon became an in-demand "territory band," traveling as far north as Lincoln, Nebraska, and as far south as New Orleans, Louisiana, keeping Kansas City as its base.

For approximately two and a half years, the McShann band became Charlie Parker's family. For the first time, Parker found acceptance as a peer within a band. The slightly older musicians doted on Parker, accepting his eccentricities and unreliability. Gene Ramey felt that the band spoiled Parker to the point where "he developed into the greatest con man in the world."[77] Although McShann was initially under the impression that Parker was no longer taking heroin (having taken Parker's word on the matter), he soon found otherwise. When Parker's heroin habit occasionally took over, McShann would advise Parker to take a few days off from the band. Gene Ramey told Parker scholar Phil Schaap that both Parker and vocalist Walter Brown required drug-related medical treatment in Austin, Texas, in 1941.[78] His fourth wife, Chan, wrote that "He was in an asylum in Kansas City years ago."[79] She may have been referring to a sanitarium, or he may have had a previously unreported emotional problem.[80] When his drug usage was more under control, Parker rehearsed the sax section and generally motivated the band, as Ramey remembered:

> The Jay McShann band . . . was the only band I've ever known that seemed to spend all its spare time jamming or rehearsing. . . . All this was inspired by Bird, because the new ideas he was bringing to the band made everybody anxious to play.[81]

Parker continued to make great musical strides within the big band format. Humbled by his saxophone section mate John Jackson's superior music-reading ability, Parker worked hard to improve his reading until it was excellent. He tried his hand at arranging for the band, and eventually (in 1941), one of his compositions, "What Price Love?" (which had a lyric by Parker), entered the McShann repertoire. (It was later recorded as "Yardbird Suite" without the words; see chapter 3).

During his stay with McShann, Parker developed the uncanny ability to communicate thoughts and ideas through his music. He enjoyed amusing the band or sending secret messages to them via certain musical phrases. He found that music could have evocative descriptive powers, and he found inspiration in his environment, whether it was nature or the nightclub: "Music is basically melody, harmony and rhythm, but I mean, people can do much more with music than that. It can be very descriptive in all kinds of ways, you know."[82] Gene Ramey remembers:

> He got into his music all the sounds around him—the swish of a car speeding down a highway, the hum of wind as it goes through the leaves . . . Bird kept everybody on the stand happy because he was a wizard at transmitting musical messages to us, which made us fall out laughing. . . . Everything had a musical meaning for him. If he heard a dog bark, he would say the dog was speaking. If he was in the act of blowing his sax, he would find something to express and would want you to guess his thoughts.[83]

As will be seen in chapter 5, Parker in the 1950s would reassert and expand his interest in music "as conversation."

It was around the time of Parker's tenure with McShann that he acquired the nickname "Bird." In one article, Parker is paraphrased as saying that over time his name evolved from Charlie to Yarlie to Yarl to Yard to Yardbird to Bird.[84] Jay McShann, however, often told a different version of how the nickname came to be. According to McShann, his band was on his way to a college job in Lincoln, Nebraska, when one of the band cars ran over a chicken in the road. Parker insisted on going back to pick up the "yardbird" to be cooked later for dinner. He even called chicken on a menu "yardbird," and eventually the name stuck.[85] Later, Yardbird was shortened to Bird. Other, somewhat different, versions can be found (usually involving Parker's supposed love of chicken), making it difficult to accurately trace Parker's famous nickname. Regardless of its origin, the nickname Bird stuck for the rest of Parker's life.

While he was in K.C. working with the McShann band (most likely in 1940), Parker met someone who would become pivotal in his musical life, trumpeter Dizzy Gillespie. Not all the accounts of their first meeting agree as to when and where it took place. As told in Dizzy Gillespie's 1979 *to BE or not . . . to BOP,* Gillespie's version and that of Bernard "Buddy" Anderson (trumpeter in the McShann group) agree that the meeting took place in Kansas City; Anderson dates it as 1940. Both agree that Gillespie was passing through on tour with Cab Calloway's big band, and that Anderson (who already knew Gillespie) sang Parker's praises and introduced the two. According to Anderson, Gillespie played only piano while Parker and Anderson played their horns. Gillespie claims to have been astounded by Parker, although Anderson remembers Gillespie showing little response to Parker, possibly due to self-pride. Parker, on the other hand, did not acknowledge any first meeting in Kansas City. Hedging the issue, he claimed to have "officially" met Gillespie when the Jay McShann Orchestra played at New York's Savoy Ballroom (despite Parker's often inaccurate memory, they opened at the ballroom at the beginning of *1942*):

> Well, the first time, our official meeting I might say, was on the bandstand (of) Savoy Ballroom in New York City in 1939 (when) McShann's band first came to New York. . . . Dizzy came by one night, I think at the time he was working with Cab Calloway's band, and he sat in with the band [McShann]. I was quite fascinated with the fellow and we became very good friends."[86]

1940 was probably also the year that his Ozarks-era friend, trumpeter Clarence Davis, recorded Parker on his amateur disc-cutter (see chapter 2). Significantly, the two songs that Parker played on the only Davis disc that survives are "Honeysuckle Rose" and "Body and Soul," the songs that had spelled disaster for him only a few years before. Once again on "Body," he tries playing double time, but on this occasion, he handles it with aplomb. Of course, this disc was for private use, and only a few people heard it at the time.

Late November of 1940 saw a cut-down version of the McShann band record at radio station KFBI in Wichita, Kansas a number of "transcriptions" for informal nonbroadcast use (these transcriptions are discussed in chapter 2). Parker was featured on most of the pieces they recorded, and his progress is evident. He plays everything from up-tempo pop songs to a "sweet" ballad with great versatility. At twenty years of age, he was already the most inspired and technically assured member of the band. His timbre was thinner and more stripped-down than that of the two major models of the time, Johnny Hodges and Benny Carter. Even though more local listeners were enjoying the band and its young alto sax soloist, the group had still not recorded commercially and thus could not yet break out of its "territory," as Count Basie's band had just a few years before. After the fall of Tom Pendergast, Kansas City had dried up as an entertainer's town. The groups of Harlan Leonard and Jay McShann were the last two important Kansas City big bands to make a break for national recognition.

Early 1941 found the McShann group on tour extensively, and on April 30, 1941, they were in Dallas, making their first commercial recordings for Decca. The eleven-piece band wanted to record their usual repertoire, which included pop songs, ballads, original compositions, blues, and "jump" tunes. They played many pieces (including Parker's "What Price Love?") for producer Dave Kapp, but he was only interested in their blues and jump numbers, especially those featuring blues singer Walter Brown. The result was that the Decca recordings (discussed in chapter 2) were not representative of the band; they did not show the band's versatility, nor did they fully document the role of the band's most inventive soloist, Charlie Parker. Parker's two solos (both on blues-based material) show how much more confident he had become since Wichita. He and the band were about to be heard nationally, and that was a start.

Return to New York

Jay McShann and His Orchestra continued to tour a wide geographical area. In Chicago, on November 18, 1941, a quartet drawn from the band recorded a series of Walter Brown vocals. With several recording sessions under their belt, the goal of the full band was New York City. A booking at the famous Savoy Ballroom was obtained, and the band drove into New York, at the end of 1941 or the beginning of 1942, opening at "The Home of Happy Feet" (the Savoy) on January 9, 1942.[87] Recently discovered recordings of a radio broadcast from the Savoy by the McShann band document the group and Parker's role in it more accurately than either the Wichita Transcriptions or the Decca studio recordings (the broadcast is discussed in chapter 2).

Parker's playing had a much more pronounced effect on New York musicians this time than it had on his first visit. Trumpeter Howard McGhee's reaction is a good example. He was working in Newark, New Jersey, with Charlie Barnet's band when they heard a McShann broadcast from the Savoy. He and the other musicians were surprised to hear an amazing but unknown alto saxophonist take multiple choruses on the pop song "Cherokee" (ironically, the song was Barnet's big hit, but he soloed upon it in a simplistic way). After their job ended, many members of the band went to the Savoy and requested McShann to repeat "Cherokee" so they could find out who the new player was. "Charlie got up to do his solo, and the mystery was solved."[88]

McShann's bassist Gene Ramey also remembered such an incident:

That Sunday, the first Sunday there at the Savoy, we had to do a matinee which started about 4:00. And so in 15 minutes, we only played two tunes. I think we played something like "Moten Swing" or something, and then we played "Cherokee." And, now, Bird started blowing—this was up there, as fast as anything that Max Roach ever played. . . . And somebody from the head office in the studio called that man on the—that had the earset on, and told him, says, let them go ahead, don't stop them, let them play. And we played 45 minutes more, just the rhythm section and Bird, with the horn setting riffs from time to time. . . . And everybody heard it. So that night, you couldn't get close to the bandstand for musicians. Everybody, man: "Who was that band? You hear that saxophone player? Who was that?"[89]

Also drawn to the band was trumpeter Dizzy Gillespie (then with Cab Calloway), who sat in with band while they were at the Savoy. If there was any misplaced sense of competition remaining from their first meeting in Kansas City, it was dispelled during this time. Parker and Gillespie began to see each other as peers, not rivals.

While the band was in New York, Parker broadened his impact on fellow musicians by jamming after-hours at his old haunt, Monroe's Uptown House. He and other like-minded young musicians fed off each other's knowledge and enthusiasm and gradually solidified a new way of approaching jazz harmony, melody, and rhythm. Some of the after-hours experimenters later said that they made their music complex to make it difficult for the less talented (or just older) musicians to sit in. In a 1953 interview, Parker graciously emphasized that he had not felt a lack in the swing era music: "Well, let me make a correction here, please. It wasn't that we were dissatisfied with it [the earlier style], it was just that another conception came along, and this was just the way *we* thought it should go."[90] One night around this time, amateur recorder Jerry Newman captured Parker playing his signature tune, "Cherokee," with the house band at Monroe's (discussed in chapter 2). The disc shows a fresh, new stylist playing with compelling authority, drive, and inventiveness.

The McShann Orchestra (now up to fourteen pieces) recorded four sides for Decca while in New York (July 2, 1942). Parker soloed on two pieces for a total of thirty measures (discussed in chapter 2). His opening phrase on "The Jumpin' Blues" caught the ear of trumpeter Benny Harris who used it as the beginning of his composition, "Ornithology," obviously dedicated to "Bird." Parker's message was spreading on records and in person.

Their successful New York debut notwithstanding, McShann and company still had to go out "on the road" to keep the band solvent and enlarge their audience. In an illustration of Parker's irrepressible spirit, McShann's vocalist, Al Hibbler, recalled Parker running down the street in Canton, Ohio, yelling "The sap is running" and saying "You can do anything you want to."[91] While McShann was touring, pianist and bandleader Earl Hines began putting out feelers about acquiring Parker for the Hines band. When Hines called, McShann said, "The sooner you take him the better. He just passed out in front of the microphone in the middle of "Cherokee!"[92] According to McShann, on a road trip to Detroit in late 1942, Parker's drug habit once again got the best of him when he lost consciousness on the bandstand:

> We couldn't feel no pulse. He had an overdose. This happened at the Paradise Theater. . . . When he came to, I told him, "Bird, you done got back on your kick again, and so I've got to let you go." Andy Kirk [the bandleader] gave him a lift to New York.[93]

Regarding his departure from McShann, Parker omitted the above incident and gave the impression that he had left the band of his own volition for artistic reasons:

But when I came to New York and went to Monroe's, I began to listen to that real advanced New York style. . . . I'd listen to trumpet men like [Hot] Lips Page, Roy [Eldridge], Dizzy and Charlie Shavers outblowing each other all night long. And Don Byas was there, playing everything there was to be played. . . . That was the kind of music that caused me to quit McShann and stay in New York.[94]

When Parker returned to New York, he had a heavy drug habit and no prospect for steady work. But his musical fortunes changed, ironically because of an old neighbor from Kansas City, Albert "Budd" Johnson. Parker would soon find himself in another band with a number of like-thinking young musicians, the most significant one being the man he later described as "the other half of my heartbeat,"[95] Dizzy Gillespie.

The Earl Hines Big Band; Partnership with Dizzy Gillespie

Pianist Earl Hines had led a big band since the early 1930s. These bands were characterized by ups and downs of musicality, shifting personnel, and stylistic changes. Hines had never set a strong direction for the group as a leader, and by 1942, the band was once again in transition. Hines's right-hand man, saxophonist Budd Johnson, was responsible for building the band up in the later 1930s, and for bringing in a handful of younger, more exploratory musicians in the early 1940s. Oddly enough, Johnson left the band in December, 1942, right before the band reached its peak in number of modernists. As reconstructed by jazz scholar Gunther Schuller, the following musicians were all in the band during March and April of 1943: Dizzy Gillespie, "Little" Benny Harris, Bennie Green, Wardell Gray, Billy Eckstine, Sarah Vaughan, *and* Charlie Parker.[96]

When Budd Johnson's tenor saxophone "chair" opened up in December of 1942, Hines's alto saxophonist George "Scoops" Carry brought Hines to a club to hear Parker. Hines was told that Parker would switch over from alto to tenor sax, and Hines was willing to buy Parker a new one. Evidently, Parker was not cleanly and decisively out of the McShann band, because Hines felt he had to approach McShann to get his release on Parker, as McShann recalled: "So Earl Hines told me, says 'Now look, Mac, listen now if you're—if Bird owe you any money, better let me know,' he said, 'cause I got the money to pay you. . . . I want him, I'm gonna get him anyway.'" After an agreement was made, and

Parker had been with Hines for some months, Hines told McShann to take Parker back because he owed everybody in the band, and the new tenor sax was gone. McShann kidded Hines: "But you told me you was gonna make a man out of him!"[97]

Parker continued to display the contradictions of a brilliant mind shrouded behind a debilitating addiction. Despite Parker's behavior problems, Hines was greatly impressed with Parker's musicianship and music-reading ability. Earl found out that Parker had a near photographic memory for music; upon running through a musical arrangement, Parker had committed the piece to memory and didn't need to look at the score later. Hines also noticed Parker and Gillespie forming a musical bond: "Charlie used to take his alto in the theater between shows. . . . between he and Dizzy, they ran over these exercises in these books they're studying up."[98] (If Gillespie and Parker were playing out of the same exercise book, chances are that Parker was playing the *tenor* sax, not the alto; the trumpet and tenor are both pitched in B♭, allowing both to read the same music without any transposition.) In Gillespie, Parker had finally found a kindred musical spirit, someone with a similar appetite for musical knowledge and technical mastery.

In the world of jazz, winds of change were in the air. A handful of young players were building on the explorations of forward looking veterans such as Art Tatum and Coleman Hawkins, and adding their own contributions developed in New York after-hours clubs such as Monroe's and Minton's. Today, the techniques of the music called "bebop" have been transcribed and analyzed and are taught in universities. In 1943, however, new harmonic, melodic, and rhythmic concepts were eagerly spread by word of mouth through a musical grapevine. Like-thinking players sought each other out to play and exchange ideas. When Charlie Parker and Dizzy Gillespie found themselves in the same band for some months in early 1943, they realized that each had something valuable to offer the other. Later, Gillespie compared himself with Parker: "At first we stressed different things. I was more for chord variations, and he was more for melody, I think. But when we got together each influenced the other."[99] In his memoirs, Gillespie amplified what he felt each brought to the music. He acknowledged that he had shown Parker aspects of music theory, harmony, and structure at the piano keyboard, then added, "Charlie Parker's contribution to our music was mostly melody, accents and bluesy interpretation."[100] Gillespie had a special interest in rhythm, and he felt that Parker was already strong in syncopation when they met. Gillespie's assessments are borne out in both artists' music of this period.

If the two musicians' early recordings are evaluated in terms of "theory" and "practice," Gillespie's improvisational work tends to be strong on the theoretical side, being well grounded in harmonic knowledge and musical structure, but somewhat uneven in coherent execution. Parker's early improvisational work tends to be strong on the practical side; musical concepts were approached from the perspective of application and expressed through authoritative performance. When exposed to music theory, Parker quickly synthesized concepts and brilliantly grasped the ideas' ramifications and applications.

While the Hines band was in New York, Parker attended jam sessions playing his tenor sax. Hines's singer, Billy Eckstine, was in attendance when Parker caused a sensation:

> One night [former Ellington tenor saxophonist] Ben Webster walks in Minton's and Charlie's up on the stand and he's wailing the tenor. Ben had never heard Bird. . . . And he goes up and snatches the horn out of Bird's hands, saying, "That horn ain't supposed to sound that fast." But that night Ben walked all over town telling everybody "Man I heard a guy—I swear he's going to make everybody crazy on tenor.[101]

Ironically, the pioneering Earl Hines band of 1943 did not record commercially because of an American Federation of Musicians union ban on recording. As of this writing, no radio transcriptions have surfaced to tell us how this mixture of old and new sounded, and specifically, how trumpeter Gillespie and tenor saxophonist Parker responded to each other in that setting. However, private small-group recordings of Gillespie and tenor saxophonist Parker were made in 1943 by Bob Redcross (friend of Billy Eckstine); until 1985, they were thought to be missing, stolen, or unplayable. In 1986, several of these discs were finally released to the public (see chapter 2), providing documentation of Parker's Hines-era tenor style. Band mate Gillespie was present on at least one piece, and Parker and Gillespie trade solos for over seven minutes on "Sweet Georgia Brown," accompanied only by Oscar Pettiford's bass. The two soloists have clearly mastered the repertoire as passed down to them, and, with each other's inspiration, are extending the language of jazz harmonically, melodically, and rhythmically. Parker sounds extremely comfortable on the larger horn and reveals even more of his Lester Young influence than had been evident when he played alto. Whereas Parker's alto sax timbre was considered thin, his tenor sound is sensuous and full. Parker's combination of timbre, harmonic sense, and melodic line sounds much like that of Wardell Gray's style of five years later.

Soon after these recordings were made, Gillespie quit the band. Parker stayed on for reasons that can only be conjectured; he certainly did not have much artistic freedom in such a large organization, nor was he enthusiastic about playing the tenor sax, which he found "too big."[102] Quite possibly he stayed on because he was unsure of his next step. While Hines and crew were in Washington, D.C., Charlie married Geraldine (Gerri) Scott on April 10, 1943.[103] It has been reported that Rebecca divorced Charlie, but Rebecca Parker stated that she was never legally divorced from Charlie, making this new marriage not legal.[104] Rebecca also claimed that Geraldine had known Charlie in Kansas City and was in fact the "other woman" whose love letters to Charlie Rebecca had discovered years earlier.[105] Geraldine later said, bluntly, "When I married him, all he had was a horn and a habit. He gave me the habit, so I might as well have the horn."[106] Hines band mate Benny Harris remarked that Parker used to pawn Geraldine's wedding ring or use it as an enticement with women. Harris also reported one of the few incidents where Parker's concerned peers tried to pressure him off hard drugs. Parker's heroin habit had him "nodding off" onstage and missing sets altogether. According to Benny Harris, "We used to get to Bird when it looked like Earl was going to fire him for goofing; fourteen of us ganged up on him in one room."[107] They started punching him lightly, telling him to straighten up. This treatment angered him and produced a temporary change in behavior, but did not alter the general curve of his decline. By his own account, Parker quit the Hines band after ten months.[108] At the time, the band was in Washington, D.C., and Parker spent time there with Gerri while working briefly with pianist Sir Charles Thompson. Not surprisingly, his relationship with Gerri didn't last, and he returned once again to the nest, Kansas City, with nothing but a horn and a habit.

Kansas City trumpeter Bernard "Buddy" Anderson recalled working in a small group with Parker playing alto sax at Tutty's Mayfair Club in 1943, post-Hines. Parker arranged and/or composed music for the band, certainly utilizing some of the innovations he and Gillespie had been working on.[109] It is likely that during this stay, Parker's acquaintance

Charles White recorded the altoist in a studio in Kansas City (see chapter 2).

It was during Parker's stay in Kansas City that Dizzy Gillespie formed a combo with bassist Oscar Pettiford to work at the Onyx Club on New York City's Fifty-second Street.[110] They sent Parker a telegram, but he evidently never received it. Parker thereby missed out on the first steadily working combo in the new soon-to-be-called bebop style. Joining Gillespie were pianist George Wallington and drummer Max Roach. Tenor saxophonist Don Byas soon came into the group, taking the role that Parker would have played. Gillespie and Pettiford participated in an April 13, 1944, Billy Eckstine recording date. Eckstine, too, had left the Earl Hines band, and this date led to Eckstine's forming his own working big band.

The First Bebop Big Band

Eckstine wanted a band that consistently reflected the new musical outlook, something that the Hines band, with only a handful of modernists, could never do. Billy reached Charlie Parker in Chicago; since leaving Hines, Parker had reportedly worked with bandleaders such as Andy Kirk and Noble Sissle. Eckstine asked Parker if he wanted to join the band that was being formed. When Parker said yes, Eckstine went to Chicago to bring back Parker and several other players to New York City. Reunited in the band were numerous young, forward looking musicians from the previous Hines orchestra, including trumpeters Dizzy Gillespie, Shorty McConnell, and Gail Brockman, trombonists Bennie Green and Howard Scott, saxophonists Charlie Parker and Tom Crump, and vocalists Eckstine and Sarah Vaughan. This new group is generally considered to be the first bebop big band. Gillespie was tapped to be musical director. He later said, "My main problem in that band was getting those guys to make time, especially Yard [Parker], and he wielded such a great influence over the others."[111] Billy Eckstine's friend and valet, Bob Redcross, remembers a particular night when the band was at its best: "One of the most memorable things I ever heard in my life was the night that they played Gary, Indiana. . . . Everybody was on. [Art] Blakey was on; John [Gillespie] was on; Bird was on; Budd [Johnson] was on; everybody. Man, they upset this place. They had people screaming and hollering."[112]

It was possibly around this time that Sarah Vaughan observed, firsthand, Parker's burgeoning interest in twentieth century "classical" music: "He used to sit on the bus or train with Stravinsky scores. And then he'd get on the stage and play something from Stravinsky, but play it his way."[113]

Although Eckstine did all he could to resist commercial and entertainment pressures upon the band, Parker evidently became disillusioned with the band's direction (and probably with the lack of individual freedom of big bands in general). Eckstine tenor saxophonist Eli "Lucky" Thompson recalled in 1981:

> Charlie saw the handwriting on the wall. He said to me, "Sister dear, there's nothing but deception here." He said, "My man B [Billy] is showing me faces that weren't part of his act." He left and I followed later. [In the same interview, Thompson explained, "We used to call each other Sister in those days."][114]

It's not known exactly when Parker left the big band, but by the time the working group was recorded on December 5, 1944, Parker was gone, replaced by his old McShann section mate, John Jackson (probably the first saxophonist to adopt Parker's style).

The Partnership Continues in New York

Parker was definitely back in New York City by September 15, 1944, for a Savoy recording session led by guitarist and singer, Lloyd "Tiny" Grimes; "Red Cross," the first composition to be copyrighted under Parker's name, was recorded at that date. Dizzy Gillespie and Charlie Parker, both now based in New York, were commercially recorded for the first time together at a January, 5, 1945, record date that included singer Henry "Rubberlegs" Williams. Williams was the unintended victim of Parker's dependence on and high tolerance for mood altering drugs:

> They sent out for coffee and sandwiches in a contain—and it was in containers, you know? Sandwiches, everybody was eatin' these sandwiches. So, I set my cup down beside the chair and dropped a benzedrine in it, you know. And I was just waitin' for it to dissolve. . . . Somehow or other, Rubberlegs gets hungry and he goes collectin' coffees and he got mixed up with mine. And about twenty minutes

later, he was all over the place, man, you never seen anything. . . .
Rubberlegs *really* got busy, you know what I mean? It was a funny
thing.[115]

Parker continued to take whatever work was available, including
stints with tenor saxophonist Ben Webster (as seen above, an early
Parker champion) and with trumpeter Cootie Williams. For most of
1945, however, Parker and Gillespie worked together whenever possible
and deepened their bond.

In the first half of 1945, Gillespie assembled a quintet to work several engagements at the Three Deuces, a nightclub on New York's
famous Fifty-second Street (they also played two concerts in New York
and one in Philadelphia). The personnel varied but always featured
Parker and Gillespie in the front line. Gillespie later called the period the
"height of perfection of our music."[116] While working at the Deuces, the
two horn players developed much of the ensemble style and many of the
compositions that their places in history would be based on, as seen in
two Gillespie-led sessions with Parker from 1945. Gillespie clearly had
the better business sense and more stable life-style of the two, so it's no
surprise that he would land the first recording contracts and that their
nightclub dates and concerts would be billed with Gillespie as the leader.
Parker evidently felt some personal and professional envy of Gillespie's
popularity, but it's not clear how much Parker acknowledged the dominant role that his addiction-derived behavior played in his limited success
in the marketplace.

During this period, Parker led perhaps his first group in New York,
a bass-less trio with pianist Joe Albany and drummer Stan Levey at the
Spotlite. In 1945, Gillespie formed his first bebop big band and took it on
a tour of the South as part of the "Hepsations 1945" package tour.
Parker was never a regular member of the band, although he reportedly
played or sat in with it briefly. Around the same time that Gillespie was
barnstorming the southern United States, Parker led an expanded group
at the Spotlite that included trumpeter Miles Davis, tenor saxophonist
Dexter Gordon, bassist Leonard Gaskin, and drummer Levey. Davis had
met Parker and Gillespie in St. Louis when the Eckstine band had passed
through, and he had come to New York in September, 1945, to study
music at Manhattan's Juilliard school. Davis later said, "I spent my first
week in New York and my month's allowance looking for Charlie
Parker."[117]

In late 1945, Parker was living with Doris Sydnor, whom he had met when she was a nightclub "hat-check girl" on Fifty-second Street. Doris remembered, "When we lived on Manhattan Avenue, he practiced his horn every day. At that time, the musicians often got together after work or during the daytime to work things out."[118] In the fall, when Gillespie had disbanded his big band, he received an offer to bring a group into Billy Berg's, a Los Angeles nightclub. Despite all he knew about Charlie Parker's addiction and its related behavior problems, Gillespie chose Parker as his partner in the front line. Thus began one of the saddest and most tragic periods of Parker's life.

The Trip to California

Gillespie was contracted to bring in a quintet for an eight-week engagement, but due to Parker's unreliability, Gillespie brought along an additional player: "I actually took six guys to California instead of five I had contracted for because I knew—them matinees, sometimes he [Parker] wouldn't be there and I didn't want the management on my back."[119] Parker's state of mind and behavior varied according to his ability to buy heroin, which was much more difficult to find in L.A. than in New York. A disturbing photo in Ross Russell's *Bird Lives!* taken at Billy Berg's around Christmas of 1945, shows an ill-looking Parker on stage with Gillespie. During the Berg's engagement, Gillespie and group performed on singer and sometime-saxophonist Rudy Vallee's radio show, *Villa Vallee*. Rudy sent a message through his father that Rudy would like to hear Parker firsthand. A meeting was arranged, and the next day, Parker and singer-pianist Harry "the Hipster" Gibson went to see and play with Vallee at his home in the Hollywood hills. By his own account, Gibson received two hundred dollars to deliver Parker in person. Gibson remembers the arrangement that Vallee chose as an old-fashioned one, and his account portrays Parker as chuckling through his horn as they played it. Parker was evidently very tactful with Vallee, who had inspired him at age eleven to play the saxophone.[120] Parker, no longer that innocent child, was now not only an accomplished artist far beyond Vallee but was also world weary and close to burning himself out with drug abuse.

Gillespie's engagement at Billy Berg's ended on February 3, and when the group was ready to fly back to New York, Parker could not be found. One account has Gillespie leaving Parker's ticket for him at their hotel, but Gillespie has stated that he eventually gave Parker the ticket and money in person.[121] In any case, Parker, deep in his heroin addiction, cashed in his ticket and remained in Los Angeles.[122] Parker began to work in Los Angeles at the Finale Club, most notably with trumpeters Howard McGhee and Miles Davis (who had traveled west with the Benny Carter big band with the hope of reuniting with Parker.) Live and studio recordings from late winter and early spring show Parker in good to passable shape. Most notable of these from a career standpoint is Parker's February 28, 1946, session for the new independent label, Dial, run by record store owner Ross Russell. This was only Parker's second date as a leader, and it was quite successful from a musical standpoint.

In February, Parker was visited in Los Angeles by Chan Richardson (born Beverly Dolores Berg), a paramour from New York, and an individual who would play a key role in Parker's life. She later reported that Parker was "trying to be real straight" during the Finale Club engagement.[123] Chan was pregnant through a liaison with another man. Parker wanted her to have an abortion; she would not, and she returned to New York in May, to give birth to a girl, Kim.

When Parker's Los Angeles heroin dealer (Emery "Moose the Mooche" Byrd) was arrested, Parker's health took a steep dive. He was generally unable to obtain heroin and turned to large amounts of alcohol in an attempt to manage his withdrawal symptoms. Parker disappeared from view until Howard McGhee found him living in an unheated converted garage. McGhee brought Parker to stay with him and his wife, Dorothy.

As his condition declined, Parker continued to pitch to Ross Russell the idea of another recording session for Dial and to ask him for advances against future royalties. McGhee himself urged Russell to record Parker soon: "We'd better do something, 'cause this cat is uptight."[124] The person who entered the recording studio on July 29, 1946, was a radically deteriorated version of the one who had arrived in California in December of the preceding year (this session was seven months to the day after Parker and Gillespie's first West Coast recordings). Parker later said, "I had to drink a quart of whisky to make the date."[125] Observers at the studio included Russell's partner in Dial Records, Marvin Freeman, psychiatrist Richard Freeman (Marvin's brother), and *Billboard Magazine* correspondent Elliott Grennard.

Breakdown

During that session, Parker was barely able to blow and finger the saxophone, and he had developed muscular spasms that resulted in involuntary jerking while he tried to play. In an attempt to stabilize Parker, Richard Freeman gave Parker six phenobarbital tablets (probably to manage Parker's spasms, but a questionable choice because Parker was already intoxicated on alcohol). Parker struggled through the session very poorly, sounding weak on the slow selections and being in no position to keep up with McGhee and the band on the up-tempo pieces. Grennard later gave a romanticized view of the recording date in a highly embellished short story called "Sparrow's Last Jump."[126]

After recording four sadly chaotic selections, Russell sent Parker via taxi back to the Civic Hotel, where Parker had been staying. McGhee and band remained at the studio to try to salvage the session by recording two additional pieces. After he got home, McGhee received a call from the Civic Hotel alerting him that Parker was walking around nude. By the time Howard arrived at the hotel, the police had already been taken Parker to a hospital. When McGhee caught up with him there, Parker was comparatively lucid and expecting to be released: "I'm fine, man. Get me my clothes; I'm ready to go."[127] McGhee had to explain to Parker that he was under arrest and it wasn't that simple. McGhee was led to believe that Parker had been arrested for public nudity.

Ross Russell, wanting to check up on Parker, had arrived at the hotel after Parker had been taken away. He was told that Parker had caused a fire in his room (earlier in Los Angeles, Parker had caused a fire in a different rented room[128]), and Russell later reported seeing a fire department truck and seeing Parker's charred mattress being carried out. McGhee, who had arrived earlier, saw no such thing and years later strongly denied that there had been a fire. Perhaps McGhee simply didn't encounter the fire vehicle, or possibly the fire had started while Parker was in his room but was not detected until after his arrest. Russell did not know to look for Parker at the hospital; he instead went through the channels of the city police but did not find Parker for days. Due to his behavior that night, Parker had been transferred to the psychopathic ward of the county jail, where Russell found him in an unfastened straitjacket and handcuffed to a cot. Parker, not yet twenty-six years old, had reached a new low.

When brought before a judge, Parker was charged with indecent exposure, resisting arrest, and suspected arson. Through the intercession of Dial partner and lawyer Marvin Freeman, Parker was sent for a minimum of six months to California's Camarillo State Hospital, the least objectionable of the treatment options that the judge had to choose from. There, Parker rebuilt his physical health through regular meals, physical work, and lack of drugs. He was visited by Ross Russell and by fellow musicians. Pianist Joe Albany was committed to Camarillo for an unexplained reason and encountered Parker in the hospital before Albany escaped from the hospital.[129] In September of 1946, Doris Sydnor, with whom Parker had lived in New York, moved to Los Angeles to be near Parker until his release. Doris took a bus to see Charlie several times a week. She recalled that he had a saxophone at the hospital, and that he played for occasional in-hospital dances, but she believed that he did little organized practicing there. As Parker's mental and physical health improved, he was allowed several passes to leave the hospital grounds with Doris. On one such outing, she became concerned about Parker's perception of reality and rushed him back to the hospital. This incident convinced her that Parker's rebuilding process was more than just snapping back from drug addiction.[130]

Parker took advantage of this forced withdrawal from the chaos of his life, as Doris recalled:

> He was really kind of inside of himself. I think he was looking at his life . . . There were people there that were very disturbed, and I think he—that was a time when he was looking at how their life affected them. . . . And Charlie said, you know, it really made him think, you know, maybe it's not good to lose yourself in one thing; that you need a more rounded life. You need, you know, you need other things in your life. Because, he—you know, music was his whole life.[131]

After some recuperation, however, Parker felt it was time to break free of the hospital setting.

> He told me one time that this man used to get up every morning and eat breakfast and go stand—look out on a hill. And so, for about three mornings, Charlie had gone out and watched him. And all of a

sudden, he had a mental vision of, like, ten years from now there would be this man, and him and whoever was behind him, watching them to see what they were looking at. He said that was when he panicked, and he felt he had to get out of there.[132]

In a December 1, 1946, note handwritten in pencil, Parker implored Ross Russell: "Dear Ross; Man—please come right down here and get me out of this joint. I'm about to blow my top."[133]

Richard Freeman worked to get Parker released in California before Parker would have to be shipped back to New York State as a psychiatric case. In late January, Parker was released into the custody of Ross Russell, who would be legally responsible for Parker. In his book, *Bird Lives!*, Russell recalls negotiating with Parker for a one-year renewal of the option on Parker's Dial contract as a way of protecting Russell's finances now that he was responsible for Parker. In a 1947 interview, Parker was paraphrased as being appreciative of Russell's efforts on his behalf:

> Ross Russell, the Dial recording man, whose help he recalls with gratitude, spoke up for him, and the authorities had Yardbird sent to Camarillo, where, after a while, he was given physical work to do and his mind and body were built up to a point they had never reached since childhood.[134]

But by 1949, Parker expressed bitterness toward Russell, saying that he had refused to sign the documents for Parker's release until Parker agreed to renew his Dial contract. Parker also reported hearing that he could have been released without Russell's help; Russell maintained that Parker otherwise would have just been shipped out to another hospital.[135] Parker was also understandably angry at Russell for releasing on record the tragic and disturbing pieces recorded during that final session before Parker's hospitalization. Parker later said of the pieces recorded that day:

> If you want to know my worst on wax, though, that's easy. I'd take "Lover Man," a horrible thing that should never have been released—it was made the day before I had a nervous breakdown. No, I think I'd choose "Be-Bop," made at the same session, or "The Gypsy." They were all awful.[136]

When Parker was finally released from Camarillo in late January, 1947, he and Doris lived in a furnished room in Los Angeles until they could return to New York City. She recalled:

> And then, I think he was feeling very lost when he came out, I think, you know, when something like that happens to you, I thing there's a fear of getting back and living again. And the fact that, you know, he wasn't using drugs then, and a fear of how people were gonna react to him. I'm sure it must be a very painful thing to have had such a complete breakdown—as he did—and lose all control. . . . There was a quality about him at that time that was kind of introspective.[137]

Parker and McGhee played in a band at the Hi-De-Ho Club, where they were recorded extensively of a home disc recorder by saxophonist Dean Benedetti. On the discs, Parker generally sounds back to his best form. Parker also recorded two sessions for Dial before flying to New York via Chicago in early April, 1947.

New York and the Classic Quintet

On April 7, Parker arrived in New York City, his home base until his death in 1955. Thanks to his relationships with two women, Doris Sydnor and Chan Richardson, his life in New York would be more stable than during his previous stay. Much of the time, he would have a home to return to, a privilege he did not always take advantage of.

He was back in New York as a well-known recording artist and a sought-after bandleader on the level of his compatriot Dizzy Gillespie. Parker once again lived with Doris Sydnor and married her in 1948.[138] His health initially was the best it had been since his youth. Doris remembers this as a particularly stable period in their lives, one during which Parker continued to practice saxophone (at least early on). Below the surface of stability, however, there were elements of chaos. After having rebuilt his health at Camarillo, Parker soon returned to heroin and alcohol abuse. According to Miles Davis, Parker briefly worked at this time with Gillespie's big band at the McKinley Theatre in the Bronx.

> On the night we opened at the McKinley, Bird was up on stage nodding out and playing nothing but his own solos. He wouldn't play

behind nobody else. Even the people in the audience were making fun of Bird. . . . So Dizzy, who was fed up with Bird anyway, fired him after that first gig.[139]

Much of the time, Parker coped amazingly well with his addiction; his creativity seemed only slightly dimmed by heroin, and he could play with more control of his instrument when he was high than most musicians could when they were lucid. Sadly, his combination of talent and tolerance for heroin led some jazz musicians to conclude that they might play better if they took the drug. Parker soon began to feel the responsibility of being a role model; in a 1949, *Down Beat* article, he stated:

Any musician who says he is playing better either on tea [marijuana], the needle, or when he is juiced, is a plain, straight liar. . . . Some of these smart kids who think you have to be completely knocked out to be a good hornman are just plain crazy. It isn't true. I know, believe me."[140]

While Parker was in California, modern jazz had begun to establish itself in New York. By the time he returned, Parker's popular and critical reputation had solidified to the point that he was in demand as a bandleader and recording artist. Parker went on to form his "classic quintet," a group that would be his main performing unit from 1947 into 1950. He chose Miles Davis as trumpeter and Max Roach as drummer. Pianist Duke Jordan and bassist Tommy Potter generally filled the other spots. Parker called a group rehearsal for an upcoming job at the Three Deuces nightclub, but he reportedly never showed up. Miles Davis has stated that when they opened at the club, Parker merely asked if they were ready to play and proceeded to play perfectly everything the group had prepared (one assumes that the repertoire consisted largely of pieces that everyone knew).[141]

On May 8, 1947, about a month after arriving in New York, Parker and a modified version of his new quintet met at Harry Smith's studio to record four sides for the Savoy label. Thus began the studio documentation of his classic quintet, recordings upon which much of Parker's reputation rests. His musical knowledge, experience, command of his instrument and contact with his imagination all came together magnificently. The quintet and its successors recorded primarily for the Dial and Savoy labels, with a few sides for Norman Granz's Clef label. Many live recordings of the quintet also surfaced after Parker's death. The personnel of Parker's quintet changed only infrequently, lending it considerable continuity.[142]

Parker's agent, Billy Shaw, succeeded in booking Parker's quintet in better nightclubs for longer engagements and at better pay than Parker had attained on his own in earlier times. Parker and his group toured the country between engagements in New York. The most extended of these engagements was at a new club, the Royal Roost. Disc jockey "Symphony" Sid Torin broadcast weekly from the Roost, and Parker's quintet is documented in a series of live recordings dating from September, 1948, through March of the next year. Torin tried very hard to use current slang and act hip; Parker tolerated Torin, but sometimes Parker couldn't resist a veiled put-down, as in this broadcast from the 1950s:

SS: Say, Bird? Charlie? Uh, [pause] Mister Parker. I didn't know whether you have this in your repertoire, but we're getting a lot of calls for ["My Little"] "Suede Shoes." Is that a little too rough, or would you rather do something else?

CP: Well, is that a request of yours directly, Symphonic Sidney,

SS: No, no it's a request—

CP: or is it for the people?

SS: [laughs]—the people, dad.

CP: For the people,

SS: Yeah!

CP: and for you, *yes*.

SS: All right—

CP: "Suede Shoes."

SS: —here it is, ladies and gentlemen, your favorite, "Suede Shoes."[143]

Much hipper and closer to Parker was Leonard Feather who still could come in for his share of ribbing from Parker, as in this broadcast from 1953:

LF: Charlie? I would like it very, very much at this point if you could give us your version of an old standard that you recorded a few years ago, George Gershwin's "Embraceable You." Would that be possible at this point?

CP: At this point, Leonard, I don't see how I could refuse you.[144]

Despite his addictions, Parker's live appearances and studio recordings generally showed great force and vitality. His level of artistic consistency as heard on the recordings is stunning. Nevertheless, even he sometimes showed signs of a diminished physical and mental state. On a recording of a January 29, 1949, live radio broadcast from the Royal Roost, Parker attempts to play Dizzy Gillespie's "Groovin' High" but is unable to articulate the melody, leaving trumpeter Kenny Dorham to carry the group. Parker drops in and out of the ensemble, misses notes, articulates the melody inconsistently and wanders in and out of the beat. Parker is not having trouble with his horn; he is physically unable to play a song he had known for four years. When Parker's turn comes to solo, he halfheartedly tries to play but drops out after just a few bars.

In 1948, the quintet was playing at Chicago's Argyle Show Bar. Parker was so intoxicated and disoriented that he urinated in the lobby's telephone booth, thinking it was a toilet, an incident that resulted in the group losing their pay. According to Miles Davis, upon the band's return to the Argyle later in the year, Parker showed his defiance of the clubowner by *intentionally* urinating in the booth and then returning to the bandstand to play.[145] Sometimes his nightclub behavior was more creatively bizarre in a dadaistic fashion. Ross Russell remembers Parker's actions at the Royal Roost in 1948: "A toy balloon was produced and inflated, and its air was allowed to escape into the microphone. A toy cap pistol was used to shoot the piano player."[146] Miles Davis also reported the incident and described in detail how he made up his mind, that night, to quit the band, tired of Parker's longstanding addiction-derived behavior.[147] Max Roach soon followed Davis out of the band.

Enter Norman Granz

In December, 1948, Parker began recording with near exclusivity for Norman Granz, a partnership that would last until Parker's death. Granz had recorded Parker in concert in 1946 while Parker was in California, and in December, 1947, Granz had recorded two studio sides featuring Parker for a special album of 78s called *The Jazz Scene*. Granz preferred to record his artists in a wide variety of musical settings, so in the next few years, Parker was heard with back-up bands ranging from a big band to a vocal group; unfortunately, Parker's working quintet was seldom recorded by Granz. Granz's distribution deal with the Mercury label (later he had his own Clef, Norgran, and Verve labels) made Parker's new records more widely available than his previous releases on Savoy and Dial.

This new recording arrangement came at a time when Parker and his manager were trying to make Parker more successful in the marketplace. Parker understandably envied Dizzy Gillespie's critical and popular success, but Parker's public behavior too often undermined the overall plan to bring him the financial success his artistry deserved. Nevertheless, an important index of Parker's increasing popularity with jazz fans was his winning, for the first time, the alto sax division of *Metronome* magazine's 1947 readers' poll, published in January, 1948 (Parker first topped the *Down Beat* readers' poll with the 1950 survey).

A key event in Parker's life came with his May, 1949, trip to Paris and its International Festival of Jazz. Parker and his quintet with Kenny Dorham, Al Haig, Tommy Potter, and Roy Haynes joined visiting Americans including Sidney Bechet, Oran "Hot Lips" Page, Tadd Dameron, Miles Davis, and expatriate Americans Kenny Clarke and James Moody. They performed concerts that presented a wide range of jazz styles in a setting that acknowledged the continuity of jazz as an art form, not as mere entertainment. Parker met French intellectuals including Jean-Paul Sartre and classical music saxophone virtuoso Marcel Mule.[148] Reportedly, Parker formulated a plan to return to Paris and study composition with Nadia Boulanger.[149] While in Paris, Parker did not show up for a pre-concert rehearsal and reportedly spent much of his time drinking and socializing.

After his return from France, Parker replaced Kenny Dorham with trumpeter Red Rodney (born Robert Chudnick), thus forming the tightest and most versatile front line in the history of Parker's 1947–50 quintet. In large part because of Norman Granz's preference for recording Parker in out-of-the-ordinary musical settings, this excellent lineup was never documented on studio recordings. However, a new Parker ensemble that both Granz and Parker *were* excited about made its first recordings in November, 1949. Inspired by his love of classical music, Parker had for some time wanted to record with a string ensemble. Although Parker's musical tastes included complex twentieth-century classical music, he and Norman Granz agreed to have arrangements made of popular songs featuring Parker, strings, and a jazz rhythm section. Parker, who loved the pop song idiom, was initially quite happy to adapt to this concept. Later, he would try to assert his concept of commissioning ambitious new works for saxophone and strings in a modern idiom.

A striking symbol of the growing recognition of Charlie Parker's talent and influence came with the December 15, 1949, opening of the New York nightclub Birdland, named in honor of Bird. For the all-star opening engagement, Parker's early influence, Lester Young, was part of the bill. Parker's initially positive relationship with the management would later turn more troubled, and he was reportedly banned from the club at least once.

Life in Flux

Early 1950 brought the breakup of Charlie and Doris's marriage. Charlie's erratic addiction-influenced behavior had become so great a strain on their relationship that Doris could not continue. In May 1950, Charlie and Chan Richardson, having renewed their relationship, moved in together. Although they never legally married, she took his name and is rightly considered his fourth and final wife. Charlie viewed Chan's daughter, Kim, as his own; Charlie and Chan then had a daughter, Pree, and a son, Baird. When Charlie and his first wife, Rebecca, had their son, Leon, Charlie was too young and irresponsible to accept the role of father and husband. This time, however, Parker tried and in many ways succeeded for a period in accepting those responsibilities and enjoying the pleasures of having a family.

The year 1950 also saw the gradual breakup of Parker's working quintet. Around May, Red Rodney had to leave the working quintet temporarily because of appendicitis. In the recording studio, Norman Granz was generally more interested in recording Parker in nonquintet musical settings, and as Parker's string ensemble began to accept concert and club engagements, Parker acquired another organized performing outlet. Parker and his agents were also finding it more profitable to send Parker out as a "single," that is to say touring by himself and picking up local musicians wherever he went.

In November 1950 Parker was booked as a single to give a series of concerts in Sweden and Denmark, and he tried to kick heroin long enough to make the tour. Unfortunately, he tried to stave off craving for the drug by increasing his use of alcohol. Despite his alcohol intake, and perhaps because of his temporary abstinence from heroin, the live recordings from Sweden document him in a highly creative frame of mind. After his Swedish concerts, Parker flew to Paris on a last-minute invitation from Charles Delaunay to play with Roy Eldridge and others at the Salon du Jazz.

Parker reportedly spent most of his time partying and drinking, and left without fulfilling his obligation, an indication of the chaos lurking just below the surface of his life. An account published in *Melody Maker* about a week after Parker's departure from Paris reported that Parker's agent, Billy Shaw, insisted that if Parker played at the Salon, the Salon's organizers would have to pay for Parker's return flight to the United States (despite the fact that the organizers of the Scandinavian tour had already done so). The *Melody Maker* writer concluded, "I am able to reveal that there is more in this than meets the eye. Suffice it to say that he felt he must return to seek shelter under the wing of his agent from a pending brush with the law."[150]

Upon Parker's return, Leonard Feather arranged for the radio broadcast of a transatlantic call between Delaunay, Eldridge, and Parker, during which Parker offered vague excuses for not honoring his Parisian agreement. Delaunay inquired, "Charlie, what happened to you?" to which Parker replied, "Sorry, Charles. I'm afraid I had to leave you." When Eldridge asked, "What did you want to leave me for?" Parker managed to say, "Sorry, Roy. I just had to go. I would have just loved to have been there" before the transatlantic connection failed.[151] Evidently all the alcohol consumed on the trip had contributed to his contracting a stomach ulcer, and soon after arriving in New York, he was hospitalized. His doctor ordered him to stop drinking, something Parker would not do for long.

Legend has that Parker was never arrested for possession of drugs, but, in fact, he was arrested at least once, possibly the "pending brush with the law" mentioned earlier.[152] Parker received only a three-month suspended sentence, probably because of his being a first-time offender. The judge, perhaps impressed with Parker's talent but not comprehending the severity of his addiction said, "Mr. Parker, if you ever have the urge to stick a needle in your arm again, take your horn out in the woods somewhere and blow."[153] Due to this conviction, Parker's "cabaret card," the document that allowed musicians and entertainers to work in New York State nightclubs, was revoked in July, 1951.[154] Without this card, Parker's ability to make a living in his hometown was severely limited (New York City and State concerts and out-of-state nightclub engagements were still possible). This too made it hard for Parker to sustain his quintet; he could still work out of town, but he had begun to find it financially necessary to make those tours by himself. Parker tried several times to re-form his quintet with Red Rodney, but Red's two narcotics arrests in the early 1950s made that impossible.

In 1951, *Ebony* magazine published an article by bandleader and singer Cab Calloway in which he outlined what he saw as the effects of hard drugs upon the jazz world.[155] Although Calloway's text carefully avoided referring to musicians by name, accompanying photos and captions clearly identified friends of Parker. When Leonard Feather asked Parker his opinion of the article, Parker said, "I'd rather say that it was poorly written, poorly expressed and poorly meant. It was just poor." After chuckling at that reply, Feather gave Parker the opportunity to say to the public that drugs did not enhance musical creativity (something that Parker had said in print several times). Parker was strangely cautious:

> LF: I certainly don't think that a musician necessarily plays better under the influence of any stimulus [stimulants?] of any kind, and I'm pretty sure you agree with me, don't you?
>
> CP: Well, um, [pause] yes, I'd rather agree with you to an extent. I think you're quoting something that I once said to you [unintelligible under next statement] . . .
>
> LF: That's right. Exactly. You said that to me quite a while ago.
>
> CP: That's exactly right. Well, nobody's fooling themselves. Never. Anymore, anyway, we'll put it that way. And in case an investigation should be conducted, it should be done in the right way, instead of trying to destroy musicians and their names. I don't think it's quite a good idea.[156]

Over time, Parker's daily involvement with his art had changed, largely because of his drug and alcohol addictions. Although Doris Parker recalled Charlie practicing often even after his return from California, Chan Parker explicitly stated that during the years they lived together, Charlie did not practice saxophone.[157] His recordings of the 1950s confirm this lack of maintenance; his improvisations tend to be repetitive and routine, with fewer moments of artistic discovery. Not helping matters was the fact that Parker could seldom depend upon a consistent backup group, whether in the studio or for live appearances.

Both because of Granz's recording philosophy and Parker's touring as a single, Parker's discography of the 1950s shows a constantly changing stream of accompanists.

Even with the breakup of his quintet and the uncertainties of touring as a single, Parker's personal life achieved some measure of stability with a home base, spouse, and children. During the early 1950s, Parker dabbled in other arts, such as drawing and painting. He took an interest in George Balanchine's choreography after seeing New York City Ballet's *Firebird*.[158] Although Chan reports seeing Charlie reading a book only once, he did occasionally write poems. The word play in the following excerpt reflects the quickness of Parker's mind:

> To play is to live and vice-a-versa
> Play to live and vice-a-versa
> Live play is vice perverse
> Live verse is play.
>
> To shun is to run
> Running is shunning
> But to shun running
> Is shining shunning of running.[159]

Parker continued to record often for Norman Granz, one of the few financial bright spots in Charlie's career. According to Chan Parker:

> Norman was very supportive of Bird, and Bird was glad to have him, and, Norman subsidized him fifty dollars a week, and, yeah, I think Norman was the best thing that had come along for Bird up to that time. I don't know how Norman profited from that, but for Bird, he had somebody that was behind him and, and Norman was recording him like mad, you know.[160]

Charlie Parker no doubt appreciated both Granz's financial support and his refusal to put on concerts in segregated auditoriums. Granz's support came at a price, however. Parker argued with Granz over recording session repertoire, and Parker was evidently dissatisfied with Granz's personality and recording philosophy as Parker acquaintance Harvey Cropper recalled: "He [Parker] didn't like Norman Granz. He said of him,

'He's made one million dollars, and he's on his way to two, yet he's the most frightened man in the world. He takes jazz musicians, and he removes them from others. He puts them in a box.'"[161]

In the 1950s, Granz recorded Parker with conventional and Latin big bands, a string section, a big band and string combination, a vocal and wind ensemble, an all-star jam session, a reunion with Dizzy Gilles-pie and Thelonious Monk, and several one-time small groups. Although Parker usually plays with polish, seldom on these recordings does he catch fire. An exception is the 1950 reunion session where he and Gilles-pie clearly inspire one another. Many of his most spirited live recordings of the period find Parker in the company of inspiring peers such as Gilles-pie, Bud Powell, and "Fats" Navarro. But even when Parker played with fire, his results in the 1950s seldom equaled the innovations and freshness of his 1945–49 work. Although Parker thirsted for new musical hori-zons, an addict's day-to-day life-style did not encourage further artistic growth. Some of Parker's popularity began to erode. Parker had won the alto sax category of the *Metronome* readers' poll every year since the 1947 survey (published in January, 1948), but the 1953 poll found him in second place to Lee Konitz. The 1954 poll put Parker in third place, behind Paul Desmond and Lee Konitz. (Parker continued to dominate the *Down Beat* readers' poll until his death.)

Parker felt no competition with the other altoists, saying in print, "I'm very moved by his [Brubeck's] altoist, Paul Desmond"[162] and per-sonally telling Lee Konitz, "I really dig the fact that you're not trying to play like me."[163] Another alto saxophonist (and singer) that Parker enjoyed was Louis Jordan. Konitz recalled Parker putting nickels into a jukebox to play Jordan's records.[164] (Parker's open-mindedness toward Jordan's early rhythm and blues music contrasts with the impression given in the motion picture *Bird,* in which the Parker-based character is disillusioned to see seemingly unsubtle rhythm and blues gain popularity.)

In her memoir, *Ma Vie en Mi Bémol (My Life in E♭),* Chan Parker wrote that during this period Parker's drinking made him mean and vio-lent. As their relationship worsened, he telephoned for the police one night, saying that he was at the point of killing his wife. With all the money Parker was making going to drug dealers, the family found itself going through hard financial times. Chan Parker recalls Charlie selling his beloved symbol of status, their Cadillac car, to buy Kim her first bi-cycle, even though Charlie had "more than five Cadillacs in his veins."[165]

As he continued to mistreat his stomach ulcers, he also developed liver and heart problems. Chan has also referred to a doctor in Philadelphia treating Charlie for she calls his *first* heart attack, indicating that his heart condition was quite serious.[166]

One bright event in their lives was the return of Parker's cabaret card. In 1953, Parker had written to the New York State Liquor Authority, stating that his inability to work in New York was detrimental to the health of his family:

> My right to pursue my chosen profession has been taken away, and my wife and three children who are innocent of any wrongdoing are suffering. . . . My baby girl is a city case in the hospital because her health has been neglected since we hadn't the necessary doctor fees. . . . I feel sure when you examine my record and see that I have made a sincere effort to become a family man and a good citizen, you will reconsider. If by any chance you feel I haven't paid my debt to society, by all means let me do so and give me and my family back the right to live."[167]

In an unusual act of clemency not previously extended other addict-musicians, Parker's cabaret card was restored to him and he was able to play in nightclubs in his hometown of New York.[168]

Life in Turmoil

Charlie and Chan's daughter, Pree, had been born with a congenital heart defect and required hospitalization several times. What Charlie did not mention in the above letter was the financially draining effect his heroin habit and chaotic life-style had on their ability to care for her. The contradiction between Parker's desire to honor and serve his wife and family and his guilt over his inability to break his destructive behavior tormented him. Chan, one the few people in Charlie's life who was strong willed enough to stand up to him, took the children and left their apartment to stay with her mother a number of times.

The greatest single blow to their lives came with the death of Pree in March, 1954, while Charlie was working as a single in Los Angeles. Charlie's early morning telegrams to Chan communicate his shock and grief.[169] After hearing the tragic news, Charlie reportedly first got drunk, then gave away his heroin. "I hope I can be a good husband . . . at least until this is over," was his comment to acquaintance Julie MacDonald at the airport as he left for New York.[170] Upon Charlie's return, Pree was buried in the same cemetery as Chan's father; he in the section set aside for Jews, Pree in the section set aside for African-American people.

That summer, the family vacationed on Cape Cod and, later in the year, they escaped from big-city tensions by temporarily taking a house in New Hope, Pennsylvania. Upon their return to New York, Charlie's drinking and behavior continued to affect their lives and his career adversely. During this general period, Parker attempted suicide twice and was admitted to Bellevue Hospital several times. A doctor at Bellevue suggested electroshock therapy for Charlie; when Chan expressed fear that his genius would be affected, the doctor asked, "do you want a musician or a husband?"[171] Beginning around Christmas of 1954, the two became increasingly at odds, and Chan and the children moved to Pennsylvania.

December, 1954, was also the last time that Parker was commercially recorded. The occasion was a session for a Norman Granz–conceived album of Cole Porter songs. Parker then went on the road as a single. His health and playing were at a particularly low point during a January, 1955, engagement in Chicago.

For the last few months of his life, Parker was based in New York City's Greenwich Village. Parker had collapsed on the sidewalk and was brought into the nearby apartment of Ahmed Basheer to rest. Although they had never before met, Basheer extended to Parker the use of the apartment. Basheer's conversion to Islam impressed Parker: "Charlie was interested in the Moslem religion. His Mohamedan name was Saluda Hakim. He knew a little Huranic Arabic."[172] Parker's life continued to have its ups and downs, but the general trend of his life was downward. Parker both spoke of the imminence of his death and tried to find musical work, a task that was made more difficult as his reputation for being late for work and missing nightclub sets grew.

His last important job came as part of an all-star band that appeared at Birdland the weekend of March 4 and 5, 1955. In addition to Parker, the group included trumpeter Kenny Dorham, pianist Bud Powell, bassist Charles Mingus, and drummer Art Blakey. Both Mingus and Dorham recalled the engagement for Robert Reisner.[173] By Mingus's account, the first night went well, with Parker playing well and everyone behaving normally. On the second night, however, Parker and Powell clashed. Powell had been hospitalized several times for emotional problems and was uncooperative and perhaps emotionally disturbed that night. He reportedly had trouble playing the same song as Parker at the same tempo and in the same key. Dorham quotes Mingus as saying over the club's public address system, "Ladies and Gentlemen, I am not responsible for what happens on the bandstand. This is not jazz." Parker proceeded to get drunk and was eventually asked to leave by the manager. He confided, "Mingus, I'm goin' someplace, pretty soon, where I'm not gonna bother anybody." Parker's coworkers did not know that the next day, March 6, marked the first-year anniversary of Pree's death, an event that placed a strain on Parker who certainly felt grief over her passing and had reason to feel guilt over his inability to care for his child.

Dizzy Gillespie told of his last meeting with Charlie Parker:

Shortly before I left for Europe, a couple of months ago, I ran into him at Basin Street. He sat down and talked to me about our getting back together again. The way he said it, it was as if he was saying "Before it's too late . . . " I think Charlie had a premonition. Unfortunately, for all practical purposes, it was already too late. If it had happened, it would have been the greatest; I don't need to say that I had some of the greatest experiences of my life playing with Charlie Parker.[174]

The Death of Charlie Parker

There are at least three different stories explaining the death of Charlie Parker. According to the standard and most widely accepted version, and one that has been told since the week of his death, Parker prepared to leave New York on Wednesday, March 9, 1955, to go to a job in Boston. On his way out of town, he reportedly stopped by the apartment of Pannonica "Nica" de Koenigswarter at Manhattan's Stanhope Hotel. De Koenigswarter was a wealthy lover of jazz and an ally of many musicians, including Thelonious Monk. According to her, Parker began to vomit blood while at the apartment. Her doctor was called in and examined Parker there. Determining that Parker had stomach ulcers and cirrhosis of the liver, the doctor recommended that Parker be taken to a hospital, advice that Parker refused to take (reportedly because he wanted to drive to Boston). As a compromise, Parker agreed to stay at de Koenigswarter's, with daily visits by the doctor. By Saturday, March 12, Parker's health was good enough to allow him to sit up and watch television. That evening, while watching Tommy and Jimmy Dorsey's show, Parker was laughing at a comedy routine, then began choking. He rose from his chair and then sat down, lifeless. De Koenigswarter reported a clap of thunder at the time of Parker's death.

Another story that has circulated for many years holds that Parker died as the result of internal injuries sustained in a fight with a fellow musician. One version of this story suggests that the usually told version of the Stanhope death was concocted to protect the musician who punched Parker.

A story that has surfaced more recently says that Parker did not arrive ill at the Stanhope but instead was *shot* there (possibly by a fellow musician). Parker's autopsy does not report a gunshot wound, however, and this story hinges on the doctor performing the autopsy either missing the wound or agreeing (possibly through a bribe; theoretically from de Koenigswarter) not to report the wound.

Of course, each of these stories could have elements of the truth. Parker could have sustained internal injuries in a fight and then wound up at the Stanhope; Parker could have been ill with ulcer problems at the Stanhope when he was shot. However, the allegation that Parker was not convalescing at the Stanhope is easily refutable. In an interview, Parker's mother clearly stated:

> I talked with them [Parker and de Koenigswarter] three days before he died. She said, "How are you? I hope to meet you sometimes." I said to Charles, "If you're sick in any way let me know." He said they wanted to give him an electric encephalogram [electroencephalogram]. "Charles," I said, "don't take it. Come home to mother. I work in the finest hospital in Kansas City, and I will have it done if it is a necessity."[175]

Of course, an electroencephalogram is not a test ordered for a patient with a gunshot wound.

All the principals are dead, so we may never confirm any of the accounts of the death of Charlie Parker. That leaves us with the music, which is as it should be.

Part 2.
The Music of Charlie Parker

Introduction to the
Musical Chapters

The following four chapters that form the heart of this book are intended as a chronological period-by-period guided tour through the music of Charlie Parker. Chapter 2 begins with his first recordings and examines his "apprenticeship" years, a time when he was in the process of assimilating and transforming his influences, plus adding to them his own artistic vision. Chapter 3 covers Charlie Parker's first years of artistic maturity, a period during which his personal musical vocabulary attained a wholeness and when his first masterpieces were recorded. Chapter 4 focuses on Parker's most productive period, whose major accomplishments include a series of reflective ballad and slow blues performances recorded with his working ensemble. Chapter 5 concludes with Charlie Parker's final years, a time when he experienced both artistic stagnation and a strong desire to expand his musical horizons, an aspiration that was largely unfulfilled at the time of his death.

Each chapter begins with descriptive material that places Parker's work of the period in context. Parker's work of the period is then organized around broad topic headings, often relating to particular Parker ensembles that suggest such groupings. Under each heading, key Parker solo improvisations are discussed both informally and more technically with regard to specific qualities, techniques, and traits (detailed below). Brief transcribed excerpts of solos illustrate these points. One representative solo per chapter is discussed in greater detail and with a greater number of excerpts. In the case of these four solos, a complete transcription of each one is included in Appendix B for readers who wish to explore them further. The compact disc sources for the musical examples are found in Appendix A.

Due to circumstances beyond the control of the author, discussion of Parker's compositional art is limited in scope. The few examples of Parker's music writing included here are short out of respect to their publisher.[1]

Before delving into discussion of Charlie Parker's individual stylistic periods, it is important to ground this study in a survey of some the subjective and objective qualities, traits, and techniques associated with Charlie Parker's mature and best-known music (especially 1945–49). It is hoped that the following material will provide context and criteria for study and enjoyment of Parker's art of any period. These factors will be discussed and returned to throughout the book.

The first group of qualities relate to some of the nontechnical aspects that untrained (non-musician) jazz listeners seem to relate to and grasp in Parker's music. These points are loosely based on nontechnical comments often found in books, articles, and discussions about Parker and are included in the belief that much of the compelling nature of Parker's music lies outside of quantifiable musical analysis.

1. Facility, virtuosity. Parker clearly had great command of his instrument. His ability to improvise with sureness at the fastest of tempos, and his ability to improvise with great complexity at slower tempos are two of the most thrilling qualities associated with his music.

2. Intensity of swing and drive. Swing is a subjective rhythmic quality characteristic of jazz, and listeners feel that Parker swung with particular power, catching them up in the forward motion of the music.

3. Inventiveness. Listeners feel that Parker improvised with notable creativity and showed great quickness of mind. He clearly interacted with his accompanists, and he included aspects of his performing environment in his live appearances. Apprehension of this aspect gives the listener a sense of Parker's process of creation.

4. Playfulness, sense of humor. Parker's music contains many emotionally whimsical flights of fancy. Probably the most easily discernible aspect of playfulness is his frequent use of quotations, i.e., his interpolation of a portion of one song into the performance of another (see also number 12, below). The more one is familiar with the melodies of pop, jazz, and classical music, the more one feels let in on a private joke when Parker inserts a quotation.

5. Bluesiness, poetic qualities. Apart from the exhilarating and playful qualities of Parker, listeners relate to the poetic depth that they feel is present. Much of this is identified as a profound sense of the blues permeating the music, whether the material is a twelve-bar blues or some other form. Among many factors, Parker's creative use of common-property blues phrases along with his cutting saxophone timbre ("tone") seem to contribute to the sense of the blues.

Of course, many of the qualities, techniques, and traits associated with the music of Charlie Parker can be notated, quantified, or otherwise described in musicological terms. This second group of more technical qualities is also intended to serve as criteria for evaluating Parker's music of any period.

6. Characteristics of repertoire. Parker's repertoire was based on 32-measure song forms and the 12-measure (or "12-bar") blues form. The song forms included both popular songs and original jazz pieces, with most of the latter based on popular songs. New melodies were commonly superimposed upon chord progressions (chord changes) based on popular songs (a popular source was the chord progression of "I Got Rhythm," hence the term "Rhythm changes") Wholly "original" (newly composed in both melody and harmony) jazz compositions by Parker were rare in his repertoire. Parker's recorded repertoire is exclusively in duple meter (4/4 or 2/4). Concert keys B♭, F, and C are the most used.[2]

7. Range of tempos. Parker was at ease and could create striking improvisations over an extremely wide range of tempos. He performed ballads as slow as quarter note = 60, or about one beat per second, a slow dance tempo. Parker sometimes performed fast pieces (often based on "I Got Rhythm" chord changes) in excess of quarter note = 300 and even approaching quarter note = 400, not only too fast for most dancers but also too fast for most musicians.

8. Range of note values. Given the tempos mentioned above, one expects and finds in Parker's solos note values from whole notes (and longer) to sixty-fourth notes. Not surprisingly, his slower performances include the shortest note values, and they tend to have the widest variety of note values.

9. Use of implied double time. Double time (also known as "long-beat" or "long-meter) is the *implication* during a performance of a tempo that is twice the reference tempo. Melodies in modern jazz often involve the subdivision of a beat into two equal parts, that is to say into eighth notes. Implied double-timing involves subdividing the beat into *four*

equal parts, in other words into sixteenth notes. This doubling of the density of notes per beat makes it seem that the performance has doubled in tempo, but in fact the measures and chord changes are still passing by at the same rate. In this book, the term "double time" will always refer to an implied but not actual doubling of tempo unless otherwise specified. In his "apprenticeship" years, Parker was already adept at this approach at slower tempos (see chap. 2) and gradually became a master of the technique at progressively quicker tempos. Again, this technique is most prevalent in slow-to-medium tempo recordings; amazingly, some of his mature ballad solos seem to imply a tempo of *four* times the original (through strings of thirty-second notes).

10. Accents, syncopation. More than most jazz musicians of his or any other generation, Charlie Parker could accent freely virtually any note falling on any part of a subdivided beat, creating compelling syncopation over a basic 4/4 meter. Parker had remarkable control at all tempos, but the richest examples of creative accentuation occur in his slow pieces. Parker's most characteristic accentuations are found at melodic points of change of direction, and most typically at those points of change that are the high points (in terms of pitch) of melodic phrases. This usage of accentuation tended to give a whiplike snap to Parker's rapid lines. (In the transcriptions, accents are generally notated only when specifically discussed in the text.) Parker was adept at creating syncopation, often by creatively placing accents on unexpected parts of a subdivided beat. He also creatively employed cross-rhythms, often in conjunction with accentuation, to imply polyrhythms.

11. Vibrato and timbre (often called "tone" or "tone quality"). Most jazz alto saxophonists who came to stylistic maturity before 1945 employed a pronounced (with regard to depth and speed) vibrato, most in evidence on sustained notes, but sometimes in evidence in passages of shorter note values. Johnny Hodges and Benny Carter are often mentioned as models in this respect. During his mature period, Parker employed vibrato sparingly, usually as "terminal vibrato" at the end of sustained tones, most often on slow pieces, and never in moving passages of shorter notes. When employed, his vibrato was slower and narrower than that of Hodges or Carter. Parker's recorded alto sax timbre is not truly quantifiable, but there seems to be consensus among critics that his functional, streamlined timbral concept differs from the richness and sensuousness of the prevalent models of Hodges and Carter. A strong model for Parker's saxophone timbre was his Kansas City mentor, Buster Smith.

In an allied area, Parker seldom used (except when suggesting a bluesy quality) the pitch-bending "scoops," "falls," and portamento, which were the stock-in-trade of most alto saxophonists before 1945, preferring to attack most notes on-pitch and leave them there.

12. Characteristics of melodic line. Space prohibits full discussion here of this broad topic, but a few points may be made. When improvising, more conservative jazz musicians of the 1920s and 1930s tended to observe the four- and eight-bar building blocks of the blues and popular song, symmetrically setting up regular periods made of equal-length (two or four measures) phrases. The more adventurous players, however, varied their phrase and period lengths, and cut asymmetrically across structural divisions. Parker built upon the latter tradition and developed it to a high order. His recorded melodic phrases run from just a note or two (see "Klact-oveeseds-tene," chapter 5) to eight measures or more (numerous examples), and begin and end at virtually any part of a measure and at any point within a structural unit.

Charlie Parker, like all improvisers, built his solos from a personal collection of melodic building blocks of various lengths. In his best work, he employed these melodic units creatively as connective components and as raw material for creation. In his more routine work (especially in the 1950s), he used them more mechanically, in lieu of real discovery. The smallest-scale of these building blocks (often called "motives" or "figures") have been cataloged by jazz scholar Thomas Owens.[3] His analysis of Parker's melodic language is quite valuable and operates particularly well on that small scale. Apprehending these short figures can be difficult for the nontechnical listener, and many jazz lovers find it easier to recognize Charlie Parker's medium- to large-scale melodic units (often called "licks"). Parker had many such pet licks of his own invention, and they become increasingly recognizable as one gets to know his musical vocabulary. The blues lick noted in "Now's the Time" and the double-time run found in "Billie's Bounce" (both in chapter 3) are easily recognizable examples of pet Parker phrases. These longer building blocks, too, were used more routinely and with less creativity in the 1950s than previously.

One prevalent medium-scale melodic unit in Parker's recorded solos is his use of musical "quotations" (in other words, melodies not of his own invention—these are also mentioned in number 4, above). Quotations of all kinds are more likely to occur in recordings of "live" performances than in studio recordings. Early in his career, Parker often quoted other jazz artists' licks and compositions. Mature-period Parker solos are more likely to contain quotations of popular songs (including common-property melodies) and Western classical music pieces than quotations of other jazz players.

13. Harmonic vocabulary. Although the music of bebop with which Parker is associated was considered to be harmonically innovative within the jazz idiom, Parker's solos are more harmonically traditional or conservative than those of his peers Dizzy Gillespie and Thelonious Monk. Monk of course was a pianist; he favored dissonant harmonies and chord voicings and employed whole-tone scales liberally. Gillespie studied harmony at the piano keyboard, and not only enjoyed fresh harmonic movement and dissonant harmonies, but also appreciated "exotic" scales as melodic resources. The commonality of study at the keyboard led both Monk and Gillespie to have a stronger "vertical" component (placing a high priority on the outlining of chords and tonal areas) in their playing than Parker, who seemed to have conceived of his solos more "horizontally" (through the imperatives of melody). Parker evidently had a keen ear for harmony and quickly grasped the melodic implications of the chord progressions and chord alterations put forth by his peers (e.g., use of the "tritone substitution" for the dominant chord, and altered dominant chords that suggested whole-tone or diminished scales). Parker's harmonic conception was derived from many sources (such as emulation of recordings and absorption of his peers' practices), and it was gained with regard to practical application, with less regard to theory in the abstract than was true for Gillespie. Although Parker's route to musical knowledge was different than Gillespie's, the audible result was no less brilliant.

Most of his solos (with the exception of some Afro-Cuban pieces) are grounded in functional harmony and the major-minor system. "Higher" intervals of the ninth, eleventh, and thirteenth are commonly found melodically and in arpeggio. "Altered" intervals of dominant-seventh chords, while regularly present, were used by Parker less often than the reputation of bebop might suggest. Some of his chromaticism (e.g., chromatic passing-tones) was evidently arrived at through the imperatives of melodic direction and was probably not theoretically conceived. Parker also derived chromaticism in part through what is sometimes called "side-slipping" (e.g., playing a phrase an interval away from [usually a semitone above] the prevailing scale), and also in part through "sequencing" (e.g., taking a motive or pattern and presenting it at various pitch levels).

A Note on the Musical Examples

The musical examples that appear in this book are in "concert" key (not transposed for the saxophone) unless specified otherwise in the text. The vast majority of the examples in this book are of Parker's work on alto sax; these sound at the pitch notated. The few transcriptions of Parker playing tenor sax sound an octave lower than written, as their clefs indicate.

To aid the reader in finding the examples on compact discs, the CD timings are given at the beginning of each excerpt. (For a few excerpts, no reliable CD version was available to the author. Timings for those examples are approximate. In some of these cases, the performance in question had been issued uncorrected for speed ["Rocker," Sly Mongoose"]; in a few cases ["Shoe Shine Boy," "Lester Leaps In," "The Street Beat"], no CD version was in the author's collection.) In one case ("Honey & Body"), the readily available CD version was issued in an incomplete form; two examples ("Body" Ex. 2 and "Body" Ex. 3) occur after the readily available CD cuts off. Timings for those two examples are of course approximate; it is hoped that the original recording will be issued on CD in its entirety.

Measure numbers for the examples begin their count from the beginning of each solo or melody statement. Since Parker usually only soloed once per song, identifying the measure in question is generally easy. In a few cases ("Honeysuckle Rose," "Sweet Georgia Brown," "Parker's Mood"), Parker solos twice; in these cases, the numbering recommences from one at the beginning of the second solo. In the case of "Just Friends," Parker is in the foreground for almost the whole piece, playing an introduction, several solos, and a tag; in that case only, measure numbers proceed continuously from the beginning of the piece to its end.

Transcriptions of solos on pieces based on popular song forms have their subsections delineated by double bars, along with bold letters (such as AABA) in boxes above the double bars. Beginnings of choruses are also marked with double bars; in the case of the four complete solo transcriptions, multiple choruses are marked with bold numbers in boxes above those double bars.

The chord symbols given in the transcriptions are meant to represent either the basic harmonies for the piece or approximately what harmonies Parker's accompanist(s) play; chords in parenthesis just above the main chord-symbol line represent some of Parker's creative interpretations of the song's harmonies; these include implied passing chords, substitute chords, and chord alterations. A capital letter by itself signifies a major triad. Chord suffixes follow capital letters and express other chord types. In this book, the following chord suffixes are used:

- -   a minor triad
- +   an augmented triad
- ○   a diminished triad
- Δ7   a major seventh chord
- 7   a dominant seventh chord
- -7   a minor seventh chord
- ○7   a diminished seventh chord
- +7   a dominant seventh chord with an augmented fifth
- -Δ7   a minor triad with a major seventh

Readers familiar with roman numeral harmonic analysis will recognize chord progressions such as "ii-7–V7–I." In simple terms for the nontechnical reader, the roman numerals describe the root and quality of various chords, and, when written in a row, they describe a chord progression.

Inspired by Lester Young, Parker (especially early in his career) used alternate fingerings to give timbral shadings to certain tones; these are marked with "o" above or below the note heads. Parker had more than his share of equipment problems with his often borrowed saxophones. The most noticeable effect was the inadvertent production of notes an interval above or below the intended note. Generally, the inadvertent notes are marked with "x" note heads in the transcriptions; the notes that Parker actually fingered are marked with conventional note heads. The only exception is when Parker only momentarily produced a note displaced by an octave and immediately recovered into the correct one. These brief inadvertent notes are written as grace notes and include the notation "o.k." for "octave key."

The transcriptions do not attempt to specify all of Parker's articulations and accents; these are usually marked only when those aspects are described in the text in connection with the example.

The tempo markings given at the beginning of each transcription are approximate. Performances vary in tempo from moment-to-moment, plus many live recordings have been issued slightly (or greatly) off pitch. When found at the beginning of an example, the notation "corrected for pitch" means that the recording was far enough off pitch to warrant a speed correction; those tempo markings reflect approximately the speed at which the piece was actually performed.

Chapter 2

1940–43

In general, Charlie Parker's "apprenticeship" years are those during which he formed working relationships with older, more experienced musicians in order to better learn his craft. These years could be said to have begun in the mid-1930s when he quit school and tried to make a living as a musician, seeking tips from other musicians and free-lancing with various groups for short periods of time. In a more traditional sense, though, his more structured jazz apprenticeship began around 1937, when he was taken under the wing of saxophonist Buster Smith, who both advised him and employed him. His apprenticeship reached a new level in early 1940 when he rejoined Jay McShann, who was then beginning to tour over a wider area with an expanded band. Smith and McShann, were "master" craftsmen in that they were slightly older and possessed knowledge and/or experience that Parker valued.

Terms like "apprentice" and "master" are borrowed from the trades and crafts but do not always have precise meaning when applied to the arts. During the mid-1930s, Parker was more of a teenage hopeful than an accepted member of the Kansas City jazz community. After his 1937 summer breakthrough (chapter 1), Parker's status gradually changed to his being regarded as a talented up-and-comer. By the time of his departure for New York in early 1939, he was ready to build upon his knowledge by playing in a regularly working and touring band, but that experience that would have to wait until his formally joining McShann at the beginning of 1940.

The earliest date for studying Parker's apprenticeship period is 1940, simply because that is the first year for which recordings of Parker exist. By then, he had already advanced beyond many of his McShann band mates and was moving into a higher level of skill. The term "apprentice" applies less to the times when he and Dizzy Gillespie became their own and one another's teachers. Still, Parker would continue to hone his skills in big bands led by older, more established musicians (most notably Earl Hines) through most of 1943. That was simply the most common way to break into the national jazz arena.

Reinforcing the use of the term "apprentice" is the fact that Charlie Parker was one of the greatest students of jazz that the idiom has known. Study of his 1940–43 recordings (especially the informally made ones) reveal just how broad Parker's sphere of listening was. A rich indicator of his early listening habits is his use of quotations, the interpolation of one melody into another piece. The quotations found in his pre-1944 recordings reveal that Parker the student drew from a wide range of sources, learned them well, and used the source materials creatively rather than simply reproducing them. During that period, he was clearly listening to many players of the previous generation and did not limit his research to his own instrument, a habit that today's students would do well to emulate. Parker was blessed with a phenomenal mind for sounds; he could readily hear another jazz artist's idea (or indeed any musical idea), absorb it, retain it, and reproduce it in whatever key he later happened to be playing in (the same was true for pop songs).

For many years after his death in 1955, Charlie Parker's available apprenticeship recordings (those made prior to 1944 on which he is clearly audible) amounted to six titles. These six official recordings with Jay McShann for the Decca company from 1941 and 1942 consist of four improvised solos, one embellished theme statement, and one chorus of quiet "fills" behind a vocal solo. Parker's officially recorded solo legacy from this period (those made for established recording companies, in Parker's case, Decca) totals about seventy-two measures (the longest solo is about seventeen and a half measures long or about twenty-five seconds in duration) and the whole (leaving aside the spare vocal accompaniment) takes just over two minutes to listen to.

Based on such a small sample, it's clear why Parker's pre-1944 musical development was not well understood. The available examples of Parker improvising were too few and too short. Fortunately, beginning in the 1970s and continuing up to the present, a remarkable number of informally recorded items featuring Parker from this period have come to light and have been made available to the public. Just one of these newly discovered discs alone ("Honey & Body") features Parker in the foreground for over three minutes, by itself exceeding the total pre-1944 Parker solo work previously available.

As of this writing, approximately thirty of these developmental or apprenticeship recordings featuring Parker solos have been released (Parker's solo participation on a few items is debated, making the number uncertain). These recordings add a tremendous amount to our knowledge of Parker. First of all, they fill in chronological gaps in his discography. Previously, we had examples of Parker's early improvisational work from only 1941 and 1942. The new releases expand documentation of his early development to the years 1940 through 1943, inclusive (and, by extension, his entire career is now documented from 1940 through 1954, inclusive). Second, the developmental recordings now display Parker in the widest possible of musical settings, from solo saxophone without accompaniment to a full jazz big band for support. Finally, the newly available recordings feature Parker soloing over a much more varied repertoire of songs and tempos than would otherwise be available.

But even if these new discoveries did nothing to fill in gaps of chronology, setting, or repertoire, they would be of great interest to the listener for the amount of time on each disc that Parker is in the foreground, either improvising or stating a given melody. In his mature work (1944 and later), Parker was not known for long solos, either in "live" settings or in the recording studio. At least six of the newly released performances feature Parker in the foreground for over three minutes each. The pre-1944 period, once characterized by exceedingly short recorded Parker solos, now contains documentation of some of Parker's longest uninterrupted work, regardless of period. At last we are in a position to examine thoroughly Charlie Parker's apprenticeship or developmental work, noting influences and describing stylistic evolution.[1]

With respect to Parker's stylistic characteristics just outlined in the "Introduction to the Musical Chapters," Parker's 1940–43 music already suggests most of the qualities associated with his mature work. These qualities are generally in a developmental state, but they are consistent with the better-known later Parker. In comparison with his band mates of the period, Parker more than holds his own with respect to command of instrument. At up-tempos, he is regularly the most comfortable of all the soloists, and at ballad tempos, he is already highly complex both rhythmically and melodically. Beginning with the earliest recordings, Parker displays a great inner sense of swing that is quite compelling. His early improvisations also reveal much of the quickness and playfulness associated with his later music. His developmental recordings already contain an essential feeling for the blues, if not at the profound depth of his later work.

There is also a striking sense of freshness to these early recordings. Parker was certainly in the midst of an exciting period of artistic discovery, but more than that, his approach to improvisation seemed to emphasize the spontaneous creation of melody in the manner of tenor saxophonist Lester Young. Of course, he employed a certain amount of prepared melodic material ("licks"), but his art had not yet become codified into a lick-based language as it did in the 1950s.

In contrast with his later career as a bandleader, during this early period Parker did not choose his own repertoire because he was usually working under the leadership of others (McShann or Hines, for example). Even when recording on his own (on the nonprofessional recordings), his repertoire fell within the common practice of the day, that is to say it was based on the thirty-two-measure popular song form and the twelve-measure blues form. Although Parker is sometimes credited as co-composer of "Hootie Blues," and arranger of "The Jumpin' Blues," compositions clearly and solely by Parker are not documented on the early recordings.[2]

Parker performed this repertoire at tempos well within the common practice, ranging from approximately quarter note = 84 to quarter note = 280, and he did not quite approach the extremely rapid tempos of his later work. He often seems more at ease than his fellow players on the faster material, though he did not yet have the up-tempo virtuosity of an Art Tatum.

Similarly, Parker's early range of note values is broad, but not as broad as his later work. From his first recording, Parker displays an interest in double-timing on slow pieces but was evidently technically unable to sustain it on faster material. By 1943 he was beginning to incorporate short bursts of double-timing on medium-swing material. Parker had already developed the tendency to accent the high points of his melodic lines. Those accents often fall on the beat, because he had not developed full flexibility to accent freely within a subdivided beat. Syncopation, whether produced by accentuation or cross-rhythm, is less varied than in his mature work.

Parker's early work employs vibrato more often and at a slightly faster rate than found in his later work; in fact, he occasionally seems nervous. He does, when "sweet" material calls for it, employ a nearly constant vibrato in the popular tradition, a practice he would soon abandon. Parker's alto sax tone evolved subtly between 1940 and 1943. Aural evidence suggests his tone gradually became less edgy, but due to the low fidelity of the amateur recordings, conclusions are difficult to make. The stripped-down and functional timbral ideal found in the early recordings is consistent with his later timbral values.

Especially in the earlier developmental solos, Parker often stops to begin a new thought at or near a formal division. The later solos within this period show more freedom to build phrases that truly cut across structural divisions. Many melodic figures that Parker continued to use in his mature work are noticeable, although his early repertoire of building blocks was more limited. Parker's practice of "quoting" one piece in the performance of another was already prevalent. As in his mature work, he was more likely to use quotations outside the formal recording studio, although some shift in the sources of the material borrowed seems to have occurred between his apprenticeship and his masterful work. Especially in his early work, Parker's use of quotations provides strong clues about his formative influences and early listening habits.

Parker the apprentice was already interested in an enriched harmonic palette and arrived at the chromaticism he desired within a framework of functional harmony. The means he employed were simply less developed than those in his mature period. Already present in his work are altered dominant chords, chord substitutions, side-slipping, and sequencing (discussed in "Introduction to the Musical Chapters"). Parker's early harmonic vocabulary is also consistent with that of his mature period in that it is oriented toward application rather than derived from theory in the abstract.

Small-Group Recordings on Alto Sax

Before 1944, Charlie Parker was recorded on four occasions (as far as is known) playing alto sax in intimate settings (ranging from solo to octet). In each case, these were informally recorded sessions undertaken strictly for the pleasure of those present and were never intended for release. Because these recordings all find Parker playing alto sax during the same period in non–big band settings, because many feature him in the foreground at greater-than-usual length, and because several songs appear in more than one session, it makes sense to discuss them together. (A discussion of Parker's concurrent alto sax work with the full McShann big band and his tenor sax recordings of 1943 will follow later in this chapter.)

Honey & Body

An ideal starting point for reaching an appreciation of Charlie Parker's apprenticeship period is what is often said to be his first recording, "Honey & Body." Consisting of both a medium-swing section and a ballad section, it exemplifies many of the musical qualities associated with early Parker. A complete transcription of this performance appears in Appendix B.

Sometime around 1940, Kansas City trumpeter Clarence Davis recorded on an amateur disc-cutter alto saxophonist Charlie Parker improvising a medley of two songs. Although the performance has been referred to under a variety of names, Davis labeled his disc simply "Honey & Body," and that is how it will be referred to here.[3] "Honey & Body" is unique in the discography of Parker in that is the only known recording of him playing unaccompanied saxophone (in this case, the alto) continuously for any length beyond a few seconds. The date of recording of this disc has been debated among Parker scholars. One claim (by the disc's last-known owner, Carroll Jenkins) states that it was recorded in 1937 when Charlie Parker was sixteen or seventeen.[4] It is known that Clarence Davis played with Parker in 1937, making this date possible. But careful listening and analysis provide important clues that indicate a later date of recording for the disc.

Unfortunately, the version of this performance that is most commonly available in the U.S. (see appendix A) fades out at the point when the needle stuck in the groove when transferring the original disc for release. Significantly, another version on audio tape that has circulated among collectors and is available as a French import (see appendix A) continues beyond that point without sticking and offers a significantly more complete performance. The complete transcription in appendix B is based on the longer version.[5] (Compact disc timings that are given to help the listener find specific moments in "Honey & Body" derive from the generally available but incomplete version on the Stash label.)

From a rhythmic standpoint, the absence of rhythmic accompaniment on "Honey & Body" means that the listener can easily grasp Parker's developing sense of "time," i.e., his conception and execution of rhythm and swing. Without accompanists to state a ground beat, Parker must, with a single melodic line, actively create a rhythmic fabric on which to organize his improvisation over time. Having done so, he may then work against that sense of meter to suggest syncopation.

From a harmonic standpoint, the absence of chordal accompaniment means that the responsibility to outline tonal areas, cadences, and chord progressions falls solely on Charlie. He cannot rely upon his accompanists to contextualize his melodic improvisation; the improvisation harmonically sinks or swims on his ability to imply tonality, cadences, and progressions. By the same token, he is not harmonically limited by his accompanists; any ingenuity or flights of fancy need not be justified by preset harmonies provided by another instrument. Thus, the state of Charlie's harmonic knowledge and imagination is made quite clear.[6]

"Honey & Body" is in two parts, and both relate to Parker's disastrous experience sitting in with Jimmy Keith's band (see chapter 1). The first part, "Honey," is an improvisation upon the chord progression and form of Fats Waller's composition "Honeysuckle Rose."[7] Upon first listening to "Honey & Body," it becomes apparent that even at this young age, Charlie Parker had a highly developed sense of swing. Even without a rhythm section, the performance has a pleasing forward motion and "drive." Parker's tone on this recording is subjectively thin, bluesy, and cutting. Positively it could be called streamlined, without the deep vibrato pulsations of a Johnny Hodges or Benny Carter, and therefore well suited to rapid lines. Negatively, Parker's tone seems a bit shrill and undeveloped, and it is not a flexible expressive tool. Vibrato, when used, is found on the notes of medium-to-long duration. Although the pulsations are not deep, they are rather rapid, and lend a slight air of nervousness. Considering his later eschewing of vibrato, he is surprisingly quick to call it into action.

When adjusted to correct pitch, "Honey" is performed at a "medium swing" tempo of approximately quarter note = 194.[8] As such, "Honey" fits in the middle of Parker's range of tempos. The basic rhythmic unit is the eighth note; the longest note value is the half note and the shortest is the triplet sixteenth. Sixteenths of any type are used rarely, and usually in embellishment figures; they are never used in "Honey" to imply double-time. As will be seen later, during this period Parker evidently could not convincingly sustain an implied double-time at this tempo. The use of accents is fairly regular and conservative; accentuation is not yet a highly developed tool for expressing syncopation. Note that he has problems getting certain notes on the saxophone to "speak"; in measures 25–28, 42, and 60 (marked "o.k."), he seems to have trouble with his octave key or in fingering the octave, producing unusual octave displacements and unusual tone qualities. This tendency may be due to a technical problem with his saxophone and will be noted in several later solos as well.

The first phrase heard on the disc is especially significant. It contains the Lester Young-derived kernel of the opening to Parker's "The Jumpin' Blues" solo (see below), which was later adapted by Benny Harris for his composition "Ornithology." Not surprisingly, Parker repeats variants of it twice in measures 60–62. Parker scholar Thomas Owens identifies the kernel as Motive 2A (an "inverted mordent"); he found about 1,400 examples of it in his survey of Parker motives![9]

"Honey" Ex. 1

In measure 16 the first appearance of an even more pervasive melodic/rhythmic unit for this performance appears, a series of repeated pitches (here, and in most cases, on D), syncopated on the "ands" of the beats. Later occurrences include measures 49, 112, and 96 (the latter on C). From a rhythmic standpoint, the on-the-beat quarter notes (containing at least one repeated pitch) found in measures 75, 89–90, and 104 may be considered at the same time. Both types (on the beat and off the beat) function more rhythmically than melodically; their function is to *swing,* the former type by stating the beat and the latter by working against one's sense of it. Listeners familiar only with mature-period Parker will find these repeated notes unusual; those familiar with the music of Lester Young will find clear precedent in Young's work (e.g., the opening phrase of his September 5, 1939, "Lester Leaps In" [master take] solo).

Parker fairly liberally plays phrases that cut across the eight-bar sections of "Honeysuckle Rose." This asymmetry is more associated with his mature (post-1943) work than with early recordings such as this. The absence of accompaniment may free him in this regard. One can also note the lack of adherence to standard two- and four-measure phrases and only occasional use of periods made of antecedent and consequent phrases. Phrases are found in a wide variety of lengths, with six measures approximately the maximum.

One of Parker's best-known practices was to quote fragments of various melodies during improvisation. One that stands out in "Honey" is the quotation of "Am I Blue?" in measures 105–9.

"Honey" Ex. 2

A particularly creative usage of the technique comes in measures 97–100, with a reference to "Honeysuckle Rose," from which "Honey" takes its name. This quotation is not only significant melodically, but also harmonically. Parker creatively takes advantage of his lack of accompaniment to sequence the fragment at three additional pitch levels, implying a chain of ii-7–V7 chord substitutions.[10] Art Tatum was considered a master of such harmonic asides, and Parker often heard Tatum perform in New York in 1939 (see chapter 1).

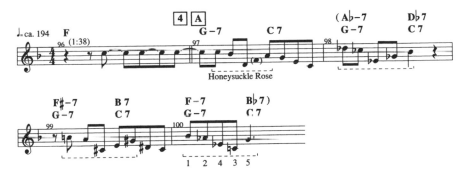

"Honey" Ex. 3

Another chord substitution, this one involving a half-step relationship, can be found in the implied ♭VI7–V7 progression in measures 55–56. Immediately following (measures 57–58; Example 4), Parker takes a four-note figure, repeats it, then transposes it up a semitone. Such departures from the prevailing tonality heighten our experience of tonality upon resolution.

"Honey" Ex. 4

After humorously tossing in a common-property "jingle" (yet another quotation), Parker clearly modulates from F to D♭ to set up "Body," based on the popular song "Body and Soul." He halves the tempo (which has slackened somewhat), and quickly begins implying double time, making the basic rhythmic unit the sixteenth note. He double-times convincingly, and, as in "Honey," one does not miss the propulsion of a rhythm section. The range of note values is greater than in "Honey" (varying from half note to thirty-second triplet), but it should be remembered that the tempo is about half the preceding.

Phrase lengths in "Body" vary considerably, with four measures being about the maximum length. Phrases begin on a wide variety of beats within a measure. The phrases' symmetry or asymmetry varies according to place. When Parker is more closely embellishing the original melody (such as in the A sections), the phrases, not surprisingly, are molded by the song's small-scale two- and four-measure phraseology. Parker seems a little freer to let phrases spin out to their natural lengths during the B or "bridge" section (measures 17–24), when he is not outlining the melody at all. On the next-larger scale, however, he clearly observes the eight-measure structural divisions (AABA) more conservatively than he would in his mature period; each section begins with a new thought, and phrases do not truly cut across those divisions.

From a melodic standpoint, the most prevalent unifying thematic element in "Body" is the original melody, which is most in evidence in the A sections. Parker works around the melody by embellishing it, paraphrasing it, digressing from it, and returning to it. There are also several possible references to other songs, and these provide clues as to the date of recording of this disc. The first reference is a modulatory phrase that leads to the B section (measure 16, beats two through four; "Body" Ex.

1). These eight notes (which form a ii-7–V7–I pattern) represent a quotation of trumpeter Roy Eldridge from a recording of "Body and Soul" led by saxophonist Chu Berry and recorded for Commodore on October 10, 1938, and probably released in early 1939.[11] It is known that Parker learned Eldridge solos[12] and that he was familiar with the Berry/Eldridge recording (see the sections "The Wichita Transcriptions" and "The Charles White Discs," below). After relying for a few years on this eight-note lick to lead into the bridge of "Body and Soul," Parker stopped using it by the mid-1940s but returned to it in 1950, this time explicitly in connection with Roy Eldridge (chapter 5). Given the quotation of Eldridge in "Body," the claims that this disc was recorded in 1937 are therefore untenable.

"Body" Ex. 1

An additional melodic clue also supports a later time period for the recording of "Honey & Body." The phrase immediately following the Eldridge quotation in "Body" is evidently a quotation of the Jimmy Van Heusen popular song "I Thought About You" (Body Ex. 1). After the C♯ pickup note, the next six notes are the same as the opening phrase of Van Heusen's song.[13] "I Thought About You" was copyrighted in 1939 (while Parker was in New York), and the first jazz recordings of it (by Benny Goodman and at least two other swing era bandleaders) were made in October, 1939. The earliest Parker could have heard the pop song on record was probably November, 1939; since Parker's own statements (chapter 1) place him on the East Coast in December, 1939, the earliest date for the Kansas City recording of "Honey & Body" is approximately January, 1940.[14]

Even at twenty years of age, Charlie Parker possessed a highly developed ability to recognize and develop melodic and rhythmic motives spontaneously created in the act of improvisation. Such a moment comes during the bridge of "Body" when a simple three-note motive in sixteenth notes is parlayed into two answering ("antecedent-consequent") phrases:

"Body" Ex. 2

Without any harmonic accompaniment, Parker nevertheless has a clear idea of the basic harmonic stations of "Body and Soul" and also has some ideas on how he wishes to elaborate upon them and modify them. Perhaps the most prevalent device (because he uses it at least three times) is the so-called tritone substitution for the dominant seventh chord at a cadence. In the second bar of every A section (measures 2, 10, and 26), Parker replaces the traditional A♭7 with a D7, a substitute chord whose root is a tritone (three whole steps, or six half steps) away from the usual chord. The resulting progression, then is E♭-7 to D7 to D♭, or ii-7–♭II7–I.

"Body" Ex. 3

This harmonic device is associated with the 1940s and bebop, but in fact was practiced by more advanced earlier players such as Art Tatum and Coleman Hawkins, both of whom Parker studied.[15] Parker very carefully outlines the chord each time, perhaps because he had a limited number of ways of navigating the substitution, or because without harmonic accompaniment, he wanted to be very explicit. Another point of harmonic interest in "Body" is Parker's implication of a ♭9 alteration to the F7 chord in measure 6. He accomplishes this through a descending line derived from the harmonic minor scale of the following B♭-7 chord. Similar use of the harmonic minor became common in jazz during the bebop era.

A good example of the still developing nature of Parker's harmonic knowledge is the expected chain of three descending chords in the last bar of the B section (measure 24): C7–B7–B♭7. On the first beat, Parker clearly outlines a C7 chord in arpeggio. What follows on beats two and three is not completely clear; if he is trying to imply the descending chords, they seem to get away from him until beat four, when he manages to right himself and lead by semitone into the first note of the next bar (the last A section). Listened to without harmonic preconception, the measure sounds surprising but effective. It is to Parker's credit that he "sells" this possible misstep with such authoritative delivery.

The Wichita Transcriptions

The so-called Wichita Transcriptions were recorded at Wichita radio station KFBI on November 30, 1940, by members of the Jay McShann Orchestra, including alto saxophonist Charlie Parker. They are called "transcriptions" because they were once thought to have been recorded ("transcribed") for later radio broadcast, but in fact jazz fans Pete Armstrong and Fred Higginson, and musician Bud Gould, recorded the band simply out of their own enthusiasm. The radio station simply offered good recording facilities and easy access through Gould's job in the house band at KFBI.[16] Parker historians knew that the session had taken place, but most assumed that the discs were long lost. Miraculously, the discs were found in surprisingly good condition by jazz historian Frank Driggs in 1959, and they were first legitimately released in 1974.

On the date, a septet (two trumpets, trombone, alto sax, tenor sax, piano, bass, and drums) recorded two pieces, "I've Found a New Baby" and "Body and Soul." On the same date (not at a later date as originally believed[17]), a similar septet recorded five pieces; "Moten Swing," "Coquette," "Oh, Lady Be Good!," an untitled blues (later released as "Wichita Blues"), and "Honeysuckle Rose." Even though the group is not quite the full McShann band (four McShann players reportedly did not attend the session), the Wichita Transcriptions add to our understanding of the group with respect to the band's repertoire and Parker's role in it better than the "official" McShann studio recordings on the Decca label. Parker is featured on all but one of the band pieces, although thirty-two measures is the most space he is given on a given performance (the discs lasted only about three minutes, so extended soloing by any one member is unlikely).

While still somewhat thin and edgy, Parker's tone throughout the Wichita recordings seems less shrill than on "Honey & Body." Some of the difference could be explained by the more professional recording techniques. Parker's vibrato seems more under control and less nervous, although it remains more in evidence than in his post-1943 recordings. Of the pieces on which he is featured, the slowest is "Body and Soul" (quarter note = ca. 106); the fastest is "Honeysuckle Rose" (quarter note = ca. 278). These tempos are within the common practice in jazz of 1940, but it should be noted that, at twenty years of age, Parker is already the most comfortable of the players at the latter tempo. Given a rhythm section, his sense of swing is even more solid than on "Honey & Body." He lets the band propel him and swings on top of their beat. Except for "Body and Soul," the basic rhythmic unit of the solos is the eighth note. Sixteenth notes are rare and are generally used in ornamentation and as pick-up notes. Parker does not attempt passages that imply double time except in the slow "Body and Soul," and indeed double-timing at medium- or up-tempo is not found in early Parker until the Charles White and Redcross discs of 1943–44 (see below). He simply did not yet have the instrumental virtuosity to "bring off" this difficult technique except at ballad tempos.

Since the two chord progressions that form the basis of "Honey & Body" ("Honeysuckle Rose" and "Body and Soul") recur on the Wichita sides, they form a good starting point for discussion. With the Wichita version of "Body and Soul," Parker and friends show that they were familiar with the aforementioned 1938 Chu Berry–Roy Eldridge version of the song by appropriating the slow-fast-slow arrangement in which the saxophone solo is played at a slow tempo, followed by a trumpet solo at twice the previous tempo (not an implied double time; for the trumpet solo, the measures pass at twice their previous rate), and concluding with the original tempo. Since Parker solos only at the slower tempo, his work on this "Body and Soul" is easily compared with the earlier "Body" segment of "Honey & Body." The two versions are similar in approach, but a few distinctions may be drawn.

Parker's solo on "Body and Soul" is the only one of the Wichita Transcriptions that features implied double time, and as in "Body," Parker seems quite at home with the technique. Parker gradually works into it and sustains it quite successfully during the second and last A sections. Compared to "Body," however, Parker devotes less space on "Body and Soul" to melodic lines that imply double time and instead refers to the original melody a little more often. Parker may have simply wished to stick closer to the tune, or perhaps the faster tempo of "Body and Soul" (twenty beats per minute quicker than "Body") made double time a little more difficult to bring off. At any rate, the greater reference to the original melody fits well with the "sweet" scooping, portamento, vibrato, and timbre that Parker adopts on this cut ("Coquette," discussed below, emphasizes even more strongly these aspects of "sweet" alto sax style). Another distinction between the earlier and later versions is the degree to which Parker outlines the chord progression through arpeggiation. In "Body," there was no harmonic accompaniment at all, so Parker chose to improvise more vertically, probably in order to make the chord progression more clear. Piano and bass *were* present for "Body and Soul," so Parker had more melodic/harmonic options; he chose to be a little less vertical. Parker's harmonic knowledge already outstripped his rhythm section's, so his sticking closer to his accompanists' chord changes means less evidence of Parker's advanced harmonic thinking. For example, in this later version, Parker does not utilize the tritone substitution progression (ii-7–♭II7–I) that had figured prominently in "Body."

Melodic quotations in "Body and Soul" once again give a clue to the young Parker's sphere of listening. As in "Body," he uses Roy Eldridge's lick to modulate into the new key of the B section (0:39). The second A section contains the above-mentioned quotation from Coleman Hawkins's 1939 "Body and Soul." Parker had done his homework well; only one note of his borrowing departs from the original (the E♭ pitch within beat four of measure 11 was played by Hawkins as a D natural). Hawkins played the phrase in measures *2 and 3* of the last A of his first chorus (measures 25 and 26 overall); Parker places the phrase in measures *3 and 4* of the second A of his only chorus (measures 11 and 12; 1:27). Parker's delayed placement results in the Hawkins phrase no longer fitting the accompanimental harmonies. Only one moment produces an outright "clash" with the chords (the first beat of measure 12; it had been a clash for Hawkins, too). Whether the displacement was planned or unplanned is unclear. The twenty-year-old Parker may have viewed the phrase as simply a fascinating lick and not known enough about harmony to understand *why* Hawkins placed it where he did; or possibly, Parker may have known what made the phrase work but elected to displace it to create a little tension (see "Just Friends" in chapter 5). In any case, the quotation, displaced by one bar, is convincing in part due to the authority with which Parker plays the phrase.

"Honeysuckle Rose" departs more radically from the earlier "Honey" than "Body and Soul" does from the earlier "Body." "Honey"

"Body and Soul" (1940)

had been performed around quarter note = 194; "Honeysuckle Rose," the fastest of the Wichita sides, was done at a much more rapid quarter note = ca. 280. One result of the tempo change is seen in Parker's emphasis on long strings of driving eighth notes instead of the greater rhythmic variety found in "Honey." The effect predicts much of bebop of five and ten years later with regard to melodic contours and swing.

Parker has two solo spots on "Honeysuckle Rose," 32 measures and 8 measures. The former begins with a quotation of Lester Young's opening to his 1937 solo on "Honeysuckle Rose" with Count Basie.[18] Parker's solo continues with a good example of the state of his accenting art in measures 9 through 12. His accents fall on the high points of note groups, initially on the beat (measures 9 and 10), then more typically of his mature period on the "ands" of the beat (measures 11 and 12). The latter practice, especially, lends a snap and a forward motion to the line.

"Honeysuckle Rose" Ex. 1

Moments later, in the B section, Parker plays a melodic/harmonic component that would be an important part of his vocabulary until the end of his career. This figure[19] involves selecting a particular pitch and approaching it ("voiceleading") first from above (by either a half or whole step), then from below (always by two half steps in succession). Parker scholar Thomas Owens speculates that Parker may have learned the figure from Duke Ellington's composition "Concerto for Cootie."[20] It should also be pointed out that the first four notes of the figure as presented in "Honeysuckle Rose" (B♭, G, G♯, and A) are identical in pitch to the first four notes of the Ellington composition. In the case of "Honeysuckle Rose" (and as will be seen in "Billie's Bounce" in chapter 3), Parker presents the figure twice, with the final note or "target" of the first presentation also serving as the initial note of the second presentation. Note how the notes lead to each circled target tone and the two presentations of the figure creatively overlap.

"Honeysuckle Rose" Ex. 2

A glimpse of Parker's harmonic thinking appears in his second solo spot in measures 23 and 24 (measured from the beginning of the chorus in question) where he convincingly side-slips up a half step (superimposing a D♭7 over the rhythm section's C7; perhaps Parker was implying a ♭VI7 to V7 cadence) and smoothly reenters, a preview of Parker's harmonic expertise to come.

"Honeysuckle Rose" Ex. 3

McShann's bassist Gene Ramey commented on Parker's practice of side-slipping a new tonal center one half step above the song's prevailing tonality.

For instance, we used to jam "Cherokee" a lot, and Bird a way of starting on a B natural against the B flat chord, and he would run a cycle against that—and probably it would only be two or three bars before we got to the channel [middle part] that he would come back to the basic changes. In those days we used to call it "running out of key."[21]

This practice was fairly common in the music of one of Parker's early influences, Art Tatum, whom Parker regularly heard during his first trip to New York City.

Nearly as fast as "Honeysuckle Rose" is "I've Found a New Baby," taken at quarter note = ca. 258. Tenor saxophonist Lester Young had recorded the song in 1937 under the leadership of Teddy Wilson, but even though the two solos share general qualities of melodic rise and fall, approach to swing, similar tempos, and the fact that both are in the same key (E♭ major), Parker's actual notes do not contain any direct quote of Young's version. The next time Parker recorded the song, however, he would make his debt to Young explicit (see "The Charles White Discs," below).

Although Parker had a wide range of listening habits and musical influences, a dominant influence was certainly Lester Young, who was based in Kansas City through late 1936. Parker may have heard him play in person and definitely studied Young's recordings (see chapter 1). When Young first recorded in 1936, he offered an alternative to Coleman Hawkins with regard to tenor sax timbre, vibrato, approach to swing, and melodic line. Young's seminal influences had been alto saxophonist Jimmy Dorsey (also one of Parker's early favorites) and most importantly Frankie Trumbauer (who, while associated with the lower "C-melody" sax, also recorded well-known solos on alto[22]). Both saxophonists featured compact timbres that were formulated before the dominance of the more rich sounds of Johnny Hodges and Benny Carter.[23] Young, with his ties to alto saxophone style, was a fitting model for the young Parker. One attraction for Parker was Young's sparing use of vibrato (usually employed only on sustained tones): "I never cared for vibrato . . . because they used to get a chin vibrato in Kansas City . . . and I didn't like it. I don't think I'll ever use vibrato."[24] Parker later tried to minimize Young's influence upon him: "I was crazy about Lester. . . . But I wasn't influenced by Lester. Our ideas ran on differently."[25] The early Parker recordings, however, reveal a considerable Young influence, and in fact Parker's pre-1944 recordings contain more references to Young than to any other musician. This is quite appropriate because Parker was one of the greatest *students* of jazz in his researching, emulating, absorbing, and, finally, transcending of his early models.

One of the Count Basie/Lester Young records that Charlie Parker took with him to study during his pivotal stay in the Ozark Mountains in 1937 (described in chapter 1) was a performance of George Gershwin's pop song "Oh, Lady Be Good!" (often called simply "Lady Be Good") with a sixty-four-measure solo by Young (for contractual reasons, the record was released under the name of "Jones-Smith Incorporated"). "Oh, Lady Be Good!" is in a thirty-two-bar AABA song form and is performed by both Jones-Smith and McShann in the key of G concert (in the key of A on Young's tenor sax, and in E for Parker's alto). Its simple harmonies do not present the more difficult modulations of a "Body and Soul," and they lend themselves to a diatonic, "horizontal" approach as favored by Young. Several authors have suggested comparing the 33 1/3 RPM Jones-Smith and McShann versions of "Oh, Lady Be Good!" by manipulating turntable speed, either by slowing down Parker's alto sax solo to 16 RPM or by speeding up Young's tenor sax solo to 45 RPM. The latter scheme (which raises the speed by 35 percent) works best because it transposes the B♭ tenor almost exactly a perfect fourth higher, into the same range as the E♭ alto. The results are striking; at normal speed, Parker's timbre, melodic contours, and sense of swing are remarkably similar to a sped-up Young. One way to conceive of Charlie Parker's brilliance at only twenty years of age is to imagine Lester Young's mind operating a third faster than usual.

Parker's solo on "Oh, Lady Be Good!" opens up with a repeated note figure of four quarter notes on the tonic, played on the beat, before rising to the major third and continuing on. This figure is borrowed from Lester Young, but not from his "Oh, Lady Be Good!" solo. Young's solo on the 1939 "Lester Leaps In" (based on the chord progression of George Gershwin's "I Got Rhythm" and in B♭ concert) likewise opens with repeated notes on the tonic (five, not four) before rising to the major third.

"Oh, Lady Be Good!"

In addition to the Lester Young borrowings already mentioned, Parker also quotes the pop song "Mean to Me" in measures 25 and 26 (1:41).

Although Parker was evidently not able to sustain sixteenth notes (four notes per beat) at medium- and up-tempos, on "Moten Swing" he attempted the next-to-most-rapid rhythmic subdivision: the eighth-note triplet (three notes per beat). In measures 9 and 10 of Parker's solo (0:58), he plays a slightly shaky and inconsistently executed run in triplets. It would be a few years more before he could bring off such a phrase with aplomb.

Thus far, transcribed comparisons have been made between Parker and Roy Eldridge, Coleman Hawkins, and Lester Young. The Wichita version of "Moten Swing" also illustrates Parker's debt to one of his early influences. As mentioned in chapter 1, Kansas City-based alto saxophonist Buster Smith served as an important firsthand musical model for the young Parker in the late 1930s. While not as innovative an artist as Young, Smith was an excellent musical role model for Parker. His alto saxophone timbre had the clarity that Parker liked, and it could take on a Southwest bluesy "wail" in the upper register. Smith employed vibrato with some restraint, and this too must have appealed to Parker. In the tried-and-true jazz tradition, Parker went through a stage of emulating his mentor, as Jay McShann observed:

> Bird worked with Buster, you know. He worked with Buster's group, and that was Bird's man. You know Bird—I remember I heard a broadcast one night, during the time Bird was working with Prof ["Professor" Smith], and so I told Prof, I said "Prof," I says, "you sure did sound good last night." He says, "What do you mean 'sound good last night,'" he says, "I didn't play last night." . . . "That was Charlie Parker you heard last night."[26]

A good sense of Parker's debt to Smith is reached by comparing Parker's version of "Moten Swing" with the 1940 version of the same song by Smith (recorded under the leadership of Eddie Durham).[27] Their respective approaches to melodic line, swing, and timbre are quite complementary. Parker scholar Thomas Owens has even found a brief three-note fragment both saxophonists play at analogous points of A sections,[28] even though Parker could not have heard Smith's recording. (Smith's was recorded in New York City on November 11, 1940, Parker's in Wichita on November 30, 1940.) Parker may have played many whole phrases that derived from Smith, but—unlike Eldridge, Hawkins, and Young—few Smith solos were recorded during the time that Parker was formulating his style, thus limiting our ability to precisely correlate the two saxophonists' work.

Probably the most unusual Parker performance on the Wichita Transcriptions is the sweet pop song, "Coquette." Parker's contribution to the song consists of twenty-four measures (sixteen plus eight) of melody statement with a fair number of embellishments. His performance is sentimental in the style of the day, and employs a more-constant vibrato that is comparatively rapid and shallow. This is the Parker who admired Jimmy Dorsey's alto sax style (indeed, "Coquette" was recorded by the Dorsey Brothers in 1928). Despite his "sweet" interpretation, Parker's embellishments speak of a more "hip" aesthetic, and he can't resist throwing in a blues lick coming into the last A section (1:02).

The Jerry Newman Disc

"Cherokee" is another nonofficial recording that was not available to most critics and listeners before 1974. It was found in the estate of Jerry Newman, who, while he was a Columbia University student, brought a portable disc recorder to several Harlem after-hours nightclubs for the purpose of capturing jazz in an informal "live" setting. He was fascinated by the established swing era players and recorded them prolifically. He also managed to single-handedly document the legendary after-hours musical explorations of such forward looking players as Charlie Christian, Thelonious Monk, Kenny Clarke, and Dizzy Gillespie. Were it not for these recordings, we would be missing much more of the transitional period between the swing era and modern jazz. How sympathetic Newman was to these explorations is not known; he most likely recorded Monk and Clarke because they were accompanying established players in their role as the "house" rhythm section at Minton's Playhouse. Charlie Parker was evidently not a strong interest of Newman's; "Cherokee" is the only item including Parker that has surfaced from Newman's estate (likewise, Gillespie was not a prime interest of Newman's and was only recorded a few times). Current discographical information cites this disc as being recorded at Monroe's Uptown House in 1942, making it contemporary with the Jay McShann Savoy Ballroom recordings discussed below. It is not known precisely when the McShann band arrived in New York, but the group began their Savoy engagement in January, 1942, making that year a likely one for this recording.[29] The exact instrumentation on "Cherokee" is unclear. A trumpeter and at least one other saxophonist in addition to Parker are audible; a pianist and bassist can be heard; and some occasional drum accents seem to be present.

At quarter note = ca. 260 (it gradually loses tempo), "Cherokee" is nearly as fast as the fastest Parker recording of this period, "Honeysuckle Rose," but still far short of the fastest tempos of his mature period. As usual, Parker is at ease and swings hard at up-tempo. The basic rhythmic unit of the solo is the eighth note, with sixteenth notes used only for embellishments and pick-ups. Double-timing is not employed, nor would it usually be at this tempo even in his mature period recordings. Accents, as expected, fall on the high points of a melodic line and usually on the beat (e.g., measures 101–8; 2:36). A short but good example of off-the-beat accents producing syncopation occurs in measures 45 and 46 (1:42), where the high points occur on the "ands" of beats and are effectively accented. Due to the limited fidelity and surface noise of this disc, Parker's alto saxophone tone on "Cherokee" is difficult to discuss in comparison with the other recordings. His tone has the streamlined, "cutting" sound we associate with him, but it is not reproduced well enough to draw any conclusions about its evolution in aesthetic or technical terms.

Parker's melodic phrases on "Cherokee" may begin on any beat or between beats. His phrase lengths vary from portions of a bar to a full ten bars. Parker's second chorus is punctuated by "riffs" from the other horns; he responds by often leaving rests in his melodic lines. The solo's phrases show some asymmetry within formal units and occasionally cut across formal divisions (especially in the first chorus, before the band's riffs mold his A sections into short units). Melodic quotations from other songs do not seem to be a factor in "Cherokee," although some may be as yet unidentified. Parker's improvisation opens with a gesture familiar from "Honey & Body" and "The Jumpin' Blues" (see above), although in those cases the underlying tonality was F, not B♭.

From a harmonic standpoint, the A sections of "Cherokee" are not particularly sophisticated for a 1930s popular song, nor do they present the improviser with particularly difficult problems. The B section, however, *is* unusual harmonically for the period and had a reputation of being difficult to improvise upon. (For an example of its daunting effect on improvisers, one need only listen to Count Basie's 1939 extended (two sides of a 78 record) version of the song; no soloist improvises on the B section, and indeed, after the first two complete AABA choruses, the A section is repeated *fourteen* times, with the B never being heard again! Significantly, Parker's model, Lester Young, only solos on the A section.)

The reason for this avoidance was the bridge's chord progression, especially the first eight measures. It cadences (via ii-7–V7–I progressions) into the keys of B major, A major, and G major before moving toward the B♭ tonic. The first two key areas particularly put transposing band instruments into unfamiliar keys. Because of Charlie Barnet's 1939 hit version of the song, big bands were expected to play "Cherokee." Parker sought out rather than avoided the song as a vehicle for improvisation; indeed, in 1939, he had a pivotal musical breakthrough while playing "Cherokee" (see chapter 1). Parker understandably viewed the song's B section as a special challenge. Gene Ramey played "Cherokee" many times with Parker in the McShann band:

> I am sure that at that time nobody else in the band could play, for example, even the channel [B section] to "Cherokee." So Bird used to play a series of "Tea For Two" phrases against the channel, and, since this was a melody that could be easily remembered, it gave the guys something to play during those bars.[30]

The B sections on the Jerry Newman disc contrast with the other sections in that they use much more repeated and preset material. As inventive an improviser as Parker already was, he clearly found the need to prepare material to get him through the difficult "bridge" of "Cherokee." The solo's second B section begins (at measure 97) with a striking and fresh linear improvisation over the first ii-7–V7–I progression. Then at measure 101, Parker embarks upon series of sequenced phrases over the succeeding ii-7–V7–I progressions; the phrase is simply an embellished version of "Tea for Two" as mentioned above (the circled notes form the "Tea for Two" melody).[31]

"Cherokee" (1942) Ex. 1

Parker found this "Tea for Two" gambit useful enough that he continued to use variations on it until his death; he employs a form of it on his last-known recorded version of "Cherokee" in 1954.

The first B section (at measure 33) begins with eight bars of a striking figure in descending sequence form over the ii-7–V7–I progressions. The figure involves a triplet that alternates a conventional fingering with an alternate ("long") fingering (marked with "o") to produce timbral and pitch shadings in the Lester Young style.[32] Parker moves away from the sequenced figure in the second eight bars of the bridge, where the chord progression leads into musical keys that are easier to improvise upon. Although Parker used this alternate-fingering gambit regularly in the 1940s, recorded evidence suggests that he dropped the pattern in the 1950s.

"Cherokee" (1942) Ex. 2

The Charles White Discs

These discs were recorded in Kansas City during one of Charlie Parker's visits to his hometown. Parker is accompanied only by Efferge Ware on guitar and Edward "Little Phil" (or "L'il Phil") Phillips playing some sort of quiet percussion. Until the early 1990s, the discs were in the possession of Charles White, an acquaintance of Parker. White originally stated that the four selections thus far released (two others were recorded but have not been found) were recorded in September, 1942, but one of the compositions, "My Heart Tells Me," was not copyrighted until September 2, 1943. The song was featured in the motion picture "Sweet Rosie O'Grady," which was released on October 20, 1943. Its earliest recording, by Glen Gray and the Casa Loma Orchestra, first entered the *Billboard Magazine* charts on November 27, 1943. Clearly, Parker could not have heard this song and recorded it until the fall of 1943, after he had left the Earl Hines band (see chapter 1, and "The Redcross Discs," below).[33] Most likely, this session took place in late 1943 or early 1944, when it is known that Parker had returned to Kansas City and was working at a local club.[34]

Three of the four songs ("Body and Soul," "I've Found a New Baby" and "Cherokee") had already been recorded in earlier versions by Parker. "Cherokee," in particular, continued to fascinate him. This version, although slower, is very similar to the earlier Jerry Newman disc;

Parker again uses the "Tea for Two" gambit (at 1:36) and the alternate-fingering triplet lick (2:38). Despite a somewhat stiff accompaniment, Parker's internal sense of propulsion provides enough swing for the whole group.

"My Heart Tells Me" and "Body and Soul" are the last two examples of the state of Parker's ballad playing until the November, 1945, session that produced "Meandering." As expected, he double-times with ease, but partly due to the rigid four-beat accompaniment, Parker's improvisations do not approach the suppleness and flexibility he would display a few years later. Like the Wichita version, this version of "Body and Soul" begins at ballad tempo, then doubles in speed, and finally concludes as a ballad à la Chu Berry and Roy Eldridge. In this case, however, Parker is the only horn player and thus is able to solo at both tempos. Parker again quotes Roy Eldridge as he modulates into the B section of "Body and Soul" (2:11).

An example of Parker's advanced harmonic concepts occurs in "My Heart Tells Me" when he chromatically sequences at various pitch levels a seven-note pattern (also used in the 1943 "Sweet Georgia Brown" recorded earlier, but discussed below). The effect in measure 52 is the implication of a ii-7–V7 progression in a new key that will lead over the barline back to the song's tonic chord via a tritone substitution (♭II7–I, or D♭7 to C).

"My Heart Tells Me"

Parker had recorded "I've Found a New Baby" in 1940 among the Wichita Transcriptions, and it's interesting to compare the two versions. This performance is in the key of F major (a whole step higher than the previous version's E♭-major). It is also taken at a slower tempo; the earlier version was at quarter note = ca. 258, while this performance is at quarter note = ca. 168. The tempo reduction is partially responsible for the most striking distinction between the two versions, namely Parker's use of double time twice in his solo. From his first recording ("Body"), Parker had shown great skill, while playing slow ballads, at constructing improvised lines that implied a doubling of the tempo. As his saxophone dexterity improved, he was able to double-time at progressively faster tempos; "I've Found a New Baby" is the fastest example of double-timing in his apprenticeship years (though it's significant that the performance gradually loses tempo). The more lengthy of the two instances comes in the second A of his fourth chorus overall (measure numbering commences after the four-bar introduction). The passage resembles later instances of Parker's double-timing in its speed and drive, but its melodic construction is rather reliant on step-wise (scalar) motion; over time, however, Parker would gradually gain more control over his double-time passages, allowing their melodic contours to have more variety.

"I've Found a New Baby" Ex. 1

Although the Wichita version of "I've Found a New Baby" is more similar to Lester Young's in key and tempo, this later version contains more explicit references to Young and is perhaps Parker's last major recorded homage to a formative musical influence. As mentioned in the "Introduction to the Musical Chapters," during his apprenticeship period, Parker often quoted the solos of older jazz musicians such as Young, Hawkins, or Eldridge when he needed help in soloing. When Parker was learning his craft, these phrases borrowed from master players of the preceding generation helped him navigate difficult harmonic passages or simply provided him with melodic material when his imagination flagged. During his mature periods (1944–55), he would be much more likely to quote pop songs or "classical" music themes than to quote his jazz predecessors. Having attained mastery himself, quotations were not needed as helps to improvisation; instead, they would take on topical or programmatic content during Parker solos. During "I've Found a New Baby," Parker quotes both Lester Young's composition "Tickle Toe" (at 0:16) and Young's improvised solo (Young's second B section) from the

1936 Jones-Smith recording of "Shoe Shine Boy" (1:56). Although Parker later minimized Young's influence, it should be evident in this chapter that Young's influence on Parker's sense of swing, the spinning of melody, timbre, and vibrato was dominant and went far beyond mere quotations. Here is the reference to "Tickle Toe" (measures 9 and 10); notice how Parker descends using G harmonic minor (measure 12):

"I've Found a New Baby" Ex. 2

The Jay McShann Big Band Sides

Charlie Parker joined Jay McShann's midsized band in Kansas City around January, 1940. Between then and July, 1942, most of Parker's recordings were made in the setting of the McShann big band (by the time Parker left, the band had grown to fourteen pieces). Because these recordings all find Parker playing alto sax during the same period in big band settings, because these performance feature generally shorter solos than the previous group and because several songs appear in more than one session, it makes sense to examine all of the McShann/Parker big band recordings in one sweep.

The Trocadero Disc

In early August, 1940,[35] university students and jazz enthusiasts Pete Armstrong and Fred Higginson recorded on a portable disc recorder the Jay McShann big band at the Trocadero Ballroom in Wichita, Kansas. The three surviving discs yield only one Parker solo, the bridge or B section on "I Got Rhythm." Parker's eight measures (about seven, actually, due to a skip in the original disc uncorrected in the transfer to CD) begin shakily but soon settle down and end in an augmented-chord figure in the style of Parker's major influence, Lester Young. In general, though, the solo is too brief and poorly recorded to yield much insight into Parker's tone, swing, or development as an improviser. The disc's importance is largely historical, since it is the earliest known documentation of the McShann band with Parker. Luckily, Armstrong and Higginson went on to record a small group featuring McShann and Parker later that year with better equipment and in a more controlled setting (the "Wichita Transcriptions" discussed above).

The Decca Sides

Until 1974, these 1941 and 1942 recordings for the Decca company by the full Jay McShann Orchestra were the sole artifacts of Charlie Parker's first style period available to most listeners. Ironically, at about seventy-one measures of solo or foreground material, these recordings now represent the *smallest* portion of his 1940–43 work available today. The Decca recordings are not truly representative of the McShann band because the group was not allowed to record its usual blend of pop songs, blues, "jump" tunes, ballads, and original compositions, nor were they able to adequately feature their strongest soloist, alto saxophonist Charlie Parker. The band was typecast by Decca as a blues band, and, indeed, three of Parker's four Decca solos are on blues (two twelve-bar blues and one sixteen-bar modified blues). In addition, the band had to shorten many of its pieces to fit the limits of the 78 RPM record, either by cutting out parts of arrangements and/or by shortening solos.

In Dallas, Texas, on April 30, 1941, two pieces featuring Parker solos were recorded, "Swingmatism" and "Hootie Blues." A McShann quintet date in Chicago on November 18, 1941, may have included Parker on one piece (see discussion below). The title in question ("One Woman's Man," a.k.a. "One Woman's Blues") only includes alto sax in accompaniment to a vocal solo, not in a soloistic role. In New York City on July 2, 1942, the band featured Parker solos on two more pieces, "The Jumpin' Blues" and "Sepian Stomp" (also known as "Sepian Bounce"). A third title from the same date, "Lonely Boy Blues," evidently includes Parker in a melody statement with minimal embellishment, not qualifying as an improvised solo.

Parker's timbre on the Dallas sessions has a new richness and depth, whether because of different equipment (mouthpiece, reed, or saxophone), better recording techniques, or a change in his concept of saxophone tone. His use of vibrato is sparing and under control, and most in evidence in the slowest piece, "Hootie Blues." His sense of swing continues to develop, as heard in not only rhythmic authority in the fastest pieces, but also in the sureness he brings to the slowest blues.

"Hootie Blues," a blues in E♭, is often referred to as a co-composition/arrangement of McShann and Parker although Parker's name does not appear on the official songwriting credits. After a sax riff possibly based on "The Donkey Serenade," Parker enters (0:35) with six notes that epitomize the blues. His stripped-down tone and more evident vibrato on notes of medium-to-long value lend an authentic Southwest bluesy "wail." He offers a double-time phrase in measure 4 (0:42), but due to its brevity and utter relaxation, his mood of restraint is unbroken. (Indeed, contributing to the phrase's appropriateness is the fact that its first six notes are based in what today is called the "blues scale.") By measure 6, he has played four short phrases with note values from a dotted half note to a string of sixteenths, all judiciously separated by rests of varying values up to two beats. Measures 7 and 8 (0:49–0:53) contain what would become a favorite lick of mature-period Parker, a descending blues run, in this case presented in an antecedent-consequent form (the first concludes down-turned, the second concludes up-turned; see "Now's the Time" and "Oh, Lady Be Good!" in chapter 3).

"Swingmatism" is a sixteen-bar extended blues in F minor. Although minor blues had not been very common in jazz (Teddy Wilson's 1936 "Blues in C♯ Minor" and Duke Ellington's 1940 "Ko-Ko" are two better-known exceptions), Parker is at home and at his most fluid here. Notable is his creative use of the minor modes of F during the pick-up and first three measures. In the pick-up measures, he ascends with the melodic minor and descends with the harmonic minor, implying a ♭9 on the C7 (or V7) chord. In measure 2, he descends again with the harmonic form this time over the tonic chord, implying an F-Δ7.

"Swingmatism"

"The Jumpin' Blues" is most famous for its opening phrase, which trumpeter Benny Harris adapted (in a new key) for his "Ornithology," which became a bebop anthem (see chapter 3). Lester Young had played a very similar passage in his 1936 "Shoe Shine Boy" solo and may have been the actual source of the phrase.[36]

"The Jumpin' Blues"

That Parker was familiar with the Young solo has been reported by saxophonist Lee Konitz:

> I was on tour with Charlie once and I was warming up in the dressing room—I happened to be playing one of Lester's choruses—and Bird came noodling into the room and said, "Hey, you ever heard this one?" and he played "Shoe Shine Boy" about twice as fast as the record.[37]

On several slower Decca recordings, Parker critics and enthusiasts have debated whether the alto sax contributions are by Parker or his section mate, altoist John Jackson. Jackson was one of the first altoists to be influenced by Parker, as Jay McShann observed:

> We made a Pabst Blue Ribbon broadcast one night and Bird was late getting there . . . Bird come in just as they had got into the first number . . . He was standing out there looking through the windows. And J. J. [John Jackson] played Bird's solo note for note. Bird said, "Man, don't ever give this cat none of my solos no more." . . . The cat [Jackson] had sat there and it rubbed off on him.[38]

Parker respected Jackson enough to name him as one of the men who'd been developing new ideas in the McShann band.[39]

A good example of the confusion possible between the two saxophonists is found on the Decca recording of "Lonely Boy Blues." There are two alto sax spots, separated by a brief McShann interlude. The first player is clearly not Parker, and indeed the tone and vibrato are reminiscent of John Jackson in the Decca/McShann "Dexter Blues." The second altoist on "Lonely Boy Blues" plays some distinctly un-Parker-like gestures (especially at the beginning) with a wailing tone rather like Parker's on "Honey & Body," and with some bluesy pitch-bends more pronounced than any other Parker recording that comes to mind. Repeated listening suggests the first soloist is Jackson, and the second one is Parker playing atypically due to the nature and requirements of a largely preset melody statement calling for little embellishment.[40] Another Decca recording with questionable Parker participation is "One Woman's Man," recorded in Chicago with a septet. The alto saxophone obbligatos behind vocalist Walter Brown are much more typically Parkeresque, although Jay McShann told Parker scholar Phil Schaap that the altoist is Jackson. Although it sounds like Parker to this author, it certainly could be Jackson. Examples of Jackson's later, clearly Parker-derived, style can be found on two Armed Forces Radio Service *Jubilee* transcriptions: Jay McShann's 1944 "Lonely Boy Blues" and "Bottle It," and especially on Billy Eckstine's 1945 "Opus X." In both cases, Jackson sounds like the Parker of several years earlier.

The Savoy Broadcast

Between the Chicago and New York Decca recordings discussed above, the Jay McShann big band was recorded nonprofessionally from an NBC Blue Network broadcast from New York's Savoy Ballroom on February 13, 1942. (The band had opened at the Savoy on January 9, 1942; the February date was McShann's first Savoy broadcast.) This material was first issued in 1991, and fills in our picture of Parker's role in the McShann band.

Even more than the Wichita Transcriptions, these recordings present the most accurate example of the Parker-era McShann big band with respect to its repertoire, solo space for Parker, and overall length of the pieces. Of the five full selections presented (not counting the brief closing theme), only two are blues. The other three pieces are an "I Got Rhythm"-derived swinger, an Ellington ballad, and a dated pop song set in swing. Parker definitely solos on four of the five pieces; his solo participation on a fifth piece is unclear (the eight-bar melody statement on "I Got It Bad" could be either John Jackson or Parker).

Not only was Parker the beneficiary of more solo opportunities, he was also given double the solo length on the two pieces that had previously been recorded for Decca, "Hootie Blues" (previously twelve bars) and "Swingmatism" (previously sixteen bars). Even with those extensions, his longest unbroken appearance is less than a minute long (five of the small-group recordings discussed above have Parker in the foreground for at least three minutes). Nevertheless, discovering any new Parker is valuable, especially material from his less-documented apprenticeship period. By definition, this was a time of his assimilation and gradual transformation of musical influences. An illustration of Parker's continuing reliance on the phraseology of his prime influence, Lester Young, is Parker's solo on "St. Louis Mood," during which every phrase is consistent with Young's musical vocabulary.

One moment that illustrates Parker's firm grip on harmony occurs during the unaccompanied break to his first solo on "I'm Forever Blowing Bubbles" (the first is in the key of B♭, the second in A♭). A less creative musical mind might have outlined a simple chord progression such as B♭–B♭–C-7–F7, but Parker, without any harmonic support, elects to take the scenic route and clearly outlines a more involved progression:

"I'm Forever Blowing Bubbles"

The Redcross Discs

Although these performances were recorded soon before the Charles White discs (discussed with the small-group alto sax recordings earlier in this chapter), Parker's use of *tenor,* not alto saxophone, on these small-ensemble recordings suggests that they be examined separately. Like the Wichita Transcriptions, the Redcross discs were known to have been recorded, but for many years, no one thought to determine if they still existed. In the early 1980s, through a misunderstanding, they were thought to be lost forever; it was not until 1985 that they were discovered by collectors, and not until 1986 that they were released to the public. Like "Honey & Body" and "Cherokee," these discs were made on a non-professional disc recorder in an informal setting. The amateur recording engineer was Bob Redcross, friend of singer Billy Eckstine, who in early 1943 held mini-jam sessions in room 305 of Chicago's Savoy Hotel. Earl Hines's band (which included Eckstine, Charlie Parker, and Dizzy Gillespie) was in town, and Redcross committed some of the music they played to disc.

From the standpoint of Parker's music, these recordings are important for several reasons. From July, 1942 (the New York Deccas) to September, 1944 (the Tiny Grimes session for Savoy, which marks the beginning of Parker's mature period recordings), Parker did not record commercially, and it was thought that there were no documents tracing the evolution of his art during this period. Parker was with the well-known Earl Hines band for approximately the first ten months of 1943, but an American Federation of Musicians ban on recording by union members prevented this unit from leaving an official record (many radio transcriptions of big bands survive from this period, but so far, none have turned up of this Hines big band). The Hines big band was an early gathering place for many forward-looking musicians who were in transition between the swing era style and that of modern jazz (or "bebop"), notably Charlie Parker, Dizzy Gillespie, Bennie Green, Wardell Gray, and Sarah Vaughan. Documents of Parker during this period fill in important blanks in his musical development, a time when he was, for the first time, allied with a group of like thinking young players. Another reason for the importance of these recordings is that they feature Parker not on alto sax, but on *tenor* sax. When tenor saxophonist Budd Johnson quit the band in December, 1942, Hines needed a replacement on that instrument, not the alto, so a tenor sax was bought for Parker. Although Parker continued to prefer (and possibly practice on) the alto, he necessarily had to make adjustments to the larger and lower-pitched horn, merging some new stylistic qualities with ones already discussed. Later in his career, Parker was commercially recorded playing tenor sax on only two occasions, so these informal discs contribute significantly to our understanding of his approach to the tenor.

Bob Redcross recorded Charlie Parker many times in early 1943. Of the 1943 discs that Redcross managed to save, eight performances with Parker on tenor sax are now commercially available. (Two additional discs of Parker playing alto sax ["China Boy" and "Avalon"] were among Redcross's collection. Parker's playing on the recordings sounds more mature and advanced than the Charles White discs; quite possibly, the Redcross alto sax discs were recorded while Parker and Redcross were touring with Billy Eckstine's big band in 1944.) The instrumentation on the discs varies widely. Parker is joined at various times by several trumpeters (including Dizzy Gillespie) and by an unknown tenor saxophonist. Rhythm section support includes at times string bass (Oscar Pettiford), guitar, and brushes played on an unknown surface. One piece even features one of the most unusual accompaniments in issued Parkeriana, a 78 RPM phonograph record.

The first item of musical discussion must be Parker's timbre on the tenor sax. As discussed earlier, his timbral concept on alto sax was outside the mainstream and was controversial for some listeners. Critics of it considered it shrill and edgy, while adherents found it fittingly stripped down and unsentimental. Probably all found his timbre compact, penetrating, and functional, but certainly none found it sensual in the sense of a Hodges or a Carter. Parker's tenor sax timbre by contrast, is full, smooth and sensual. Revealing the influence of Lester Young, Parker's tenor sax timbre is not generally treated with a constant vibrato, rasp, or growl as with many tenor players of the Coleman Hawkins school. Aural evidence on these low-fidelity discs suggests that Parker's tenor sax sound had somewhat more weight than Young's, much like that of Wardell Gray's of five years later. Indeed, Parker and Gray were section mates in the Hines band during part of 1943. Parker had a large influence upon Gray's sense of melody and harmony; he may have also had an effect on Gray's timbral concept.

Parker's use of vibrato on tenor is interesting. As one would expect, he uses it quite sparingly, however there is one exception: held notes in the upper register are sometimes treated with a pronounced vibrato of uncharacteristic speed and depth, a practice associated with the Coleman Hawkins school of tenor playing. Parker once again exhibits a strong internal sense of swing whether he is rhythmically accompanied by bass or guitar or just by brushes on some surface. As expected, the basic soloistic rhythmic unit is the eighth note, with the exception of a number of striking double-time passages.

"Sweet Georgia Brown" is performed at a "medium swing," approximately quarter note = 256, although the tempo varies. Parker's two lengthy solos are bursting with ideas and represent some of his best work of the period. His long eighth-note lines swing with compelling power, tremendously aided by the young but already accomplished bassist, Oscar Pettiford. Parker also seems inspired by the presence of trumpeter Dizzy Gillespie who not only solos inventively, but also audibly urges Parker on. With only two instruments, Parker and Pettiford admirably hold together the improvisations, although in one section, they seem "turned around" in the form.[41]

A few techniques drawn from tenor saxophonists of the previous generation are present in "Sweet Georgia Brown." Perhaps used humorously is the growl or rasp associated with Coleman Hawkins (perhaps via Chu Berry) found in the second solo at 5:23 (timings are continuous from the beginning of the first solo). Another technique is the frequent use of alternate fingerings in the Lester Young style to produce timbral and pitch shadings. Probably the most clear example of that technique comes in the first solo at 0:34.

"Sweet Georgia Brown" contains many brief examples of a melodic device that would become characteristic of Parker's post-1944 work, the "chromatic passing tone." These tones are nonharmonic tones (outside of the prevailing scale or harmony) that continue a downward or upward melodic line by chromatically filling in between two tones that *are* part of the prevailing scale or harmony. In the following example from Parker's first solo on "Sweet Georgia Brown," the asterisks show the alternation of chord tones and chromatic passing tones:

"Sweet Georgia Brown" Ex. 1

In strings of eighth notes, these chromatic passing tones tend to occur between beats (as they do above) and thereby may be used to place chord tones *on* the beat.[42] In the above example, on-the-beat chord tones that are adjacent to chromatic passing tones are marked with asterisks.

"Sweet Georgia Brown" also offers numerous glimpses of Parker's harmonic thinking, specifically in the ways that he obtained chromaticism. In the first solo, he creatively uses melodic sequencing to provide chromatic interest. Beginning with the last beat of measure 72 on the pitch F, he presents a seven-note pattern (also used in "My Heart Tells Me," above) that is immediately sequenced modally down a perfect fifth, then sequenced chromatically (except for the last note) up a semitone. As in "My Heart Tells Me," the figure implies a ii-7–V7 progression that leads down by half step (via a tritone substitution) to the tonic chord (A7 to A♭, in this case).

Also interesting from a harmonic standpoint is his treatment of the

"Sweet Georgia Brown" Ex. 2

C7 chord functioning as a V7 in the key of F minor (see also the studio recording of "Swingmatism," above). In order to obtain desired chromatic alterations to the V7 chord, Parker uses the fifth mode of three F minor scales. In the first solo, he employs F melodic minor ("ascending" form, although his melody descends) to supply the ♭13 (measure 90) and F natural minor to provide the ♭9, ♯9, and ♭13 (measure 92). In the second solo, Parker employs F harmonic minor to obtain the ♭9 and ♭13 (measure 60).

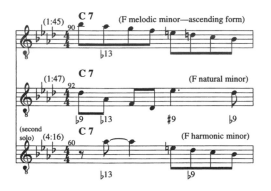

"Sweet Georgia Brown" Ex. 3

The Redcross disc of "Body and Soul" contained the only substantial ballad-tempo playing from Parker on these sides. Unfortunately, the beginning and end of the disc were too damaged to play through, so the CD version picks up during the guitar interlude and later omits the return to the ballad tempo. In general, the performance follows the Chu Berry and Roy Eldridge's slow-fast-slow scheme, although Parker and the guitarist imply double time before actually doubling the speed. Note that the guitarist (probably the same one as on "Three Guesses") does not keep the AABA form straight:

Form:	A A B A	guitar interlude	B A	B A	A
Tempo:	ballad tempo	ballad tempo	implied double time (loses speed)	true doubling of tempo	ballad tempo

---------- on CD ---------

From Parker's first ballad recording ("Body"), he had demonstrated the ability to imply double time; on the Redcross version of "Body and Soul," he has several passages in implied *quadruple* time (thirty-second notes). Despite playing a horn that he found "too big," Parker showed that, at twenty-two years of age, he possessed technique and rhythmic sureness that surpassed nearly every jazz musician of the time (Art Tatum would be a likely exception). Clearly, Parker was feeling more confident about bringing off such passages at ever-increasing tempos. These brief flurries anticipate more lengthy and sustained passages in thirty-second notes on his classic ballad recordings of 1947 (chapter 4). One such moment in "Body and Soul" begins at 0:38 on the CD version. Although the guitarist, through implied double time, seems to be playing at a medium tempo (quarter note = ca. 156, he gradually loses speed), the basic tempo of this section is around quarter note = 78. Parker uncorks a stunning run that is a developmental version of what would become one of his most famous licks (see "Billie's Bounce," chapter 3). Note the characteristic accentuation on the high points of the melodic line and the voice leading figure from "Honeysuckle Rose" solo, above.

"Body and Soul" (1943)

Implied double time is also evident on "Indiana" and "Embraceable You." The latter was recorded with Parker playing along with a 1942 recording of the Gershwin song as played by pianist Hazel Scott. This is the first document of Parker playing what would become a staple in his mature period repertoire. Scott played the song in F concert (G on the tenor), as altoist Parker often later did (although it transposed to D on the alto). The novelty aside, this is a very successful performance. After the rubato introduction, Scott takes the tune at a comparatively bright quarter note = ca. 124. Parker creatively embellishes and paraphrases the original melody before straying from it and indulging in some effective double-timing.

"Boogie Woogie" is played without any harmonic support. The only person playing when Parker solos is Bob Redcross himself playing "brushes" on some surface, possibly a snare drum (a voice at the beginning of the performance says "Bobby boy. . . . You got them skins"). The piece is so titled because Parker uses the riff melody of Count Basie's 1937 recording of "Boogie Woogie," though he more extensively quotes Gene Krupa's 1941 recording of "Drum Boogie." Other melodic borrowings include "London Bridge" (1:06) and a clever quotation of Ben Webster's opening to Duke Ellington's 1940 "The Girl in My Dreams Tries to Look Like You" (1:35). The disc begins with twelve measures of Parker, then sixteen measures of Parker and trumpeter Billy Eckstine riffing, before settling into five complete choruses of twelve-bar blues in the key of G. Parker's clarity of harmonic thought is demonstrated in the third blues chorus, where he not only ably sketches the basic progression without a bass, piano, or guitar, but also neatly outlines alterations on the IV7 (C7; measure 29) and follows with a arpeggiated series of descending minor-ninth chords (A-9 and B♭-9; measures 30–32) leading to the ii-7 (B-9).

"Boogie Woogie"

He fittingly ends (after riffing with Eckstine) with the same common-property "jingle" (3:33) that ended the "Honey" section of "Honey & Body" (described above), thus neatly joining the first and last recording sessions examined in this chapter.

"Three Guesses" is based on Rhythm changes in the key of B♭. An unknown tenor saxophonist takes first solo; Parker begins his solo approximately 1:28 into the disc. Unfortunately, the rhythm guitarist does not keep the thirty-two bar AABA form straight, and Parker's solo winds up like this: AABA AAA AABA. Parker gamely tries to lead the guitarist into the B section several times to no avail (it's hard to believe that this inconsistent musician was Earl Hines's guitarist, Hurley Ramey, as is usually listed). To a great degree, these form problems limit the continuity of Parker's solo; every eight bars, he has to second-guess the guitarist. During his first B section (1:50), Parker appropriately quotes the saxophone soli of Duke Ellington's "Cottontail" (another "I Got Rhythm" variant). When Parker finally gets another "bridge" many measures later, he authoritatively uncorks a two-bar double-time run (3:18). At 2:24, Parker plays a series of Lester Young-like "honks" in the lower register. This phrase would soon be recorded as "Mop Mop," but it was actually a common-property riff Parker knew from Kansas City.[43]

"Three Guesses"

Parker was already incorporating the above riff into an original song then called "The Devil in 305" (the room number at the Savoy Hotel). When he next visited the recording studio (at the session that marks the beginning of his "mature" style periods), "The Devil in 305" would be titled "Red Cross," a (mistitled) tribute to Bob Redcross.

If jazz historians had to assess the stylistic contributions of Charlie Parker strictly on the basis of his commercial and amateur recordings made by the end of 1943, they would today finally find a sufficient body of work to do so. He might be seen as an advanced but nevertheless transitional figure between the swing era style and bebop (the way that some view Charlie Christian and Jimmy Blanton, both of whom died in 1942) who stopped recording before the full flowering of the new style. His debts to Lester Young, Buster Smith, Coleman Hawkins, Art Tatum, and others would be traceable, and his own burgeoning contributions to a new musical direction would likely be recognized. Of course, Parker continued recording; we know how his style evolved, the nature of his post-1943 innovations and the extent of his influence on other players. But an appreciation of his mature work should not take away from the inventiveness and uniqueness of his apprenticeship recordings.

During that apprenticeship period, Parker combined and then developed ideas from the most advanced of his swing era predecessors. His influences and original ideas were in flux as they would be at no other point in his career. Partly because of this artistic flux, Parker's 1940–43 recordings are particularly vital examples of Parker because they present him at his most spontaneous; he had not yet codified his musical vocabulary, and he took an impromptu approach to the spinning forth of melody, much like his prime influence, Lester Young. In addition, Parker's work of the period is marked by a stunning pace of growth, a strong sense of discovery, and a rare appetite for new ideas. Each recording exhibits new facets of Parker's evolving art. The spontaneity and discovery found in these recordings reward the listener in unique and satisfying ways; for all these reasons, Parker's apprenticeship recordings stand on their own within Parkeriana.

Chapter 3

1944–46

Although brief, Charlie Parker's 1944–46 period is wide ranging. It signals Charlie Parker's first expressions of maturity and mastery, contains his first recorded masterpieces and also includes his poorest and most unfortunate recordings. With the recordings of this period, Parker could no longer have been considered merely a "transition" figure from the swing era to bop, the way that Charlie Christian and Jimmy Blanton sometimes are. During this time, he and Dizzy Gillespie honed their innovations, first as "sidemen" under others' leadership and then on their own nightclub and record dates, culminating with Parker's first recording as a leader.

The beginning of this period is dated partly out of circumstance. After Parker was recorded by Bob Redcross and Charles White (see previous chapter), he does not seem to have been recorded until September, 15, 1944, (see the Tiny Grimes session, below). By that 1944 record date, most of Parker's characteristic musical qualities were in place, making 1944 a good starting point for his first "mature" musical period. The end of the period is dated by Parker's 1946 physical and emotional breakdown. This event, brought on by his addiction to heroin and alcohol, resulted in his hospitalization and his not being recorded until early 1947.

In 1943, after leaving the Hines band, Parker had returned to Kansas City, worked regionally with Carroll Dickerson, Andy Kirk, and Noble Sissle; toured nationally (with Gillespie) in Billy Eckstine's bebop-influenced big band; and then returned to New York City and began to work on Fifty-second Street. Parker's period with Eckstine was the last time Parker would work regularly in a big band setting; he much preferred the freedom of small ensembles.

Because of the gap in recorded documentation between the Red-cross/White recordings and the Grimes date, the transitional artistic steps Parker took in that period are not clear. It is known that by late 1944, Charlie Parker had largely finished transcending his swing era influences to present a coherent approach to melody, harmony, and rhythm. As expected, these "mature" (post-apprenticeship) recordings find Parker displaying the virtuosity, swing, inventiveness, playfulness, and bluesiness so much associated with his other mature work. In addition, the more technical elements of tempo, note values, double time, accentuation, vibrato, harmony, and melody outlined in the "Introduction to the Musical Chapters" come largely into focus by 1944. The element of repertoire does change somewhat toward the end of this period in that Parker, as bandleader, was more able than in the past to choose the pieces he recorded and performed. Many of Parker's pet "licks" are in place by the end of this period, signaling a slight shift away from his earlier spontaneity in weaving fresh melody. Nevertheless, the sense of discovery mentioned in the last chapter is still quite strong, albeit sometimes with an edge-of-one's-seat intensity.

Charlie Parker and Dizzy Gillespie were speaking a recognizable and new musical vocabulary, and a sufficient number of other players were embracing their artistic direction to form entire groups of like-thinking modern jazz musicians. For better or worse, this musical vocabulary became known as "bebop" (originally rebop) or simply "bop." The musical explorations of the early 1940s that had taken place in Harlem after-hours clubs such as Monroe's and Minton's and that continued to develop in Earl Hines's band and on New York's Fifty-second Street had finally borne fruit. Participants in these after-hours sessions differ as to their motivation in creating a new jazz style. Some, like Kenny Clarke or Thelonious Monk, spoke of a competitive drive to improve jazz and to keep less sophisticated or older musicians away. (Clarke later revised his characterization of the musicians' motives.)[1] In a 1953 interview with John Fitch (radio name: John McLellan), Parker minimized the role of dissatisfaction with older jazz in the development of modern jazz:

> JF: Then, whom do you feel were the really important persons, besides yourself, who evidently were dissatisfied with music as it was, and started to experiment?
>
> CP: Well, let me make a correction here, please. It wasn't that we were dissatisfied with it, it was just that another conception came along, and this was just the way *we* thought it should go.[2]

In another interview that included Fitch, saxophonist Paul Desmond asked him, "Did you realize at that time what effect you were going to have on jazz, that you were going to change the entire scene in the next ten years?" Parker's reply was, "Well, let's put it like this: No, I had no idea that it was that much different." [laughs].[3]

Although Parker was officially supportive and accepting of earlier styles of jazz, he may have felt that bebop had not really evolved from those styles. A 1949 *Down Beat* article by Michael Levin and John S. Wilson quotes Parker extensively:

"Bop is no love-child of jazz," says Charlie Parker. The creator of bop, in a series of interviews that took more than two weeks, told us that he felt that "bop is something entirely separate and apart" from the older tradition; that it drew little from jazz, has no roots in it.[4]

Although hesitant, Parker was "pushed further" to define bop:

The beat in a bop band is with the music, against it, behind it. It pushes it. It helps it. Help is the big thing. It [bop] has no continuity of beat, no steady chug-chug. Jazz has, and that's why bop is more flexible.[5]

It's intriguing that Parker called preceding styles "jazz" and differentiated them from his music, "bop." Certainly most of Parker's peers felt that modern jazz had evolved from the earlier styles. One month after the above article appeared, Dizzy Gillespie was quoted in *Down Beat* as disagreeing with Parker: "Bop is an interpretation of jazz. It's all part of the same thing."[6] Given that Parker was "pushed" by the authors, he may have felt pressured to make distinctions that he would not have ordinarily made. It should also be remembered that this was a time when the modern jazz musicians were still struggling to establish their legitimacy.

In 1947, Parker referred to New Orleans jazz as "ancient," and this and other statements he made suggest that he did not understand the previous jazz styles very well, or was not as sympathetic to them as his highly diplomatic public statements suggested. In a 1947 *Down Beat* "Blindfold Test," Parker reviewed a record by saying, "You want my honest opinion? Okay. Well, that's music—that's very good Dixieland. . . . I like Dixieland, in a way; I mean, I can listen to it—it's still music. There's a status of appreciation you can reach if you listen for it."[7] In a 1953 interview for radio, Parker was a little more tactful: "Well, I like

Dixieland, I like good Dixieland, it's all right, you know, but I just don't—I don't play it because I most likely wouldn't make a good job at it anyway, I just think it [music] should go another way."[8]

An example of Parker's sense of jazz history is found in the same interview. In it, he gave his view of the chronology of jazz styles:

> Dixieland, I think, was introduced in '14 or '15, and then, the swing era came in about 1928, and lasted until 1935, '36. . . . But, during that time, this [the beginnings of modern jazz] happened in 1938, just a little bit before '45 . . . Dizzy Gillespie, Thelonious Monk, Kenny Clarke. It was Charlie Christian, '37, I guess. There was Bud Powell, Don Byas, Ben Webster, yours truly.[9]

Parker's sequence departs a little from the usual datings for the changes in jazz styles (he was often inexact in placing past events in time, so it's hard to say how intentional or how accidental these dates may have been). For example, 1928 might be considered early for the birth of the swing era, but certainly Don Redman and Duke Ellington were well on their way to forging the arranging concepts that formed the basis for the swing style. Also, Parker placed the end of the swing era right at the time that most white Americans were just becoming aware of swing as a style (Benny Goodman's pivotal Palomar Ballroom engagement was in 1935). Most striking is his placing the birth of modern jazz in 1937 or 1938, a period when Charlie Christian and Jimmy Blanton had yet to record, and when Dizzy Gillespie's recordings primarily revealed his indebtedness to Roy Eldridge.

Small Group Recordings

The recording session that brought Parker back into the studio once again (amazingly, the first time for an actual record company since July 2, 1942) was a quintet date for the Savoy label led by guitarist and vocalist Lloyd "Tiny" Grimes. Through 1945, Parker participated in many recording dates led by swing style leaders who were sympathetic to the new sounds being heard on New York City's Fifty-second Street, resulting in mixes of the established and the new styles.

In this case, Savoy wanted two commercial vocals for the "A" sides of two 78s and two jazz instrumentals for the "B" sides. Parker improvises strongly on all four titles and shows his new mastery, in particular, on the ballad "I'll Always Love You Just the Same," Grimes's B♭ blues

"Tiny's Tempo," and the first piece clearly and solely composed by Parker, "Red Cross." As was noted in the last chapter, Parker had developed this piece during his tenure in the Earl Hines Orchestra, originally calling it "The Devil in 305." Like so many Parker "original" compositions, the amount of actual music writing is minimal and mostly found in the A section (the B section consists of the sequential repetitions of a short riff). Although the song is based on the "I Got Rhythm" chord progression, Parker does have one new wrinkle in the A section, a half step harmonic aside from B♭ to B (0:09):

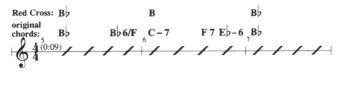

"Red Cross" (Take 1) Ex. 1

An example of Parker using fairly lengthy pre-prepared material is found during the B sections of Parker's solos on both takes of "Red Cross." The lick is presented most straightforwardly in the first take:

"Red Cross" (Take 1) Ex. 2

Parker's fascination for half-step relationships both chordally (D to E♭, G to A♭) and melodically (over each barline; circled) is evident. The fact that his accompanists don't follow him chord-wise up the half steps doesn't detract from the effectiveness of this passage; in fact, the resulting dissonances are entirely consistent with bebop chromaticism. Parker would use this same B section gambit in his studio recording of "Shaw Nuff" (see below).

Studio Recordings with Dizzy Gillespie

Parker spent most of 1945 free-lancing in New York City, often in the company of Dizzy Gillespie. Indeed, all but one of Parker's six commercial recording sessions of 1945 were made with Gillespie. Further, most of the reputation of the striking partnership of Bird and Diz derives from sessions they made in a fourteen-month period dating from January, 1945, to February, 1946. After that time, the two played together very irregularly and recorded commercially together only twice.

A January 4 Clyde Hart date presented Parker and Gillespie on record for the first time to the general public, but a more important artistic breakthrough for modern jazz came with Dizzy Gillespie's February 28, 1945, session for Guild, the first Gillespie-led session with Parker (Gillespie had already recorded two sessions under his own name). Despite another mix of swing era and modern jazz players, Gillespie and Parker forcefully present the new style. One can imagine the radical effect that their playing had on musicians and the public alike. The Gillespie compositions are well crafted and arranged and do not consist of just the minimum of written material, as Parker's "Red Cross" had. The introduction of "Groovin' High" has much of the restless rise-and-fall quality that would typify bebop. Its theme (based on the chord changes to the song "Whispering") is presented in E♭; an interlude puts Parker's solo D♭; eventually, a slower coda (adapted in part by Tadd Dameron for his "If You Could See Me Now") ends the piece dramatically (by then, back in E♭). Parker's break and half-chorus solo show remarkable poise and balance, with a pleasing swing .

Likewise, "Dizzy Atmosphere" (based on "I Got Rhythm," but in A♭) is more than just a quick head, including as it does an introduction, theme statement (the A sections' melody possibly derived from the traditional African-American song "Hambone"), "shout chorus," and coda. Parker's solo is a gem, étudelike in its clarity. Perhaps some of its freshness and relative lack of cliché is due to the key; Parker usually played Rhythm changes in B♭, and may have had less preset material in this key. His opening four bars look like this:

"Dizzy Atmosphere"

Note Parker's implied chain of descending minor chords in measures 3 and 4, and how often he leads smoothly from one measure to another by step (half step in bars 1 to 2, 4 to 5, 5 to 6, and by whole step in bars 7 to 8). Interestingly, the descending chords resemble a passing-chord figure played by an early Parker influence, guitarist Efferge Ware, in 1940.[10] Despite the rhythm section's somewhat stiff feel (evidently the more modern drummers Max Roach, Shelly Manne, or Stan Levey were unavailable), Parker seems unaffected; his propulsion comes from within. This Gillespie session is also notable for Parker's lyrical eight-measure improvised bridge on "All the Things You Are" (0:42), his first recording of one of his favorite soloistic vehicles and the harmonic basis for his masterpiece of 1947, "Bird of Paradise" (see chapter 4).

Gillespie led another recording session for Guild featuring Parker on May 11. This time, all but the versatile drummer Sid Catlett were solidly in the new style, making for a more unified group sound. The compositions again show great care and attention in writing and arranging. Parker and Gillespie's tight ensemble statements illustrate their affinity for one another and why Parker later called Gillespie "the other half of my heartbeat."[11] Gillespie is solely credited as the writer of "Salt Peanuts," and "Shaw Nuff" is usually credited to both Gillespie and Parker. In a 1949 article, Parker blamed Gillespie's managers for miscrediting his compositions, saying "they stuck his [Gillespie's] name on some tunes of mine to give him a better commercial reputation."[12] The article paraphrases Parker as referring to "Shaw Nuff," "Anthropology," and "Confirmation" as his own compositions with no Gillespie contributions.

Parker is thrilling in both his ideas and his swinging execution of them. His playing shows some remnants of his old Kansas City sound in its thinness and occasionally wobbly vibrato ("Hot House" and "Shaw Nuff"). During the B section of the vocal chorus on Gillespie's novelty "Salt Peanuts" (1:09), Parker continues to develop the ii-7–V7 lick that was first noted in the Redcross version of "Body and Soul" (chapter 2) and will be fully formed in "Billie's Bounce" (below). "Shaw Nuff" (usually credited as being written by both Parker and Gillespie) is again based on Rhythm changes, this time in the usual key of B♭. Parker's solo seems a little frantic rhythmically in that his placement of notes in relation to the beat is inconsistent. Ironically, that frantic quality at this up-tempo supplies some of his solo's excitement. At the beginning of his B section (1:01), he rips through the same worked-out pattern noted in "Red Cross." The final selection featuring Parker, Tadd Dameron's "Hot House" (based on Cole Porter's "What Is This Thing Called Love?"), is taken at a slower swing tempo that allows everyone to relax. During his second A section (1:07), Parker displays the ability to double-time with more assurance than just a few years before.

Parker and Gillespie continued to play together whenever possible. Theirs was the most vital partnership in jazz of the time. While working at the Three Deuces nightclub with Gillespie, Parker, Al Haig, and Stan Levey, bassist Dillon "Curly" Russell observed the telepathy between Bird and Diz firsthand:

> We were playing down at the Deuces one time, and this half-way drunk come up and ask us for the usual drunken tune, "Melancholy Baby." And they got to the turnaround after the first eight bars, and Bird and Diz played the exact notes on the turnaround. And when they finished, they turned around and laughed like the devil! Because, that shows how their mind was workin'. Completely. We had never played this tune. The guy just wanted us to play it, he gave us five dollars, so they called it off, and here they played the same notes. Note for note. And, you know, things like that make you wonder about these guys, "do they think alike?"[13]

Around this time, Parker, Gillespie, and drummer Max Roach worked at the Onyx Club. Roach discovered a new aspect of Parker's instrumental expertise:

> One day, I walked into the Onyx Club—late—strutting, of course, and Bird was sitting there on the drums. They were all waiting for me: Charles Parker, Dizzy Gillespie, waiting for Max, little Max. It's something, when you think of it. When I walked in, he said to me— Dizzy just kinda glared—but Bird said to me, "Hey, Max, can you play this exercise on your drum set?" He had his saxophone placed across his lap. He played a Charleston beat on the left foot, the hi-hat cymbal, which is: "chick, [pause] chick." And in the left hand, he played a shuffle beat: "chick-cha-chick-cha-chick-cha-chick-cha-chick-cha-chick." And on the right hand, he played the simple— what we call swing beat on the ride cymbal: "ching-chick-cha-ching-chick-cha-ching-chick-cha-ching." And he played a quarter note on the bass drum. That's the regular time: "boom, boom, boom, boom, boom." Now, all this together creates a wonderful sound. So he played it. And then he got up off the drums and said "can you do

that?" I sat down, and for the life of me, I couldn't do it. He reduced me to (the) absolutely nothin.' Now, this was Charles Parker, and I didn't know he played drums.[14]

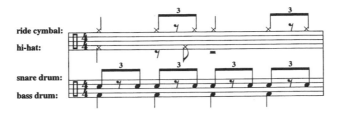

"Parker Drum Exercise"

Charlie Parker's First Date as a Leader

An important milestone in Parker's career came on November 26, 1945, when he led made his first records as a leader for the Savoy label. Beginning with this session, one can gradually develop a sense of Parker's own musical direction through his choice of musicians, choice of repertoire, and approach to the organization of the sessions themselves.

Unlike any of Parker's previous 1944–45 sessions (including those under Gillespie's leadership), both the bassist and the drummer were solidly in the new style. Unanimity of rhythmic conception is essential in any form of jazz, and the playing on this session swings more consistently than the two Gillespie dates with Parker. Parker's choice of trumpeter was also significant. Instead of using his peer, Dizzy Gillespie, Parker called on the nineteen-year-old Miles Davis to share the front line with him. Parker and Gillespie had a vital partnership; among modern jazz musicians, only Gillespie could match Parker in brilliance. Davis was not selected to be an improvisational match for Parker but as a complement or contrast to him. At this early stage in Davis's development, Parker heard something promising in the trumpeter's playing. Despite Davis's potential as an improviser, he had many inconsistencies in tone production and especially in technical execution of ensemble passages. The fact that Gillespie had to play trumpet on one particularly difficult number underscores Davis's technical limitations of the time. In addition to selecting Davis for his talent, possibly Parker may have been asserting his independence from Gillespie. Ironically, although Parker had passed up Gillespie as the date's trumpeter, he wound up asking Gillespie to play accompanimental piano when the first keyboard choice, Bud Powell, was unavailable![15]

Parker's choice of material is also revealing. Although Gillespie was a fine blues player, he had selected no blues for his recording sessions with Parker. Parker, on the other hand, recorded two blues (both in F) on his first record date. In doing so, Parker asserted his Kansas City roots. One blues, "Billie's Bounce," is a real bebop tune in its melodic contours and rhythms. The other, "Now's the Time," is largely based on the repetition of a simple six-note lick (rather like "You're in the Army Now"), making this piece much simpler for Parker to put together. "Thriving on a Riff" (credited to Parker as author; probably titled by Teddy Reig of Savoy) is virtually identical to what would soon be known as "Anthropology" (credited to both Parker and Gillespie; Parker claimed he was sole author of this piece). Parker had also prepared a fourth and final piece, his "Ko Ko."[16]

If Parker's choices of personnel and repertoire were significant, so was his manner of organizing the session. Parker approached his first record date as a leader with casualness bordering on chaos. Although his intended pianist, Bud Powell, had unexpectedly left town, Parker improvised by tapping Gillespie to comp chords for him. Perhaps because Gillespie was not able to convincingly solo on piano, Parker also asked pianist Argonne Thornton to join the session. Because Miles Davis could not technically navigate the tricky ensemble passages in "Ko Ko," Gillespie was also called upon to play trumpet during the introduction and coda. The fact that the shifting piano and trumpet roles caused a nightmare for discographers that lasted for years is of no importance to the success or failure of the music. But, in addition, Parker brought a saxophone/mouthpiece/reed setup that was clearly not working. During the first three takes of "Billie's Bounce," Parker's reed squeaked unacceptably and the sax itself was evidently not in good shape. Teddy Reig, Savoy's producer, told Bob Porter, "Bird was having trouble with his horn. We tried everything to get it straight. Bird even poured a pitcher of water into the horn to try to get the pads wet."[17] After several takes were marred by squeaks, it was decided to take a break and get Parker's saxophone repaired. When Porter asked Reig if he had accompanied Parker to get the horn repair, he replied "Of course! You think I'd leave Charlie Parker alone in midtown? What am I crazy?"[18] Of course, what Reig is referring to is Parker's drug-related lack of accountability. The same forces of addiction that made his behavior undependable when left on his own also led Parker to sometimes pawn his saxophone for money and have to play on borrowed horns in poor shape.

The first piece attempted that day (and the one that was interrupted for horn repair) was "Billie's Bounce." Each of Parker's solos on the five takes has elements of great beauty and freshness; Parker is clearly at home with the blues. Readers who have a reissue of the complete session might listen for Dizzy Gillespie's shouts of encouragement after Parker blows a particularly funky phrase on the penultimate fourth take (1:02). Parker begins his solo on the originally issued fifth take with a concise phrase that was learned by a generation of saxophonists, such as Wardell Gray who used it to open his famous solo on "Twisted":

"Billie's Bounce" (Take 5) Ex. 1

During his second chorus (fifth take), Parker uncorks a fleet double-time run (1:11) that would from then on be one of his favorite ii-7–V7 patterns[19] (noted in an earlier form on "Salt Peanuts," above, and the 1943 Redcross version of "Body and Soul" described in chapter 2). Following is a comparison between the lick as found in Parker's solos on "Billie's Bounce" and "Body and Soul." (In order to make the relationship between the two clearer, the rhythmic notation of the "Body and Soul" has been augmented, and both examples are presented as played in their *saxophone* keys, not in "concert" key.)[20] Notice how many notes from the "Body and Soul" rendition of the lick turn up in the "Billie's Bounce" version. The two most significant additions to the "Billie's Bounce" excerpt are circled. The addition of these notes allows a second, overlapping presentation of the voiceleading figure first discussed with regard to the 1940 "Honeysuckle Rose" in chapter 2. Parker's control of accents at high speed had increased markedly since the earlier examples, and this time, Parker displays his increasing skill in creative accentuation by emphasizing the melodic high points of measure 33, thereby creating cross-rhythms of groups of three against the basic duple pulse.

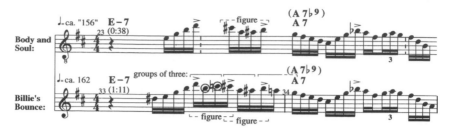

"Billie's Bounce" (Take 5) Ex. 2

Like the previous example, thousands of saxophonists over the years considered memorization of this lick to be a must. In later years, Parker himself tended to use this lick unconsciously, and it turned into one of his clichés.

Parker then turned to the riff-derived "Now's the Time." Each of the two complete Parker solos is a concise masterpiece. On take three, he plays an earthy blues melody that he would return to often.[21] Because he phrased this pet lick slightly differently each time, it's been regularized in the notation here to aid subsequent recognition. With frequent use, this phrase would become one of Parker's most characteristic and best-loved licks.

"Now's the Time" (Take 3)

On the originally issued take four, he plays a variant of the pair of downward blues runs noted in the "Hootie Blues" description in chapter 2. Although bebop in general, and Charlie Parker's music in particular, were often considered to be abstract, Parker had a constant undercurrent of earthiness that might surface at any time. In a few notes, Parker could suggest the essence of the blues.

After waxing "Thriving on a Riff" ("Anthropology") with Thornton on piano, Parker turned to the fourth prepared selection, "Ko Ko." Miles Davis was incapable of playing the complex and rapid introduction on the spot (Parker tended to spring new material on his group right in the studio), so Dizzy Gillespie was tapped to play that section on trumpet

Charlie Parker as a child

(Left to right) Charlie Parker (alto sax) and Gene Ramey (bass), circa 1940. (Duncan Scheidt Collection.)

(Left to right) Harold West (drums), Curly Russell (bass), Charlie Parker (alto sax), and Dizzy Gillespie (trumpet) at Town Hall, May, 1945. (Frank Driggs Collection.)

Charlie Parker at Camarillo State Hospital, 1946 or early 1947. (Francis Paudras Collection.)

(Left to right) Tommy Potter (bass), Charlie Parker (alto sax), Max Roach (drums), Miles Davis (trumpet), and Duke Jordan (piano) at the Three Deuces, 1948. (Photograph: William P. Gottlieb.)

(Clockwise from top) Billy Bauer (electric guitar), Eddie Safranski (bass), Charlie Parker (alto sax), and Lennie Tristano (piano) recording with the Metronome All-Stars, January 3, 1949. (Photograph: Herman Leonard.)

(Left to right) Buddy Rich (drums), Ray Brown (bass), Charlie Parker (alto sax), Max Hollander (violin), Mitch Miller (English horn), and Milton Lomask (violin), November, 1949. (Frank Driggs Collection.)

(Left to right) Art Blakey (drums), Charlie Parker (alto sax), and Kenny Dorham (trumpet) at Birdland, March 5, 1955. (Photograph: Marcel Zanini.)

"Now's the Time" (Take 4)

before sliding behind the piano to comp. "Ko Ko" is as much a sketch for improvisation as it is a composition. Of the entire performance, only sixteen bars are "written"; most of the piece is improvised. Often in jazz, that's all that's necessary. Played by Gillespie (trumpet), Parker, and Max Roach, the scheme for the introduction looks like this:

A (8 measures)	B (8 measures)	C (8 measures)	D (8 measures)
muted trumpet	muted trumpet		muted trumpet
alto sax		alto sax	alto sax
brushes on snare	brushes on snare	brushes on snare	brushes on snare
written	improvised	improvised	written
eight measures	eight measures	eight measures	eight measures

The written A and D sections are unlike any other Parker writing in their harmonic and rhythmic ambiguity.[22] Even Max Roach had to work hard to play the introduction: "The introduction to 'Ko Ko,' I know, was a struggle because rhythmically, you know, it was [sings]. It started on the upbeat, and it was almost like a disguised downbeat. 'Where was one?' was always the question."[23] Parker did not pursue this abstract direction for entire songs, although these passages are different from other bop writing and effectively anticipate Ornette Coleman's more boppish pieces.

After the introduction on the second (and only complete) take, Charlie Parker then launches into a breathtaking two-chorus solo (with Gillespie rushing back to the piano to comp) based on the harmonies and form of Ray Noble's "Cherokee." Today, we can prepare ourselves for "Ko Ko" by listening to Parker develop his approach to "Cherokee" in two amateur recordings from the earlier 1940s (chapter 2). But in 1945, only a handful of listeners and musicians had ever heard Parker on his favorite test-piece. This solo, more than any other Parker had yet put on disc, announced Parker's brilliance as an instrumentalist and a musical mind to the world. Parker, to be sure, used some familiar material in his solo. The rapid tempo and difficulty of the B section harmonies require rigorous preparation that do not significantly detract from the overall freshness of the solo. Readers who have heard Parker's solo on "Chero-kee" recorded at Monroe's in 1942 (discussed in chapter 2) will find the following bridge section passage familiar:

"Ko Ko" (Take 2) Ex. 1

It is, of course, a variation of the lick involving the alternate or "long" fingerings noted in both the apprenticeship period recordings of "Cherokee." As Parker begins his second chorus, he plays a surprising quotation, the clarinet part from the New Orleans jazz staple, "High Society" (1:16):

"Ko Ko" (Take 2) Ex. 2

Parker was not an organized student of jazz history, but he had inquisitive listening habits as has been noted in chapter 2. Before 1944, Parker was more likely to quote from the jazz world (swing era musicians like Eldridge, Hawkins, Young, Krupa, Ellington, et al.) than in his mature work. This quotation in "Ko Ko" is unusual in part because of its source; New Orleans jazz was not part of Parker's early listening sphere. In 1945, "traditional" jazz was experiencing a revival, and Parker may have picked up this lick from the revivalists rather than from an early recording. He had already referred to this melody during this recording date during his solos on "Warming Up a Riff" (0:17) and on the first take of "Thriving On a Riff" (1:13). (Around 1949, Parker began quoting Louis Armstrong's 1928 "West End Blues" solo in his blues improvisa-tions: see chapter 4.)

At the bridge of the second chorus (1:41), Parker again plays his "Tea for Two" variations discussed in chapter 2. Instead of presenting the pattern simply from beat one, with regular accents on beats one and three of each measure, he waits a beat and then rearranges the pattern to produce accents that fall on beats two, four, one, three, one, three, four, two—producing a much less symmetrical and more boppish scheme.

"Ko Ko" (Take 2) Ex. 3

After Parker, Max Roach takes a half-chorus solo, which is followed by a return of the introduction material acting as a coda. In a demonstration of how modern jazz was misunderstood in the mid-1940s, when *Metronome* magazine reviewed "Ko Ko," it was rated "C+" ("fair"); the reviewers referred to Max Roach's "horrible, utterly beatless drum solo."[24]

Two other selections were incidentally recorded that day, the so-called "Warming Up a Riff," which is an in-progress warm-up for "Ko Ko," and "Meandering," an improvisation on the chords to "Embrace-able You" (in E♭). The latter ends abruptly during the Thornton piano solo (once thought to be by Gillespie), when the musicians exceeded the three-plus-minute limit of the 78 RPM. It could have been issued as a complete performance if the producer or Parker himself had anticipated the extreme length of the thirty-two-bar form at that tempo and arranged for a shortened second chorus. In its reflective qualities, "Meandering" documents Parker's further development as a ballad player and forecasts his ballad masterpieces made for Dial in 1947 (see chapter 4).

The California Recordings, Part One

Soon after Parker's Savoy session, Gillespie took a group including Parker to Los Angeles to open at Billy Berg's nightclub on December 10, 1945. The group that met in Los Angeles for the job was: Dizzy Gillespie, trumpet; Charlie Parker, alto sax; Al Haig, piano, Milt Jackson, vibes (an added starter to fill out the group when Parker, as a result of his drug addiction, might be absent); Ray Brown, bass; and Stan Levey, drums.[25] Tenor saxophonist Eli "Lucky" Thompson was eventually added at Billy Berg's request for the same reasons that Gillespie brought Jackson. Berg also requested that the band include some vocal selections to make their sound more commercial; according to Ray Brown, Parker obliged by writing "a couple of charts where the whole band was singing."[26]

Gillespie's California band did not record commercially for any record label. However, the basic quintet, with or without added starters Jackson and Thompson, is documented in four informally recorded selections from late 1945 and early 1946. The selections ("Shaw Nuff," "Groovin' High," and "Dizzy Atmosphere" from an Armed Forces Radio Service date and "Salt Peanuts" as broadcast from Billy Berg's) offer our best glimpse of the California band with Parker. Not restricted by the three-minute 78 RPM record format, three of the four pieces, not surprisingly, run a bit longer than the original studio recordings. Their longer solos and in-person excitement display much of the vitality of the early Gillespie-Parker partnership. All four songs had been recorded by Gillespie and Parker in 1945 and were at the heart of the California band's repertoire. Other likely selections in the group's repertoire include Charlie Parker's "Confirmation" and Thelonious Monk's "Round About Midnight" (both recorded by Gillespie in California at a recording session that Parker failed to show up for; see below), Gillespie's "Blue 'n' Boogie" (featured by Parker at the Finale Club, see below), most of the pieces from the 1945 Gillespie and Parker sessions discussed above, and Gillespie's "A Night in Tunisia" (below).

On January 24, 1946, in Los Angeles, Parker made his first appearance of many over the years at Norman Granz's ongoing Jazz at the Philharmonic (JATP) concert series. Parker would later record exclusively for Granz's labels, and Granz would subsidize Parker to a limited extent. This concert is significant in part because it is the first recorded documentation of Parker and his early idol, Lester Young, playing together. The drummer of the evening, Lester's brother Lee Young, was hearing Parker for the first time: "And Bird sounded, to me, the way Lester sounded when he was playing alto."[27] Lee Young's assertion in another interview that Lester played more technically on the alto sax than later on his tenor is seconded by saxophonist Benny Carter: "He had a definition and a mastery that I don't think he ever felt necessary to display on the tenor."[28]

On this particular night, both Parker and Gillespie were scheduled to appear in the first half of the program to allow them enough time to play their usual date at Billy Berg's. In his excellent liner notes for the complete set of Parker's recordings for Granz, Phil Schaap relates how Parker arrived just in time for the last number of the first set, "Sweet

Georgia Brown," reportedly because he had been out obtaining heroin.[29] During "Sweet Georgia Brown," one can hear Parker being greeted by someone with "Say, man, where you been?" (1:08). Gillespie exited as planned during intermission, but Parker stayed on, evidently willing to arrive late at Gillespie's gig. As has been noted, Gillespie was prepared with an extra player or two to round out the group at Berg's.

On the faster pieces, Parker's rhythmic sense has a wild edge-of-your-seat quality, and his solo lines show subtle signs of disarray. Perhaps his reportedly intoxicated state accounts for his uncharacteristically imprecise execution. Parker's timbre during the concert is edgy and has a tendency to minor reed squeaks. He avoids use of vibrato on medium-to-short notes, but he does use it on notes lasting two or more beats.

"Sweet Georgia Brown" finds Parker loosely quoting tenor saxophonist Budd Johnson's "Yellow Fire" solo (2:01; recorded in 1940 with Earl Hines), another example of Parker's encyclopedic stock of licks from many sources and his ability to call up those musical phrases at will. Pianist Arnold Ross reports an odd moment, evidently on "Blues for Norman": "And on this one tune, I remember Bird stepped forward and he didn't play for a whole chorus. He just stood there with his horn in his mouth."[30] When he does solo, he seems to extend his solo for a few choruses too many, perhaps waiting for the usual JATP riff accompaniment to clear out before concluding. Even Parker is not immune to the frantic JATP atmosphere as he tries a honk, a bit of rasp, and an altissimo note.

Oh, Lady Be Good!

Given that Charlie Parker had carefully studied Lester Young's recordings of the 1930s, it was fitting that they should both participate in a performance of George Gershwin's "Oh, Lady Be Good!" that evening (complete solo transcription in appendix B). Among his 1944–46 works, Parker's solo on "Ko Ko" (above) is probably more famous than his solo on "Oh, Lady Be Good!"; certainly it has been more frequently cited, transcribed, analyzed, and anthologized. But compared to "Ko Ko," "Oh, Lady Be Good" offers an especially varied basis to evaluate the state of Parker's harmonic, melodic, and rhythmic arts of this period.

Much like Lester Young's 1936 version, Parker's 1940 recording of "Oh, Lady Be Good!" with Jay McShann (see chapter 2) was taken at a medium-up swing tempo (quarter note = ca. 230), and Parker had responded with some Young-like gestures. The 1946 JATP rendition is taken at a slower groove tempo (quarter note = ca. 138), and Parker this time demonstrates his transcendence of his influences and his arrival as a unique improvisational voice. This thirty-two-bar AABA pop song in 4/4 time was written in and here performed in the concert key of G major, putting Parker in the key of E on his alto sax. The key signature of four sharps presents Parker no technical problem.

Parker's "Oh, Lady Be Good!" solo includes a wide variety of note values from long (dotted half note) to short (thirty-second notes). The latter, of course, is found only in the briefest embellishments and is not sustained. The basic rhythmic unit for the first chorus is the eighth note. Perhaps responding to the other musicians' riffing, Parker double-times extensively during the second chorus, making the basic rhythmic unit the sixteenth note. His first double-time phrase (2:13; over a ii-7–V7–I progression) demonstrates both his fluid technique and his penchant for accenting at the high points of a melodic line.

"Oh, Lady Be Good!" (1946) Ex. 1

Although a few phrases marginally cut across the song's AABA structural divisions, Parker generally observes the piece's eight-bar units. *Within* the units, Parker creatively expresses himself with asymmetric phrase construction. These phrase lengths vary from just one or two notes (measures 26 and 27) to approximately three measures long. Although Parker was more likely to indulge in musical quotations in live settings such as this, his "Oh, Lady Be Good!" solo is notable for its lack of references to other songs. Parker's high level of melodic invention no doubt accounts for much of the freshness of the solo.

Unusual for Parker are the very effective scoops and falls that give this solo so much of its bluesy nature. Parker was a master at suggesting the blues in very few notes, as this pair of phrases from early on in the solo illustrates:

"Oh, Lady Be Good!" (1946) Ex. 2

A favorite blues lick of Parker's (noted in "Hootie Blues" in chapter 2 and "Now's the Time," above) begins the first B section:

"Oh, Lady Be Good!" (1946) Ex. 3

Parker's balance between the abstract and the earthy can be seen in the final A section when, after neatly exiting some double-timing, he returns to the basics with another favorite blues lick:

"Oh, Lady Be Good!" (1946) Ex. 4

From a harmonic standpoint, Parker displays an astute sense of substitute and passing chords. Parker had picked up pianist Ross and bassist Billy Hadnott's chromatically descending passing chords in measure 4, and in the parallel spot of his second A section (measure 12), Parker follows suit:

"Oh, Lady Be Good!" (1946) Ex. 5

To conclude his first chorus, Parker superimposes a lyrical ii-7–♭IIΔ7–I progression over his accompanists' usual ii-7–V7–I cadence (a substitution he occasionally employed; see "Donna Lee" take 2 in chapter 4). Note the careful top-to-bottom 7–5–3-1 arpeggiation (substitute chords in parenthesis):

"Oh, Lady Be Good!" (1946) Ex. 6

Probably due to the horizontalizing effect of the background riffing, Parker is less interested in implying substitute chords in the second chorus. His rapid double-timing does not, however, deter him from clearly outlining the basic chord changes and some tasty alterations of them. Ever resourceful, he even takes a simple tonic chord and, having arpeggiated it from the third of the chord (3–5–7–9), proceeds to embellish it effectively with chromatic "lower neighbor" tones (the circled pitches a half step below the following E, B, G♯, and E chord tones):

"Oh, Lady Be Good!" (1946) Ex. 7

In the liner notes cited above, Phil Schaap writes that none of the on-stage musicians wanted to follow Parker's solo. After an unplanned bass solo, some of the musicians reportedly urged Lester Young to go out and solo next on this piece that was highly identified with him. Although already entering into his "slow-motion" saxophone period, Young shows that he, too, has new things to say on "Oh, Lady Be Good!"

Parker and Young were slated to participate in a recording date for Dial, a new Los Angeles label. The session was to be led by composer-arranger-pianist George Handy, but Young was not available on one date and didn't show up for another. At the latter session (February 5, 1946), Parker and Gillespie recorded Handy's "Diggin' Diz," which would be their last studio recording for nearly two years. Gillespie salvaged another Handy date on February 7, bringing in his Billy Berg group (minus Parker, who did not show up) to record several pieces that were probably from the band's repertoire at Berg's. These included "Confirmation," an important Parker composition that he himself would not wax until 1953. While still in Los Angeles, Gillespie also recorded four Jerome Kern songs in a setting that included strings and winds. This date preceded Parker's first string recording by about three and a half years and may have whetted Parker's appetite for a more orchestral setting.

After his engagement at Billy Berg's had ended, Gillespie returned to New York City while Parker stayed behind. Parker soon began working on his own in Los Angeles, primarily at the Finale Club. The one surviving live recording of that band features a lineup of Parker (alto sax), Miles Davis (on trumpet, who had traveled West with Benny Carter's band specifically in order to reunite with Parker), Joe Albany (piano), Addison Farmer (bass), and Chuck Thompson (drums). The repertoire consists of pieces associated with Parker and Gillespie ("Anthropology," "Blue 'n' Boogie" and "All The Things You Are"), with Parker and Davis ("Billie's Bounce"), and a new composition not yet commercially recorded, "Ornithology."

The latter was a co-composition of Parker and trumpeter Benny ("Bennie") Harris over the chord progression of the pop song "How High the Moon." The opening phrase of "Ornithology" derives from the beginning of Parker's 1942 solo on "The Jumpin' Blues" (a phrase that may have derived from Lester Young; see chapter 2). Although "The Jumpin' Blues" is in the key of F and "Ornithology" is in G, the nearly identical melodic contours of the two phrases is evident in this comparison:

"Ornithology" (1946)

At the time of the Finale recording, the last four measures of each A section (measures 13–16 and 29–32) were left open for improvisation. Soon Parker would fill the latter measures in with a simple triplet figure (see below).

A fair number of Charlie Parker's 1945–46 recordings described thus far have some out-of-control element to them, be it a squeaking reed, wobbly vibrato, rhythmic imprecision, or octave key problems. Despite his phenomenal ability to play well when high on drugs, most of the problems of execution might be attributed to Parker's heroin and alcohol addictions. Even the problems with his equipment trace back to his addiction; he played on borrowed and inferior saxophones often because he regularly pawned his own horn to get money for drugs. Although Parker's health was generally worsening due to his difficulties obtaining heroin, he sounds quite relaxed on the Finale Club selections, playfully quoting "I Hear a Rhapsody," "Happy Birthday" and his own Savoy label solos from "Billie's Bounce" and "Now's the Time."

Davis, playing with a trumpet mute throughout, sounds more confident and secure than on his 1945 recordings with Parker. The seldom recorded Albany is particularly interesting; although his sense of swing is on the heavy-handed side, his comping and melodic solo lines are highly creative and display considerable technique. Albany's solo on "Ornithology" is an effective assemblage of small, independent fragments. During the Finale engagement, Parker and Albany had a run-in:

> Bird was singing to me like I wasn't comping right, so I did it every which way, and finally I did what I thought was backwards, comping out of time, and I still didn't please him, so I turned around and said "____ You, Bird," and that was the end. He fired me.[31]

Albany was soon replaced by pianist Michael "Dodo" Marmarosa.

During the initial Finale engagement (it would soon close and later be reopened by trumpeter Howard McGhee), Parker approached the founder of Dial Records, Ross Russell, with recording in mind. Although the music of Gillespie and Parker was not generally well received in L.A., Parker "had been told that Igor Stravinsky and Arnold Schoenberg had made their permanent home in Southern California, and he now saw the area in a new light."[32] Parker outlined optimistic plans to settle in Los Angeles, live the healthy life, and compose "seriously." The result of this pitch was a one-year, twelve-side contract (a "side" was one side of a 78 RPM record) with Dial. Although the working relationship between Parker and Ross Russell was sometimes contentious, Russell's respect for the integrity of the music would produce a striking series of Parker masterpieces for the Dial label.

The first of these Dial sessions took place in Los Angeles on March 28, 1946. The personnel was largely drawn from the pool of Finale Club musicians. Chaos entered the organization of another Parker recording session when he scuttled an attempted rehearsal the night before at the Finale Club. Reportedly, he asked the musicians to wait and then spent two hours looking for his heroin connection, Emery "Moose the Mooche" Byrd. Bassist George "Red" Callender then quit over Parker's behavior. If the recording session had a shaky beginning, things smoothed out when the group assembled in the studio. The supporting musicians who finally did participate in the session for Dial were Miles Davis (trumpet), Lucky Thompson (tenor sax), Dodo Marmarosa (piano), Vic McMillan (bass), Roy Porter (drums), and Arvin Garrison (electric guitar, on three of the titles).

Parker's improvisations on this session show a new level of consistency and predict his best work of 1947 and 1948. Gone are the frantic qualities that surfaced in some of his faster performances of 1945; replacing them are a new balance and poise that do not conflict with Parker's great powers of invention and surprise. Several factors may contribute to this overall impression. First, due to the large number of soloists in the band, no one solos at great length. Parker responds to the time restriction by producing succinct improvisations of classic balance. Second, none of the tempos of the four pieces recorded match the breakneck speed of some of Parker's work with Dizzy Gillespie of 1945; the medium tempos chosen favor a more reflective Parker (Parker's accompanists may not have been able to function at up-tempo as well as Gillespie or Max Roach, perhaps necessitating the more relaxed tempos). Finally, without the friendly competition of Gillespie, Parker's partner for most of his recordings of the past twelve months, Parker may not have felt as inclined to attempt the dramatic, virtuosic musical statement. (Although they would occasionally reunite for concerts, nightclub dates, and recording sessions, a sustained Gillespie-Parker partnership was over.)

Although Parker had promised to compose new music for the date, he merely chose three preexisting songs and sketched out one original tune on the way to the session.[33] That new piece (based on the AABA form of "I Got Rhythm") would be titled "Moose the Mooche" and was named for his Los Angeles drug connection. This is one of Parker's finest original melodies of any era, and it is all the finer because he composed both the A and B sections instead of improvising the bridge, as was becoming his tendency. Much of the piece's effectiveness derives from

Parker's use of a single rhythmic motive to unify the composition, an unusual technique for Parker:

"Moose the Mooche" Ex. 1

Parker employed the motive (and variations upon it) eighteen times in the statement of the melody, choosing to maintain the basic rhythmic pattern while varying other elements. Although the original motive begins on the "and" of beat 2, Parker also begins the motive on the "and" of 3 and on the "and" of 1. Parker began the motive on eight different notes and ended it on seven different notes. Along the way, the overall melodic contour is presented in six different shapes. Parker also varied the placement of the motive within the song's eight-measure section. Particularly inventive is the way he used the motive in the transition between the second A section and the bridge. Note how the motive is shifted in time, beginning on the "and" of beat 2 (bar 15), the "and" of beat 1 (bar 16), and the "and" of beat 3 (bars 17–18), and also note how two new melodic contours are produced:

"Moose the Mooche" Ex. 2

"Moose the Mooche" is one of Parker's high points of melodic composition.

The next selection to be tackled was "Yardbird Suite," an instrumental version of "What Price Love?" a melody, chord progression,[34] and lyric Parker had written while with Jay McShann. Although Parker generally tended to only write new melodies over preexisting forms, "Yardbird Suite" (its title is evidently a pun on the piece *Firebird Suite* by Igor Stravinsky; Parker had heard part or all of the ballet score several years before) is a wholly original composition in both melody (A *and* B sections) and chord progression. This piece is best known in its instrumental incarnation, but in the 1940s, singers Carmen McRae and Earl Coleman learned the lyric from Parker. The vocal version, "What Price Love?" first recorded by Coleman in 1948, begins:

It's hard to learn how tears can burn one's heart,
but that's a thing that I found out
too late, I guess, I'm in a mess.

My faith is gone, why lead me on this way?
I thought there'd be no price on love,
yet I have to pay.[35]

In measures 6 and 7 (0:53) of Parker's solo in the fourth (master) take of "Yardbird Suite," Parker plays in passing the melody that he would record the next year as "Cool Blues," also in the key of C. (For a discussion of the derivation of "Cool Blues," see chapter 4).

By 1946, a growing number of saxophonists all over the United States had discovered Charlie Parker's music and were learning its ways through the transcription of his solos. Saxophonist Lee Konitz was later asked by Lennie Tristano how it felt to play Parker's solo on "Yardbird Suite," one that Konitz (already a professional musician) had memorized and played in private practice:

I feel that I have to use every ounce of energy in my body to play this properly. . . . I learned this solo off the record . . . because it's perfect music to me. And through playing the notes, I was able to absorb some of the essence of the feeling that he used.[36]

After Parker and group had tackled "Yardbird Suite," they turned to the Benny Harris-Charlie Parker composition, "Ornithology." The composition was still in transition; the above mentioned improvisational measures 29–32 of the Finale Club version were replaced for this recording with a simple written (or merely worked-out) triplet figure seen in the upper part. By 1948, these bars would be finalized with the chromatic turnaround figure seen in the lower part. (At that later date, the previously open measures 13–16 were also set; it's not clear whether Parker or Harris wrote the additional music that finalized the song into the version played ever since.)

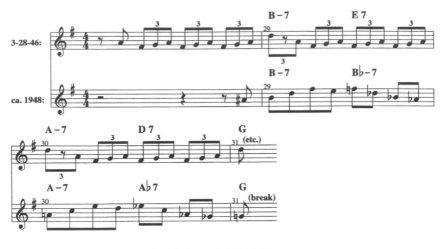

"Ornithology" (1946/1948)

The last piece to be recorded on this date was Dizzy Gillespie's "A Night in Tunisia," probably part of the Gillespie group's repertoire at Billy Berg's. Typical of Gillespie, "A Night in Tunisia" is a wholly original composition with a well-worked-out arrangement including an introduction, an interlude, and a four-bar "break" for the first soloist. During the first take, Parker filled that four-bar section with a stunning fantasia in sixteenth notes. After the take, Parker said, "I'll never make that break again;"[37] in fact, Parker played basically the same break on each take. Due to mistakes from the other musicians, that take was not judged to be suitable for release, although, years later, a short excerpt of it was released as "Famous Alto Break."

"Famous Alto Break"

Despite Parker's claim, analysis of his solo breaks on this and the other two surviving takes of "A Night in Tunisia" show that he had already worked out his opening improvisational gambit: all three breaks are nearly identical. This lack of variation does not take away from the brilliance of his solo break; no other instrumentalist in jazz at the time would have conceived of and executed that passage.

If Parker's first date as a leader for Dial was productive and smoothly run, his next date for the company was quite the opposite. The human body that entered the recording studio on July 29, 1946 (just seven months to the day after his and Gillespie's first West Coast recordings), had radically deteriorated from the one that had arrived in California. After his drug connection, Emery Byrd, had been arrested, Parker tried to stave off heroin withdrawal symptoms by drinking large amounts of alcohol. He later said, "I had to drink a quart of whisky to make the date."[38]

Parker had been working with Howard McGhee at the reopened Finale Club. McGhee had watched Parker's health deteriorate, and he urged Ross Russell to record Parker again soon. Ross Russell characterized Charlie Parker as insisting that he was ready to record, despite Russell's concerns about Parker's deteriorating health. Parker evidently promised to write "half a dozen" new pieces for the record date and asked for advances against future record royalties.

By the time of the recording date, Parker had developed muscle spasms that caused his arms to twitch as he blew the saxophone. Dial partner Marvin Freeman's physician brother, Richard, attempted to medicate Parker, and the recording date went ahead. Two fast pieces ("Max Is Making Wax" and "Bebop") and two ballads ("Lover Man" and "The Gypsy") were chosen. On the up-tempo numbers, Parker is unable to keep up in the ensemble passages; when it comes time to solo, he can only produce halting, surreal fragments of melody. On the slow pieces, Parker manages a little more continuity, but his efforts are just as disturbing to the listener. Typical of these moments is the opening of "Lover Man" in which, after a short introduction from the rhythm section, Parker misses his entrance and has to be cued by the pianist Jimmy Bunn. When Parker does enter, his timbre is thin due to his inability to support the saxophone airstream and is marked by a weak vibrato in the older style that Parker had consciously shunned.

Parker's condition was so bad that only one take of each of the compositions was attempted. The responsibility to hold the shaky session

"Lover Man"

together fell to Howard McGhee, and he did so through the consistent level of his playing. As was noted in chapter 1, Parker was sent back to his hotel and later was arrested, an episode that led to the lowest ebb of his twenty-five years. McGhee, showing his professionalism and preparedness, completed the date with two fiery trumpet-plus-rhythm sides.

These sides were the last to be recorded by Parker for seven months. As detailed in chapter 1, Parker experienced a physical and emotional breakdown that evening and was committed to California's Camarillo State Hospital. Although the selections recorded that day seemed unreleasable, Ross Russell fairly quickly put out "Lover Man" and "Bebop" (Parker reportedly never forgave him), and soon the jazz world heard the depths to which Parker had sunk. Amazingly, some young jazz players enthusiastically learned Parker's halting "Lover Man" solo note for note, not realizing that his playing represented a personal disaster and musical low point.

Parker's breakdown ended a period marked by both his first undisputed masterpieces and his most discouraging recorded efforts. Through his recordings with Dizzy Gillespie, and especially through his first recordings as a leader, Parker had established himself as a major new jazz voice. Parker had reached a striking level of virtuosity and ability to swing at furious up-tempo, and demonstrated convincingly the continued relevance of the blues even as jazz became more complex and sophisticated. While ironing out inconsistencies in tone production and technical execution, Parker continued to gain flexibility in both double-timing and creative accentuation of his melodic line.

Importantly, Parker was no longer dependent on the phraseology of his apprenticeship period influences for improvisational material. His melodic, harmonic, and rhythmic explorations had borne fruit in the form of a distinct and unique musical vocabulary. Remarkably, he had accomplished all of this despite an increasingly debilitating heroin addiction. With so many musical factors in place, Charlie Parker was in a position to create his best work; his health was the only likely impediment.

Chapter 4

1947–49

With Charlie Parker's release from Camarillo State Hospital came the most musically productive period of his life. This period may be dated from the beginning of February of 1947 (his first posthospitalization recording) until the gradual breakup of his working group in spring of 1950. Central to this period is that working group, Parker's classic quintet, which was formed in 1947. Although this chapter is titled "1947–49," it will follow the evolution of Parker's working quintet into 1950. New noncombo developments in Parker's career that began at the end of the 1940s (especially the bulk of his Norman Granz recordings) will be discussed in chapter 5.

This period of Parker's development is his best-documented one. His discography shows Parker being recorded on nearly eight times the number of dates from 1947 through 1949 than he had been recorded from 1944 through 1946. This fact allows Parker's development as an artist to be traced much more accurately than ever before. The quality and consistency of Parker's recorded work was also at an all-time high during this period. Much of this may be attributed to the advantages of having a working group with a regular personnel, a first for Parker. His health was more stable than before his hospitalization, and few of his studio or live recordings show impairment of his reflexes. These riches of quantity and quality ironically place a premium on the need for this chapter to be extremely selective. There is simply no way that all of Parker's highlights of this period can be included, given this book's concentrated nature.

Parker's qualities of virtuosity, swing, inventiveness, playfulness, and poetic bluesiness reached new highs during this period. With Parker's return to the jazz scene, a new sense of poise and flexibility is evident in his improvisations. Parker seemed to have undergone a final evolutionary step in his mastery of what jazz musicians call "time." On the extreme up-tempo pieces that form an important part of his reputation as a virtuoso, Parker displayed an even more relaxed relationship to the beat than previously, leading him to swing more satisfyingly than ever.

Parker had been documented in earlier chapters as raising his upper limit of the tempo at which he could sustain double-time passages. During this period, his control of this skill reached a new height. At the slow ballad tempos that Parker had more recently mastered, his ability to accurately subdivide the beat into smaller units (sixteenth or thirty-second notes, for example) attained an amazing degree of mastery. Understandably, at the same time he also raised the absolute tempo at which he could fluently play rapid swing pieces. At fast or slow tempos, Parker had further developed the ability to accent virtually any note falling on any part of a subdivided beat, lending a whiplike snap to his rapid runs. Of course, a few other jazz instumentalists from the previous generation had played as rapidly as Parker, although they did not always have an easy, swinging relationship to the beat; Art Tatum, and Coleman Hawkins spring to mind as examples. Parker's contribution lay as much in *how* he played as in *what* he played. He not only played rapidly, he also played accurately (in his words, "clean") and with great swing. In describing modern jazz, Parker said, "I think the music of today is a sort of a combination of the Midwestern beat and the fast New York tempos."[1] There is much to Parker's assessment. If the swinging Lester Young (who came to musical maturity in Kansas City) exemplifies the "Midwestern beat," and the virtuosic Tatum and Hawkins exemplify the "fast New York tempos," Parker proved that swing need not be sacrificed in the pursuit of virtuosic complexity.

The out-of-control elements of "time," equipment, and vibrato of Parker's 1945–46, playing as noted in chapter 3 are not highly significant factors in the 1947–49 period. Their absence gives Parker's music of this period more subjective polish. Many of these elements (such as reed squeaks, octave key problems, or wobbly vibrato) may have been a result of Parker's intoxication and to the unreliability of the borrowed saxophones that Parker often used (during this period, he is known to have owned Conn, Selmer, and King saxophones, in that order). Parker's health upon his release from hospitalization was initially better, he certainly was making a better living playing music, and his daily life was arguably more stable. These factors of equipment, health, and life-style may contribute to Parker's seeming greater control of his tone production and consistency of saxophone timbre during this period. Ross Russell, not a saxophonist, reported that Parker switched from harder- to more moderate-strength reeds around the time of his classic quintet recordings. In general, Parker remained true to his ideal of a stripped-down and streamlined sound with minimal vibrato.

From 1947, Parker would usually take the role of bandleader on recordings and live appearances, and thus his repertoire fully reflects his choices. Except for the Dizzy Gillespie pieces he had learned during his partnership with the trumpeter, Parker only occasionally performed pieces by other jazz writers. The demands of record dates generally provided the impetus for new, copyrightable material. As expected, he often composed new melodies set to preexisting chord progressions and forms, and in the case of AABA forms, he often wrote only the eight-bar A sections, leaving the B sections to improvisation.

From a melodic standpoint, during this period Parker became a master of spinning out fanciful lines and letting them find their own lengths, without regard to symmetry or sectional divisions. He continued to enjoy, particularly outside of the recording studio, tossing in quotations of various pieces. Parker's best solos of the period (especially on the slower pieces on which he could leisurely create) had a great freshness and sense of discovery about them. Toward the end of the period, however, Parker's art showed signs of becoming melodically repetitive, a tendency that would increase in the 1950s. Parker's outlook on harmony did not markedly change post-Camarillo, although his understanding of harmony certainly deepened as he continued to absorb music theory from his more studious colleagues.

The California Recordings, Part Two

After Charlie Parker was released from Camarillo State Hospital, he was recorded at a party at the Los Angeles home of trumpeter Chuck Copely. Although Parker sounds understandably a little rusty on these few selections, there is also a freshness and lack of cliché to them. On the version of "Cherokee" known as "Home Cookin' II," Parker begins to fall into his favorite "Tea for Two" gambit during the bridge section (1:31), but instead of finishing the cliché, he moves on with fresh improvisation instead of set licks. Parker's best recordings of this period continue this preference of melodic invention over stock phrases.

Ross Russell had planned an all-star septet date for Dial to be recorded before Parker's departure from Los Angeles, but Parker instead wanted to record with the singer Earl Coleman. Parker's motivation in hiring Coleman is unclear; it's likely Parker was being supportive of the young singer, and perhaps he felt the vocal selections would appeal to a broader public. Russell has stated that he did not want to jeopardize the septet session he had in mind, so he proposed an earlier, separate date to record Coleman. For this February 19, 1947, recording session for Dial, a preexisting rhythm section was chosen, namely the Erroll Garner rhythm section that Parker had been fronting for Sunday matinees at Billy Berg's.

The tempos of the Coleman sides are slow, and although Parker contributes some moments of beauty, neither he nor the other musicians seems very inspired. After Coleman recorded two selections using four takes each, Parker and the trio had enough time to wax two instrumental selections. As soon as the quartet tackled the first instrumental selection, the mood changed markedly and Parker blew with a real sense of joy and freedom. These two selections are Parker at his most characteristic: young (still only twenty-six!), physically healthy, and bursting at the seams with ideas. One of the instrumental tracks was "Cool Blues," a riff blues in C credited to Charlie Parker. Its melody is similar to a figure found in Duke Ellington's 1932 "Blue Ramble" (also in C).[2] "Cool Blues" is also similar to a set-closing theme (conceivably derived from Ellington's earlier melody) reportedly used several years beforehand by bassist John Kirby's sextet.[3] Ellington, Kirby, or some other source could have been the root of this riff melody credited to Parker.

A week later (February 26, 1947), Parker reentered the studio to record the all-star septet date that Ross Russell had proposed. Parker was joined by Howard McGhee, Wardell Gray (tenor sax), Dodo Marmarosa (piano), Barney Kessell (electric guitar), Red Callender (bass) and Don Lamond (drums). A rehearsal for the session had been held the day before. According to Russell, Parker was late to the session, seemed hung over, and supplied only one of the four original compositions he had promised. The one tune, a blues, was written in a taxi on the way to the rehearsal. Ross Russell recalled:

No one could read Charlie's notation. When Howard [McGhee] tactfully pointed out mistakes in the musical spelling, Charlie crumpled the music paper, threw it on the floor, picked up the horn, and played out the theme. . . . The rest of the hour was spent struggling to master its insinuating line.[4]

Parker would refer to the piece as "Past Due," perhaps a reference to his lateness to the session. Russell retitled it "Relaxin' at Camarillo" when he released it. At the studio the next day, Howard McGhee brought three additional compositions to add to Parker's one, thus reaching the standard four selections per recording session.

The composition "Relaxin' at Camarillo" is notable for its tricky rhythms. The circled notes on the "ands" of the beat (those followed by rests) give the opening phrase a considerable syncopated punch.

"Relaxin' at Camarillo"

Later, when Parker had returned to New York City, his views on the two Dial sessions described above were paraphrased in an interview with Leonard Feather. "He made two Dial dates before returning to New York: one was with a group of musicians unfamiliar to him, and he wasn't too happy about it, but the other was a trio date with Erroll Garner which he believes was great."[5] Who were the musicians "unfamiliar" to Parker? Clearly not McGhee, Gray, Marmarosa, or Callender, each of whom Parker had worked with or whom he had hired for gigs or record dates. Remaining would be Kessell and Lamond, both of whom were chosen by Ross Russell. Setting aside any question as to their musical appropriateness to the group as a whole, it seems that Parker wished he had had more familiar players in those slots. In addition, Parker may have been dissatisfied with the all-star format; with so many soloists, no one gets to stretch out.

Howard McGhee landed work for a quintet at the Hi-De-Ho Club in Los Angeles. Saxophonist Dean Benedetti recorded the group regularly over a two-week period (March 1–13, 1947) on his portable disc-cutter. This group of Parker recordings, long believed lost, was finally issued in 1991. It offers an another of view of Parker's brief post-Camarillo period in Los Angeles, before his return to New York City.

A survey of the group's repertoire is of particular interest. Only four Parker compositions (including one co-composition) were certainly played by the group; Dizzy Gillespie and Howard McGhee are represented by three compositions each. The largest single source for the repertoire was the "book" of the popular and well-established Coleman Hawkins, with whom McGhee had played. Compositions by jazz artists aside, more "Tin Pan Alley" pop songs in general and ballads in particular are represented than in most live recordings of the period led by Parker or Gillespie. Sixteen of the pieces recorded by Benedetti at the Hi-De-Ho are unique in Parker's discography, with no other versions known to survive.

One of the earliest occurrences of a favorite quotation of Parker's comes up during the March 8, 1947, recording of the Hi-De-Ho group. During the song "Wee" (0:58), Parker plays the opening bars of Exercise 23 from *25 Daily Exercises For Saxophone* by Hyacinthe Eleonor Klosé, an example of how almost any material was fair game for a Parker solo. In this case of "Wee," the quotation is in B♭, but because at various times he played the quotation in different keys, the opening of the exercise is presented in the original key of C.

"Klosé Exercise 23"

In early April, 1947, less than a month after the Hi-De-Ho engagement ended, Charlie Parker flew to New York City via Chicago. Upon his return, Parker spoke quite critically of the Los Angeles jazz scene to critic Leonard Feather.

> What made it worst of all was that nobody understood our kind of music out on the coast. They *hated it,* Leonard. . . . As I left the coast they had a band at Billy Berg's with somebody playing a bass sax and a drummer playing on the temple blocks and ching-ching-ching-ching cymbals—one of those real New Orleans style bands, that *ancient* jazz—and the people liked it! That was the kind of thing that helped to crack my wig."[6]

The statement about New Orleans style jazz is unusual for Parker; seldom did he go on record as being critical of any style of jazz or any particular group or individual. The jazz world was at the time experiencing a rediscovery of New Orleans-derived music (often called "Dixieland" and now more generally "early jazz"), and certainly Parker was encountering the music much more often than he would have only a few years earlier. Older musicians who had been playing in the 1920s were now being rediscovered by jazz fans and critics, and younger players were emulating the earlier sounds. A construct that was popular in jazz until the late 1960s held that jazz was constantly improving; that further harmonic, melodic, and rhythmic sophistication and complexity advanced jazz; that each new style superseded the previous one, e.g., New Orleans jazz was made obsolete by the swing style that was then superseded by modern jazz. The devotées of early jazz styles felt that the music had classic qualities of simplicity, directness, honesty, and joy that were lacking in later styles, especially modern jazz. Certain critics, some listeners, and a very few musicians built up the differences between the earlier and current styles into a partisan rift that was very heated in the press at the time.

The Classic Quintet and Its Successors

Studio Recordings

Since Parker's departure in December, 1945, modern jazz had become much more firmly established in New York. Over the same period, Parker's fame had grown; he was no longer an underground phenomenon but was actively sought by club owners. These factors allowed Parker to form his first truly regularly working group, his classic quintet. He chose two of the musicians from his last New York recording session (November 26, 1945), Max Roach and Miles Davis. Rounding out the group usually were pianist Duke Jordan and bassist Tommy Potter. The group was relatively stable: Davis was in the group until late December, 1948; Roach was present until at least mid-1949; Tommy Potter continued well into 1950. (The term *classic quintet* is most often applied to Parker's 1947–48 group with both Davis and Roach. As the original quintet personnel gradually departed and were replaced by others, the overall sound of Parker's quintet remained similar. Therefore, both the classic quintet and its evolutionary successors will be discussed here.)

The question arises: why did Parker choose Miles Davis for the trumpet chair in his working group when other trumpeters with more dependable dexterity and tone production were available? Clearly, he could not use Dizzy Gillespie because both players were intent on leading their own groups. Howard McGhee, who had traveled from Los Angeles to New York City with Parker, certainly had the technique to play the music, but he had returned to California.[7] Able trumpeters McKinley "Kenny" Dorham and Red Rodney were able and probably would have jumped at the chance to join Charlie's new group; for unknown reasons, they were not tapped for Parker's quintet until 1948 and 1949, respectively. The ideal trumpeter for Parker's quintet probably would have been Theodore "Fats" Navarro. By 1947, Navarro had already formed a vital, coherent, and recognizable style. His high standard of dexterity plus his approach to melody, timbre, and articulation formed the mainstream of modern jazz trumpet playing at least until 1960. Several live recordings of Parker with Navarro show the two to be ideal partners in a modern jazz ensemble, and one recording in particular (see "The Street Beat," below) shows Navarro inspiring Parker to some of his most creative playing of the time. Navarro was in and around New York in 1947 but for unknown reasons was not hired for the Parker quintet.[8] In hiring Davis, perhaps Parker wanted a trumpeter whose style would complement rather than match Parker's and would be as different from Dizzy Gillespie's as possible. As suggested in the last chapter, Parker probably heard the potential in Davis's partially formed style. Since they had played last together in Los Angeles, Miles Davis had not only firmed up his trumpet technique but also had continued his evolution toward an individual trumpet style. Among Davis's best solo work with Parker are the open-horn solos found on take B of "Dexterity," and take C of "Bongo Beep," and the muted solos on take C of "Bird of Paradise" and the take B of "Embraceable You" (all recorded for Dial).[9] Davis also sounds particularly confident on the session he led for Savoy with Parker on tenor sax.[10]

Parker's working quintet lies at the heart of this period, and a survey and the evaluation of its music, primarily the studio recordings mentioned above, forms the core of this chapter. For the first time in his career, Parker was consistently in demand to record under his own name and was regularly in control of personnel and repertoire. A strikingly large share of Parker's artistic reputation derives from this small body of work. The ensemble sound is consistent (although Parker plays tenor sax on one session, and guests are added on several others), the performances are generally first rate and Parker specifically is brilliant, striking an artistic balance between virtuosity and poise. The grouping of several years of quintet recordings together reveals much with regard to Parker's musical values and tendencies. Because recordings from many sessions are discussed side by side, recording dates and record companies are cited in parentheses for each quintet piece discussed.

The classic quintet with Parker, Davis, and Roach always present recorded thirty-eight pieces for the Savoy and Dial labels in 1947 and 1948 (Davis was present, but sat out for one of the thirty-eight selections; trombonist James "J.J." Johnson was added to the basic quintet for six pieces). For the sake of completeness, to the thirty-eight studio recordings should be added five more compositions recorded for Norman Granz's Clef label (later Norgran) in 1949, for a total of forty-three. These five Granz recordings are based around Parker's working quintet with Kenny Dorham in place of Miles Davis, and they are stylistically consistent with the earlier sessions. In general, recording sessions of Parker's time produced a standard four releasable pieces or "sides." The five Savoy classic quintet dates hold to the norm, but the three Dial dates produced six sides each. The two Granz dates produced irregular numbers of sides. (Note: the Savoy and the Granz labels identified the alternate takes of a particular song with numbers [take 1, take 2, etc.]; Dial [beginning in 1947] identified its alternate takes with letters [take A, take B, etc.].)

All forty-three of the quintet-based pieces reveal much about the state of Parker's art as an improviser. For the purposes of describing the working group's repertoire and Parker's tendencies as a composer, however, four pieces (the ones with Parker on tenor sax) that were recorded by the quintet at a session led by Miles Davis are not relevant here because the pieces were not composed by or chosen by Parker. Of these thirty-nine quintet studio pieces that do reflect Parker's choice, thirty-one were "composed" by Parker, although four of these have no set melody for their choruses. These four are simply improvisations over chord progressions *selected* by Parker (see also discussion of the authorship of "Donna Lee," below).

Of the thirty-nine pieces, fourteen are 12-bar blues. Their extent of real melodic composition varies; eleven pieces are fully composed, consisting of twelve bars of set melody. Of the remaining four pieces, two simply involve the statement of a basic phrase three times (a tried-and-true blues technique), one sandwiches improvisation between two short phrases to form the head, and one has no composed theme at all for its chorus (although it has a short composed introduction). From a rhythmic standpoint, three of these blues feature "Latin" drum and bass patterns for all or some of the melody statements. Supporting the idea that Parker was not nearly as interested as Dizzy Gillespie in the rhythmic complexities of Afro-Cuban music, Parker quickly drops the Latin accompaniment patterns for the solo sections of each of the three pieces.

The twenty-five nonblues pieces that Parker chose are based on Tin Pan Alley pop song forms or are consistent with that tradition. Most are 32-bar AABA forms, although there are variations (one is 36 bars long, one is a double 64 bars in length, another is 69 bars long; some could be described as having ABAB', ABAC, or ABCB forms). Six of the AABA-based pieces use only eight bars of composed melody for the A sections with eight bars of improvisation for the B.

As can be seen above, the blues and pop song forms used by Parker's quintet broke no new ground. The above mentioned practice of composing only eight bars or not having any fixed theme at all fit in well with Parker's casual approach to recording; he could write only the minimum amount of material for each recording session and present those pieces at the sessions themselves. (Unlike Parker, Davis presented pieces whose melodies were completely written, and Davis held rehearsals before his recording session.)

The need for new material for recording was the driving force in Parker's composing; he did not break in the new tunes on the job before recording them. Indeed, live recordings of the quintet show that (with one possible exception) Parker's new compositions only showed up in his nightclub repertoire *after* being recorded. A surprisingly large number of the Parker "compositions" by his quintet (twenty-one) are documented only in the studio versions, underscoring the notion that the demand of the studio was the chief raison d'être for many of the pieces. Of course, Parker could have drawn on many compositions by his peers, but one could understand if perhaps he generally wanted to feature his own material on record and thereby derive royalties from sales.

Although Parker generally took the path of least resistance with regard to composing, in 1947 and 1948 he composed and recorded two pieces that showed greater than usual forethought and preparation. Each piece is based on the "I Got Rhythm" chord progression in F, and in the typical Parker fashion, only about eight measures of writing is involved (the A sections are written, the B sections are improvised). What is unusual about the pieces is that both involve contrapuntal melodies (two interdependent melodic lines that sound simultaneously) for the trumpet and alto saxophone. Improvised counterpoint was common in New Orleans jazz, but written counterpoint has never been common in jazz. Of course, written counterpoint *has* been common in Western classical music, especially during the Baroque period. As discussed in chapter 1, Parker by the mid-1940s had been exposed to classical music and—as discussed later in this chapter (with regard to "Dexterity")—he was specifically impressed by the work of Baroque composer Johann Sebastian Bach, who wrote a large body of contrapuntal music. What spurred Parker to so briefly employ this texture is not known, but anytime he took extra time in constructing a new piece, the results tend to be interesting.

The first of these contrapuntal compositions was "Chasing the Bird" (5-8-47; recorded for Savoy). As a first effort at contrapuntal composition, this is a largely successful piece. Its weakness might be in that the trumpet part is not as well thought-out as the sax part. Parker achieved a better balance of interdependent parts in his second contrapuntal piece, "Ah-Leu-Cha" (9-18-48; Savoy).

The range of tempos found in the repertoire of the quintet's studio recordings is extremely wide. The slowest ballads (e.g., "Don't Blame Me") are around quarter note = 65. The fastest swing performance ("Bird Gets the Worm" take 3) is approximately quarter note = 370. As expected, there are few notes in the latter performance shorter than an eighth note, precluding any double-timing (subdividing the beat into four equal parts). At more moderate tempos (as fast as quarter note = 230; quite brisk for other players), Parker often includes double-time passages in sixteenth notes. Parker had become so adept at double-timing that on take B of "Quasimado" [sic] performed quarter note = ca. 144, all but two of the sixteen measures are played with a double-time implication. The slowest performances (such as the ballads discussed below) include sustained passages in thirty-second notes that could be said to imply *quadruple*-timing (implying a tempo that is four times the reference tempo).

Parker's control of articulation had also reached a new height during this period. He could accent at great speed, as the up-tempo "Bird Gets the Worm" (take 1; 12-21-47; Savoy) thrillingly illustrates in a passage that must be heard to be appreciated (the circled notes and chords in parentheses are examined below in the discussion of his harmonic practices).

"Bird Gets the Worm" (Take 1)

Parker's ability to creatively accent virtually any note on any subdivision of a beat, a skill best demonstrated in slower tempo pieces, is discussed below in the section on his ballad performances of the period.

As implied earlier, Charlie Parker's alto saxophone tone production and timbre show more control and consistency in the quintet recordings. The earliest of these were made at a time when he usually played a Conn saxophone; for his December 17, 1947, date for Dial, Ross Russell reported that Parker used a new French Selmer saxophone. On that date, Parker's timbre has a particular fullness and richness in its midrange. On the Miles Davis date that featured Parker playing tenor sax, Parker's tenor timbre is consistent with his earlier work on that horn (see chapter 2) in that it is streamlined, without pronounced vibrato, rasp, or growl. It is not perhaps as lush and sensuous as before, sounding a little more blunt and less incisive; Parker was reportedly playing on a borrowed horn. Miles Davis had specifically wanted Parker to play the tenor, and, indeed, a trumpet–tenor sax front line became increasingly popular in bop and hard bop styles.

In his quintet studio recordings, Parker reached complete mastery over his improvised melodic line. On the large scale, his control over phrase lengths and the phrases' placement within musical form is remarkable. This nine-measure phrase from the classic quintet recording of "Constellation" (take 5; 9-18-48; Savoy), stunningly executed at up-tempo, unwinds at unusual length and creatively cuts across the sectional division between the two A sections.[11]

"Constellation" (Take 5)

On the small scale, the above example is also a good illustration of Parker's mature (post-1944) usage of chromatic passing tones (first discussed with regard to "Sweet Georgia Brown" in chapter 2). As expected, most of those tones (marked with asterisks) fall on the "ands" of the beats and are often involved in creating descending melodic lines. In fact, the above example is characterized by two melodic descents of more than an octave (marked by the circled notes in measures 38–40 and 43–46), which are linked by a shorter ascending passage (measures 41 and 42).[12]

Parker's willingness to let phrases find their own lengths apart from the customary four- and eight-bar conventions is superbly illustrated in Parker's opening statement from the first take of his composition "Klactoveeseds-tene" (11–4–47; Dial). These sixteen measures begin haltingly with short, seemingly disconnected phrases that lead to a longer, five-measure phrase. What initially seemed like a collection of unrelated gestures comes together into a remarkably effective whole.[13] (Note also the marked voiceleading figure noted first in "Honeysuckle Rose" [chapter 2] and later in "Billie's Bounce" [chapter 3].)

Although bebop in general and Charlie Parker's music in particular were often considered to be abstract and intellectual, Parker's playing had a constant undercurrent of earthiness that might surface at any time. In just a few notes, Parker could suggest the essence of the blues, one of the essential roots of jazz (see "Parker's Mood," below). Another example of Parker maintaining contact with his roots is demonstrated in his tenor saxophone break on "Little Willie Leaps" (played identically on takes 2 [0:35] and 3 [0:32]; 8-14-47; Savoy). Both Parker's tenor sax tim-

"Klact-oveeseds-tene" (Take A)

bre and the break's overall contour are somewhat reminiscent of his major influence, Lester Young. Parker's unique contribution, however, is seen in his characteristic chromatic passing tones (marked with asterisks). Also characteristic of Parker is the break's arpeggiated leap up to a high note, followed by a largely stepwise descending line (discussed above with regard to "Constellation"). Note in particular the chromatic descent over the interval of a perfect fifth from high C to F, as noted by the circled notes below.

"Little Willie Leaps"

One aspect of Parker's melodic bag of tricks is not prominent in these recordings, and that is his creative quotation of various songs while improvising. As noted earlier, Parker tended to employ this technique sparingly in the recording studio, and that generalization holds true for the quintet studio recordings. Live quintet recordings were a different matter, as will be seen below.

Charlie Parker's solos on the quintet studio recordings illustrate a new level of harmonic sophistication. As discussed earlier, unlike Dizzy Gillespie, Parker's harmonic knowledge was based more on practice than on theory. If he did not come upon his harmonic concepts through study at the piano, he nevertheless quickly grasped concepts gleaned from study of recordings and from his peers, transforming them and making them his own. A common harmonic device since the 1940s has been the iii-7–VI7–ii-7–V7 turnaround (a turnaround is a chord progression that jazz musicians place at the end of songs to add harmonic interest to an otherwise static segment). An average modern jazz player might navigate the turnaround chord progression with this melodic lick (which, incidentally, is nearly identical to measures 2 and 3 of Miles Davis's composition "Little Willie Leaps"):

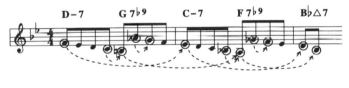

"iii VI ii V I"

The lick clearly outlines the basic chord/scale relationships; for each new chord (each beat 1 or 3), the melody rests on the third of that chord. Each beat three finds the melody leaping from the third to an altered chord timbre (the "♭9") before arriving at the root of the chord. The lick has very strong harmonic voiceleading in that many of its tones lead by half step or whole step to subsequent tones (the dotted lines, when traced from left to right, delineate the voiceleading). The average player might learn this phrase and then regularly repeat it verbatim, turning it into a cliché. In Parker's classic quintet performance of "Dexterity" (take B; 10-28-47; Dial), Parker begins the lick in the common manner but chooses a more spontaneous approach to phrase's conclusion. Note how much less formulaic Parker's version turns out to be. (Once again, the dotted lines trace from left to right the voiceleading.)

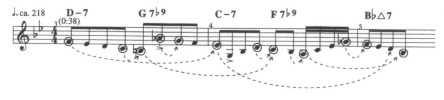

"Dexterity" (Take B)

The harmonic clarity and precision of this and many other Parker improvisational excerpts are reminiscent of the same qualities found in Johann Sebastian Bach's solo sonatas, and they recall Parker's statement about being "impressed with Bach's patterns," and how the patterns of jazz "had already been put down, and in most cases, a lot better."[14] Perhaps Bach served as an ideal or model for how harmonically clear and explicit a single melodic line could be.

Like most of his colleagues, Parker enjoyed implying "substitute" chord changes to lend harmonic variety to a solo. A clear example of this practice occurs in the second take of "Donna Lee" (5-8-47; Savoy) at the end of Parker's second chorus. One expects the usual iii-7–VI7–ii-7–V7 turnaround, but Parker takes a more scenic route, suggesting the colorful iii-7–♭iii-7–ii-7–♭II△7 progression in parentheses (the pretty ♭II△7–I substitute was first noted in chapter 3 in "Oh, Lady Be Good!"):

"Donna Lee" (Take 2)

Another example of Parker implying substitute chord changes may be found in the excerpt of "Bird Gets the Worm" above. The basic B♭-7–E♭7 progression has been elaborated into the richer B♭–B♭-△7–B♭-7–E♭7 seen in parentheses (the circled notes mark the voiceleading that delineates the substitute progression).

Classic Quintet Ballad Performances

Of the ten quintet-based studio recording sessions for the three record labels, only the dates for Dial included any ballad performances based on American popular songs. Interestingly, these always came at the end of each Dial session, suggesting that Parker only had so much material prepared and that the pop songs were used to fill out each session (these Dial dates included six compositions instead of the usual four, setting up the need for additional material). Up to this time, only one of the five Parker-led recording sessions had produced any complete slow instrumental ballad performances, those pieces being the disastrous "Lover Man" and "The Gypsy" (chapter 4). The other ballads that have been mentioned in this book so far were either not issued at the time (such as "Body and Soul" and "Meandering") or were on sessions not led by Parker. As of the beginning of 1947, the jazz record-buying public did not know that Charlie Parker was one of the greatest interpreters of ballads in American music.

Parker's freshest up-tempo solos (such as "Just Friends," chapter 5) are marvels of an instantaneous linking of conception and execution, but Parker also had the ability to coast his way through up-tempo solos (albeit on a high level that was the envy of many a musician), free-associating through a vast repertoire of his characteristic phrases (or "licks"). This aspect of Parker's playing is more associated with his live recordings of this period than with his studio work. Perhaps the nature of performing a show for a live audience sometimes led Parker to make virtuosic statements that were constructed of dependable musical components. Conversely, perhaps the relatively concentrated atmosphere of the recording studio allowed Parker to feel free of audience expectations and therefore more thoughtful in constructing his up-tempo solos.

When playing slower material either "live" or in the studio, however, Parker was often at his most reflective and relaxed. The slowly arriving harmonic deadlines of ballads and slow blues give the improviser more time to create, perhaps partially explaining the sense of fresh discovery often found in Parker's ballad-tempo improvisations. It was significant, then, that Ross Russell of Dial gave Parker free rein to record the ballads that Parker knew and loved. These examples of American popular song were generally part of his nightclub repertoire; all six of the songs are documented in live versions played by Parker. They are "Bird of Paradise" (based on the chord progression and form of "All the Things You Are"), "Embraceable You," "My Old Flame," "Don't Blame Me," "Out of Nowhere" and "How Deep Is the Ocean?" Interestingly, because he makes only fleeting use of the songs' original melodies, Parker and Dial could have in some cases retitled the performances and, in the common practice, received songwriting and publishing royalties.[15] To this group of reflective ballad performances should be added a ballad-tempo twelve-bar blues that Parker recorded for Savoy, "Parker's Mood." The blues is one of the most important American popular music forms, and this performance has much in common with the six ballads with regard to melody, harmony, and rhythm.

The seven pieces (preserved in fourteen complete takes and one nearly so) exemplify the state of Parker's art of 1947–48. From rhythmic, melodic, and harmonic perspectives, they sum up many of his musical accomplishments and are special within "Parkeriana" because they find him at both his most richly complex and at his most thoughtful. Further, for some listeners, the slower tempos may more easily reveal the artistry of Charlie Parker than the more up-tempo classics. For all these reasons, the slower performances of 1947–48 merit a special discussion among the quintet pieces in general.

A similar format is followed for most of these selections. In each case, an introduction leads to the first chorus; for two pieces, the intro also serves as a coda. Parker then takes over for a chorus of improvisation (two on "Parker's Mood") with a general implication of double time from him. He either ignores the original melody ("Embraceable You" and takes B and C of "Bird of Paradise") or states it, departs from it and returns to it at will. One or more of the other instrumentalists then solo. In most cases, Miles Davis (generally muted) joins Parker for a few bars of impromptu harmony or collective improvisation to close the piece. "Parker's Mood" is again an exception as Davis does not play on the piece at all; unusually, Parker there returns for an additional solo. Parker has his bassist walk (pluck the strings on all four beats) on each selection; by contrast, most jazz ballads of today are stated in "two" with the bass playing on the first and third beats until the improvised solos. The time limits of the 78 RPM record urged Parker to get to his improvisation pretty quickly, and perhaps the pervasive walking bass best fit that technology-enforced routine. The six ballads and one blues are similar in tempo. All but one piece are slower than quarter note = 90. The two takes of "Bird of Paradise," taken at quarter note = ca. 114 and 116, stretch the limits of "ballad" tempo but belong in the ballad category here due to their adherence to the above format, especially in their pervasive double-time feel.

One of the most striking and thrilling aspects of Charlie Parker's art was his ability to play very rapidly without sacrificing swing and accuracy. One might think that these ballads, being rather slow in tempo, might lose some of the excitement derived from the sheer velocity of Parker's up-tempo pieces like "Ko Ko." Yet, Parker, in his flexibility, could lock into the beat on a variety of levels with no sacrifice of power and vitality. One could say that these ballads were originally performed by nonjazz interpreters with the quarter note as the basic rhythmic unit (the simplest level). Jazz performers from Louis Armstrong on considered that ballads needed at least a subdivision of the beat into two parts (the eighth-note level) to swing satisfyingly. Improvisers such as Art Tatum and Coleman Hawkins were considered virtuosos to be able to double-time (divide the beat into four parts, the sixteenth-note level) on ballads. By the time of his 1947 classic quintet recordings, Parker was able to quadruple-time (dividing the beat into eight parts, the thirty-second-note level) with a high degree of swing at ballad tempos, thereby attaining the same stunning velocity of notes as on his up-tempo displays of virtuosity. His flexibility in referring to the basic beat on at least four metrical levels gives these performances the widest range of note values and, not coincidentally, the widest range of emotional content in "Parkeriana." This flexibility also allowed him great creative control of accentuation even in the most rapid passages.

Parker's general timbre on the slower material is consistent with the other quintet recordings of the time; the most noticeable departure is his slightly more prominent vibrato, not surprising given the longer note values occasionally found in the seven titles. At its most pronounced, however, Parker's vibrato is not as deep or constant as Johnny Hodges's or Benny Carter's.

From a melodic standpoint, the six ballads and one blues are rich in invention. Parker constructs his phrases asymmetrically and across sectional divisions, using a wide variety of phrase lengths. Parker's own small-scale melodic building blocks are of course present, and certainly Parker uses some of his larger-scale "licks"; nevertheless his improvisations are relatively free of cliché. Parker is not under pressure to deliver blistering up-tempo runs, and he takes advantage of the opportunity to relax and be more thoughtful. These fantasias are reflections of the spontaneity, freedom, and brilliance that was Charlie Parker at his best.

Because Parker felt great liberty to state, embellish, paraphrase, and depart from the songs' melodies, his opening melody statements show great invention and spontaneity. In this example, the original melody of "Out of Nowhere" (upper stave) is contrasted with Parker's version of it on his first take of the song (11-4-47; Dial). Notes in common between the melody as written and Parker's statement of it are circled. Note how Parker's rapid double- and quadruple-time inventions meld smoothly with his embellished statements of the tune.

"Out of Nowhere" (Take A)

One of the most famous and most striking examples of Parker's melodic invention is his solo on take A of "Embraceable You" (10-28-47; Dial). For years, Parker scholars and fans alike had marveled at how Parker utilized variations of his own (seemingly improvisational) opening six-note motive to unify the first eight measures of his solo. Older jazz players had attained continuity by creatively embellishing and paraphrasing a song's melody while soloing (some of them found this technique to be expedient as a way of dealing with difficult chord changes, but the effect is the same). In their quest for fresh and continually evolving improvisation, and to accept the challenge of improvising over difficult harmonies, advanced swing style and modern jazz players had largely abandoned references to a song's melody during solos (Thelonious Monk was certainly an exception to this trend). This approach emphasized forward motion over development, and in the hands of merely average improvisers, the large-scale unity of a solo was sometimes lost.

A technique that honors both invention and continuity is motivic improvisation (called "thematic improvisation" by jazz historian Gunther Schuller).[16] It involves the creative manipulation and development of a motive (a term often used instead of "figure" when the musical material is employed for melodic development) from any source in the course of improvisation. These motives may be arrived at impromptu, or they may be fragments from the melody of the song being played. Common means of manipulation used by composers include the ornamentation of the motive, augmentation or diminution of it (using longer or shorter note values), adding or subtracting notes from the motive, preserving the contour of it while increasing or decreasing its overall range, sequencing the motive (transposing it to higher or lower pitch levels), inverting it or presenting it in retrograde (upside down or in reverse order), and preserving the motive's rhythmic pattern while varying the melodic content. Improvisers, operating in real time as they do, must have quick reflexes to utilize these techniques while creating.

On the first take of "Embraceable You," Parker begins with a six-note motive (marked "1" in the example) that does not resemble Gershwin's original melody. He immediately embellishes the motive via a quick fill-in run up to the highest note ("2"), and without pausing, sequences the motive at a higher pitch level ("3"). That transposed version is then embellished ("4"). The six notes next appear transposed lower as the beginning of a longer phrase ("5"), then a rapid double-time run ensues that concludes surprisingly with the motive expanded in range and transposed again ("6"). The effect is a remarkably well-integrated eight measures that embody both coherence and spontaneity.

The source of Parker's six-note motive was not known to most Parker listeners until the 1980s, when jazz critic Gary Giddins discovered a 1939 pop song by composer Dana Suesse and lyricist Sam Coslow, "A

"Embraceable You" (Take A) Ex. 1

Table in a Corner." Like "Embraceable You," it was written in the key of F, and its chord progression is similar to that song. In this example, "A Table in a Corner" is compared with Parker's opening statement on "Embraceable You." Notes in common between the original song and Parker's improvisation are circled. The former's chords move at half the speed of the latter, so Parker's work has been rhythmically rewritten to coincide with the original song.

"Embraceable You" (Take A) Ex. 2

Parker was aware of the compatibility of the two songs and had the skill to superimpose "A Table in a Corner" upon "Embraceable You." The mere act of quotation was not his real accomplishment; many jazz artists from Louis Armstrong to the present have enjoyed use of the device. It was his ability to creatively use composerlike techniques while improvising in order to gain unity within the solo. That Parker drops the six-note motive after just eight bars does not weaken the balance of the solo. In fact, Parker goes on to find, examine, and depart from several other motives during the chorus (e.g., 0:52, 1:20, 1:35, 1:58), all of which add further unity to the solo. Because use of thematic improvisation was not the norm in modern jazz of the 1940s, this take of "Embraceable You" is notable not only for its effectiveness but also for its uniqueness. Other Parker ballads of this period have brief moments of such motivic development, although their brevity necessarily lessens their unifying potential.

Parker's essential feeling for the blues was always ready to be tapped whether he was playing an actual twelve-bar blues or a thirty-two-bar pop song form. Parker recorded many actual blues pieces in the modern jazz style, that is to say twelve-bar blues played at medium-to-fast tempos featuring relatively abstract melodies and substitute chord changes. Although he was a master of the more earthy slow blues, only once in Parker's discography of the 1947–49 period (both studio and live recordings) do we find Parker, as bandleader, choosing to perform a blues at a tempo less than quarter note = 100. The reason for the lack of this type of material in his repertoire is unclear. One could speculate that slow tempos in general were not considered commercially viable in either the record or nightclub businesses, but indeed Parker's love of the ballad-tempo popular song is richly documented in both professional studio recordings and amateur live recordings. One could imagine that the record companies he worked for influenced him to not record slow blues; in such case, one would expect proportionately more slow blues to appear in the many live Parker recordings. Even if we discount Parker's radio broadcast repertoire as being perhaps not strictly under his control (discussed below), there are nevertheless no slow blues in the many 1947–49 nonbroadcast live recordings that remain. Although some of the above factors may have influenced Parker, the fact remains that by this point in Parker's career, he chose his own repertoire most of the time. For reasons unknown, and despite the fact that he excelled at slow blues, he did not choose to play them often either in the studio or in live appearances.

Parker's Mood

The one slow blues referred to above is "Parker's Mood," recorded in five takes for the Savoy label on September 18, 1948. The occasion was a session with Parker's classic quintet featuring Miles Davis on trumpet, Max Roach on drums, Curly Russell on bass, and John Lewis sitting in on piano. For this blues, Davis was present but did not play. The format for "Parker's Mood" is as follows: an introduction consisting of a short out-of-tempo statement led by Parker and a brief tempo-setting introduction led by Lewis is followed by two improvised choruses by Parker. A chorus by Lewis and a third and final chorus of improvisation by Parker then lead to a coda based on the introduction that ends the performance. A complete transcription of the originally issued take 5 appears in Appendix B.

Of the five takes, numbers 1 and 3 were false starts. Takes 2 and 5 are complete takes, and take 4 is nearly complete; these three will be discussed here. (Early reissues of "Parker's Mood" incorrectly label takes 2, 4, and 5 as being takes 1, 2, and 3 respectively.) Parker's work is notable on each of these latter three lengthy takes; except for some saxophone tone production problems late in the third attempt, any of these three takes had the potential to be the original issue. Take 2 is the slowest (quarter note = ca. 65), take 4 is the fastest (quarter note = ca. 87), and take 5 is in between (quarter note = ca. 81).

The three takes of "Parker's Mood" provide an excellent case study in Parker's improvisational process. At home with the blues at reflective tempos, Parker here is at his creative best in creating both unity and variety. Within each individual take, Parker achieves unity through motivic development—taking melodic and rhythmic ideas and developing them over time. He also achieves variety within each take by knowing when to move on with fresh melodic and rhythmic material.

Although Parker expected only the final take to be heard by the public, listeners with access to the alternate takes can appreciate musical unity and variety on a different level, that is, by comparing takes. Parker clearly valued variety and spontaneity, and was not content to merely repeat himself, as seen in his very different opening gestures to takes 2, 4, and 5. Parker begins take 2 with a bluesy idea that ends on the root of the tonic chord. On the fourth take, his more abstract six-note phrase ends on the third of the chord. The fifth and final take opens with a bluesy phrase in triplets that neatly outlines the tonic chord.

Although space only permits lengthy discussion and transcription of take 5, takes 2 and 4 have much to reward the listener. These earlier takes find Parker attaining unity within each take by stating and developing in the first four measures of the opening the one-measure motives

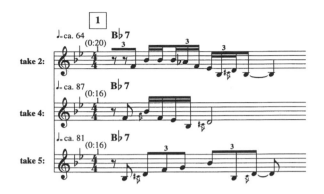

"Parker's Mood" (Takes 2, 4 & 5)

seen above. This motivic development, although not as extensive as found in the "A" take of "Embraceable You," nevertheless goes a long way toward unifying the opening moments of takes 2 and 4 of "Parker's Mood."

In take 2, Parker plays the opening motive or idea (which ends on the root), then proceeds in the second bar to embellish it and end the phrase on the root of the subdominant. The third bar finds Parker extending the idea and ending it on the seventh of the tonic chord in bar four, totaling three versions of the idea in all.

On the fourth take, Parker examines his opening phrase four times before moving on. He begins with the six-note phrase seen above (coincidentally the same length as the motive in "Embraceable You," take "A"), which ends on the third of the tonic chord. In the second bar, he adds one pitch to end the phrase on the root of the subdominant, and in the third bar, he repeats the first presentation of his idea verbatim. Finally, Parker in the fourth bar moves the motive higher in pitch and ends it on the ninth of the tonic.

In the case of the originally issued and best-known take 5 (complete solo transcription in appendix), Parker opens with a longer two-bar phrase (part of which is presented above) that outlines the tonic chord in a bluesy fashion and then repeats it with some variation, forming an antecedent-consequent (or "question-answer") scheme.

Parker's next gesture illustrates how he reexamined musical ideas from take to take, varying them and, in this case, developing one. In bar 6 of take 4, Parker had played a short descending melodic idea or motive of seemingly no more than passing interest, and had moved on. In bar 5

"Parker's Mood" (Take 5) Ex. 1

of take 5, Parker returns to the motive but this time embellishes it and changes a few of the notes in the descent. Most improvisers would be satisfied with just the slight embellishment, but Parker plays with the motive, repeating it, varying it melodically and—most importantly— rhythmically. Each presentation of the motive is creatively placed on a different beat. In the following example, the idea as first played in take 4 is labeled "motive" in bar 6 of take 4 (only the relevant part of that solo is included). Take 5 shows how Parker developed his motive; these presentations are labeled 1 through 4, with the five notes of the original motive circled.

"Parker's Mood" (Take 5) Ex. 2

In comparing the various takes of "Parker's Mood" as done just above, the listener of today can appreciate a kind of motivic or compositional unity between and among the versions that was not planned by

Parker. Although we can conceive of the various takes as adding up to an artistic whole, Parker only expected one take to be heard by the public. He was in the process of creating a master take of "Parker's Mood" which would be artistically inspired and technically acceptable for release. To this end, Parker utilized his keen powers of memory and creativity to revisit musical motives from earlier takes and develop them toward that master take. Even though his perspective was different than ours, comparing the takes of "Parker's Mood" can give us a rich appreciation Parker's creative process.

Another example of the practice of motivic development between takes is found in comparing take 2 and the originally issued take 5. In measure 9 of the second take, Parker played a two-measure phrase whose melodic essence is a long descent from D in the middle of the staff to the B♭ below middle C, as marked by the circled note heads in the example below. In take 5, also below, Parker revisits the idea but begins his descent a bit more than one beat later. He pauses momentarily on the pitch G in bar 10 before extending the idea into the eleventh bar, reaching the low B♭ three beats later than he had in take 2. The comparison between takes is insightful because it illuminates Parker's keen mind, highly developed aural skills, and compositional outlook in the creation of a solo.

"Parker's Mood" (Take 5) Ex. 3

In each take, Parker's third chorus (after the piano solo) is accompanied by a implied double-time hi-hat pattern from Roach which reinforces Parker's near constant double-time implication. As has been seen in the above discussion of Parker's ballads of the period, he even felt comfortable *quadruple*-timing in sixty-fourth notes at this tempo. This burst over a iii–7 to VI7 progression is from the originally issued take 5. Note the typical accenting at high points of the melodic contours that lends such a strong rhythmic snap to the example.

"Parker's Mood" (Take 5) Ex. 4

Parker didn't have to blaze away in rapid note values to show that his mind was operating at a clock speed at least double that of most swing era players. This simple example from his second solo (after the piano solo) of take 5 finds him dancing over the rhythm section, all the while mentally subdividing the beat into sixteenths:

"Parker's Mood" (Take 5) Ex. 5

In "Parker's Mood," Parker displays his harmonic awareness without ever losing the essence of the blues. He of course grew up in Kansas City, a town known for excellent blues instrumentalists and singers. His models for saxophone style, Lester Young and Buster Smith, were fine blues players, as were many of the members of the Jay McShann band in whose ranks Parker came of age. What most of these musicians didn't have (and arguably might not have needed in order to play the blues, pre-1940) was the depth of harmonic knowledge that Parker had attained by this time. Certainly the combining of the earthy with the complex was one of Charlie Parker's biggest contributions to music. The opening of Parker's second solo on take 5 illustrates how Parker used his harmonic knowledge to first paint the primary colors of the blues and then to expand its palette. For the first two bars, he outlines the tonic and subdominant chords (the chord degrees are numbered in the example) in a way fully consistent with the soulful essence of the Southwest blues. He then pursues a more abstract two-bar double-time run that culminates in a substitute ii-7–V7 progression (F-7–B♭7; measure 4) over the rhythm section's simpler V7 harmony. The purpose of this progression is to lead more colorfully into the coming subdominant harmony. A brief but pungent moment comes on beat three of the fourth bar with a descending run based on the whole-tone scale, implying either a B♭+7 or the tritone substitution E9♭13. Despite the rapidity of this passage and the whole-tone scale, Parker never loses the spirit of the blues.

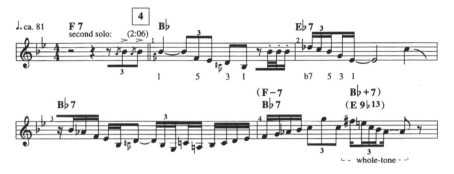

"Parker's Mood" (Take 5) Ex. 6

By the time the coda brings the performance to an end, Charlie Parker's contributions to the interpretation of the blues are evident. One need not sacrifice funkiness for harmonic, melodic, and rhythmic complexity.

Live Recordings of the Quintet

A survey of Parker's 1947–49 studio recording sessions by (or based on) the quintet suggest great stability of personnel; for eight of the ten sessions, Charlie Parker, Miles Davis, and Max Roach were all present. The studio recordings, however, trace only one facet of Parker's working quintet. In order to fully survey the evolution of the group's personnel, one must turn to the live recordings by Parker's group. Judging from a recent Charlie Parker discography,[17] his working quintet (occasionally with a few added starters) was recorded live on at least thirty-six occasions from late 1947 through early 1950. Of these, Miles Davis was present for just under 40 percent of the sessions.

When Davis quit the group in late December, 1948, he was replaced by trumpeter Kenny Dorham. The group had just begun a weekly late-night broadcast from New York's Royal Roost nightclub, so Dorham's tenure with the group is well documented at just over 40 percent of the live sessions. Dorham was short-changed, however, in the studio recordings upon which the quintet's reputation is largely based, in part explaining why he is not as strongly associated with the group as is Miles Davis. At the time of Dorham's tenure with the group, Parker was in the first year of a recording contract (discussed at greater length in chapter 5) with jazz aficionado and producer Norman Granz that would continue until Parker's death. Granz wished to record Parker in a wide variety of musical settings, thereby deemphasizing the studio documentation of this edition of Parker's quintet. Only two sessions based around the quintet with Dorham were recorded by Granz; these sessions produced only five compositions. Although Dorham had occasional inconsistencies in his tone production and articulation, he brought a more assured technical facility to the band's trumpet role. Max Roach recalled, "And when Kenny Dorham joined the band, the band, to me, actually began to grow as far as playing the figures that Bird had written. I think that Kenny came much closer to dealing with them than Miles did."[18]

A particularly significant addition to the band was pianist Al Haig. Haig had developed a modern jazz piano style independent of Bud Powell (both Haig and Powell spoke of their admiration of the other's playing and may have influenced each other), and of course had already worked extensively with Parker and Gillespie. Haig could solo convincingly at the fast tempos that Parker favored and was a fine ballad player and accompanist. Like Dorham, Haig is well represented in the live quintet recordings but is only present on the same two studio sessions based on the quintet (on which he plays very well).

A few distinctions may be drawn between the quintet's studio and live recordings. In the less time-restricted live settings, Parker and group played pieces a little longer than they had on the time-limited 78s, perhaps averaging four minutes instead of three. In general, live versions of the group's medium- and up-tempo numbers are often performed a little faster than the original versions. Subjectively, Parker seems more thoughtful on the studio recordings; his solos are often gems of concentrated fresh invention. In the nightclub, Parker did not have to be so succinct. Therefore, the live recordings often display a side of Parker that was more spontaneous and extroverted. On one hand, the live setting fostered an energetic and freewheeling quality in Parker's playing; on the other hand, live recordings of the working quintet (especially late in its life) too often find Parker coasting, content to repeat his trademark licks without being very thoughtful.

Parker's live repertoire also varied from his studio recordings. In clubs especially, Parker featured, in addition to his own compositions, quite a few of the Dizzy Gillespie pieces, such as "Dizzy Atmosphere," "Bebop," "Salt Peanuts," "Groovin' High," "Oop Bop Sh'Bam," and "A Night in Tunisia," that Parker knew from his 1945 work with Gillespie. Among the other prolific modern jazz writers, Tadd Dameron was usually represented only by "Hot House," and Thelonious Monk usually only by the set-closing "Fifty-Second Street Theme." When Miles Davis was in the band, Parker included a few Davis tunes, such as "Donna Lee"[19] and "Little Willie Leaps," with some regularity, but Parker did not choose to revisit the Howard McGhee tunes he had played in Los Angeles. Parker also seldom looked back at composers of the generation before, such as Duke Ellington, Benny Carter, Coleman Hawkins, Lester Young, and Billy Strayhorn. Most of the live recordings of the quintet come from WMCA radio broadcasts hosted by "Symphony" Sid Torin made during an extended run at New York's Royal Roost nightclub. These offer a less-than-representative view of Parker's repertoire in that no ballad performances were included on the air (perhaps the radio station only wanted to broadcast quicker, energetic material). In addition, judging from Torin's announcements, certain pieces may have been included *more* often because they were often requested by listeners, or because they were recent releases by Parker's group.

One aspect of Parker's art that jumped out during his live performances was his practice of creatively quoting various pieces while improvising. Their inclusion in a performance might come about for several different reasons. Parker might make a quotation strictly on a free-association basis: the song he was playing and the song to be quoted might have similar chord progression, or he might find himself improvising a line that suggested another song and follow the line through. More strikingly, Parker also used quotations in a narrative fashion to comment on the goings-on in the nightclub or to reflect fairly literally on his thought process as he played. If one knew the words to the song he was quoting, one might pick up on Parker's meaning. According to his fourth wife, Chan: "I mean, he sent messages all the time through his horn, and I got every one of them. . . . Yeah, I mean, if he wanted somebody's attention, he'd play 'Over There.' [sings:] 'Over There.' He'd send me a million messages. And he was so pleased that I heard them."[20] Indeed, several live Parker sessions, one of which was recorded by Chan Parker, document Parker quoting "Over There" in the middle of solos.[21]

Earlier in the 1940s, Parker's sphere of listening had expanded to include Western "classical" music, and by the 1947–49 period, Parker's musical quotations revealed these new listening habits. Parker scholar Thomas Owens has identified many of Parker's quotations from classical music.[22] A few of the composers and their works from which Parker quoted during this period are: Frédéric Chopin, *Minute Waltz;* Igor Stravinsky, *The Rite of Spring;* Gioacchino Rossini, *William Tell;* Ferde Grofé, *Grand Canyon Suite;* Edvard Grieg, *Peer Gynt;* and Richard Wagner, *Tannhäuser.*

Parker's use of the classical music material is always resourceful; his inner ear, reflexes, and technique were so highly developed that he could recall a classical music theme and instantaneously apply it to the pop song chord progression at hand. Parker's classical music quotations were not as likely to have a narrative function as his pop song quotations; the classical music themes he quoted usually did not have the built-in associations that the lyrics of pop songs provided, although Parker may have occasionally used a classical music title or programmatic association in a narrative fashion.

In early May, 1949, Charlie Parker and his quintet (Dorham, Haig, Potter, and Roach) traveled to Paris for the *Festival International de Jazz.* Near the beginning of his solo on "Salt Peanuts" (the shorter of two versions recorded in Paris),[23] Parker greeted his audience by quoting the bassoon part that opens Stravinsky's *Rite of Spring* (*Le Sacre du printemps*), which premiered in Paris in 1913. Parker was evidently having trouble with his horn or with his ability to produce notes; the notes with "x" note heads reflect octave-displaced notes that Parker inadvertently produces. (Parker occasionally revisited this quotation in his performances. Two later examples are during "Cool Blues" [3-25-52] and "The Song Is You" [7-26-53], both in the key of C).

In Parker's apprenticeship period, he revealed his early influences and listening habits clearly by often quoting the major jazz artists of the preceding generation from whom he had learned (Lester Young, Roy Eldridge, Coleman Hawkins, and others). Having long since assimilated his influences and become a virtuoso in his own right, Parker no longer found it technically necessary to use his influences' licks to navigate cer-

"Salt Peanuts"

tain chord progressions; one result was that Parker seldom quoted other jazz players after he reached musical maturity. A significant exception to this tendency was his striking quotation of Louis Armstrong's 1928 introductory cadenza to "West End Blues" during a live performance of Parker's blues "Cheryl" as played by the last edition of Parker's quintet (see below) on December 25, 1949. Although Armstrong was not one of Parker's direct influences, Parker may have been recalling this famous solo from his formative years. More likely, Parker had recently heard the Armstrong recording in connection with a then-current revival of interest in early jazz (Parker had, in the past two years, appeared in the same setting with Baby Dodds, Sidney Bechet, Joe Sullivan, and others).

"Cheryl"

In late summer 1949, trumpeter Red Rodney (born Robert Chudnick) joined the quintet, and Parker finally had the tight two-horn ensemble sound he had needed but not had since he and Dizzy Gillespie had gone their separate ways. Although heard on a handful of excellent live recordings from late 1949 (such as "Cheryl," above) and early 1950, the top-notch quintet that featured Red Rodney, Al Haig, Tommy Potter, and Roy Haynes never recorded commercially. This lesser-known edition of the group was probably the most consistent of all versions of the 1947–50 quintet with regard to playing Parker's music with fire and precision. Rodney had been introduced to Parker by Dizzy Gillespie in 1945 and was well prepared to take over the trumpet chair. In some ways, Rodney occupied a similar musical niche in the trumpet lineage as did Fats Navarro: both had technique and tone production approaching Gillespie's coupled with a lyrical melodic gift somewhat comparable to Miles Davis. Around this time, former Lester Young drummer Roy Haynes replaced Max Roach at the drums. Red Rodney remembered Parker's satisfaction with their new drummer: "And Bird would lean over to me and say 'Whooh! Got all the right moves. Listen to that guy. Oh, we got a winner here.' "[24]

As 1950 arrived, however, the laissez-faire concept upon which Parker's quintet was based was showing its limitations. The group's repertoire consisted of the same Parker and Gillespie compositions and usual sampling of Tin Pan Alley pop songs as always. Without quintet recording dates to provide the impetus to compose, no new Parker compositions had entered the quintet's "book" since March, 1949, and the effect of presenting the same material night after night began to take its toll, as Red Rodney recalled:

> There was a lot of frustration for me, because we didn't rehearse, we didn't get new tunes, we didn't—and I kept asking, "Come on, let's get some new tunes, let's get—let's play different things." Same thing over and over. Almost the same tunes in the same places every night, he got so complacent. And, "Ah, we'll rehearse tomorrow." But we—of course tomorrow never came. And it *was* frustrating, of course. . . . I felt cheated. [long pause] It's a hell of a thing to say, you felt cheated playing next to Charlie Parker, but I started feeling cheated because we weren't playing newer things.[25]

Along with this stagnancy of repertoire, Charlie Parker's improvisational work with his quintet became increasingly repetitive. While still usually forceful and authoritative, his solos became less spontaneous and were increasingly assembled from Parker's huge vocabulary of licks, a vocabulary that was being added to at a much slower rate than just a few years before. A significant impediment to Parker's continued improvisational and compositional development was his gradual withdrawal from the regular saxophone practice and study of jazz that had characterized his youth and early adulthood. Parker was again abusing heroin and alcohol, and the discipline required for regular practice and study was difficult to sustain.

According to pianist Lennie Tristano: "In 1949, however, Bird told me that he had said as much as he could in this particular idiom. He wanted to develop something else in the way of playing or another style. He was tired of playing the same ideas."[26] One live recording, reportedly made at the New York nightclub Birdland, probably in late 1949 or early 1950,[27] gives some hints of a "new way of playing" in Parker's solos. Although this group is not strictly an edition of the working quintet, its personnel is strongly related, and so the ensemble is logically discussed here. Definitely present are Parker, pianist Bud Powell (who had recorded with the classic quartet in 1947), and trumpeter Fats Navarro. Close listening suggests that the drummer is Roy Haynes of the working quintet, and Haynes's quintet section mate, Tommy Potter, is a good guess for the group's bassist.[28] The personnel is near ideal; from a purely musical standpoint, Navarro and Powell provide Parker with the brilliance and inventiveness that Parker needed to challenge him. If not for Navarro and Powell's physical and emotional health problems, this could have been the ultimate quintet, had it been a working group.

On the up-tempo pieces, Parker and Navarro often creatively duel in lengthy four-bar exchanges, and Navarro seems to bring out the best in Parker.[29] One of the best sequences comes in "The Street Beat," where Parker's chromaticism derives from interval-based architecture. The first phrase in the following example (measures 65–66) descends in augmented triads and ascends in diminished triads, both of which are harmonically ambiguous. (Each note in parentheses is an "enharmonic" equivalent of the note immediately preceding; the intent is to aid in the recognition of the augmented triads.) The second phrase shown (measures 67–68), a bit simpler in its construction of minor triads sequenced down by half steps, supplies chromatic interest in much the same way and is very effective at high speed.

After Navarro's answering four bars on "The Street Beat," Parker immediately tries another chromatic gambit with this phrase constructed

"The Street Beat" Ex. 1

largely of minor thirds (diminished triads are composed of two minor thirds). Note how the upper notes (circled) descend by half steps. Although Navarro's "fours" are not notated here, listeners will hear him immediately try to imitate this phrase:

"The Street Beat" Ex. 2

Parker was clearly interested in the chromaticism that these and other intervalically conceived patterns could provide. On a live version of "Dizzy Atmosphere" from the same nightclub recording, Parker plays the initial phrase (measures 65–66) from the first "Street Beat" example twice, beginning around 2:11 into the piece (during the second A section of Parker's fifth solo chorus of "Dizzy Atmosphere"). Moments later on the same piece (around 2:15), Parker plays a chromatic phrase consisting of augmented triads ascending by whole steps (derived from a whole-tone scale). These patterns cut across the prevailing tonality and will be further discussed in the next chapter (see "Rocker" and "Sly Mongoose").

Early Norman Granz Studio Recordings

During this period, while Parker was still leading his quintet, producer Norman Granz approached him about recording a single selection for a deluxe album of 78s to be called *The Jazz Scene*. Parker had of course known Granz since Parker's first trip to California, a time when Granz had recorded Parker live at the Philharmonic Auditorium in Los Angeles in early 1946 (chapter 3). The American Federation of Musicians had announced a January 1, 1948, strike against the recording industry and Granz hoped to record as much material as possible before the deadline. Granz obtained from Dial Records a release for Parker's services for five hundred dollars.[30]

On one evening in December, 1947, Granz assembled two groups in two halls within New York's Carnegie Hall. He recorded Parker in the smaller recital hall with a one-time-only group consisting of pianist Hank Jones, bassist Ray Brown, and drummer Shelly Manne. The group tackled an improvisation upon the chords to the swing era standard "Topsy." Eventually titled "The Bird," the loosely organized performance had no written theme and lasted an unusually long 4:44, necessitating a 12″ 78 RPM disc. "The Bird" is one of Parker's more haunting performances for several reasons. The piece is based in C minor (one of very few Parker pieces truly based in a minor tonality), and some of the unresolved mood of Parker's solo may derive from his melodically emphasizing the major 6th degree of the minor scale (A natural) when on the tonic C-minor chord. As the key signature below shows, the minor sixth, A♭, occurs naturally in C natural minor; the more striking A natural requires an accidental sign when it occurs (A natural *is* found in the Dorian mode and the melodic minor [ascending] scale). This practice of emphasizing the major sixth degree was a favorite of Parker's dominant influence, Lester Young. In the following example from the beginning of Parker's second solo, melodic occurrences of the major sixth degree (the pitch A natural) are circled.

"The Bird" Ex. 1

Note that the pitches with "x" note heads are overtones (acoustically related pitches that may have an indistinct or veiled timbre) that sounded through the accidental "overblowing" of Parker's horn, producing notes higher than those intended (the standard note heads reflect the pitches that Parker fingered and intended to sound). His saxophone evidently had a mechanical problem, as verified by the many earlier passages when Parker's horn briefly sounds notes an octave *lower* than intended (due to Parker's old octave-key problem, as noted in earlier chapters). The sudden emerging and disappearing of these overtones make for unexpected twists to the melody, and, along with the notes' unusual timbre, lend a strange quality to this piece. Here in Parker's first solo, his melodic line unintentionally drops an octave (the standard note heads reflect what Parker fingered and intended; the "x" note heads reflect what came out).

"The Bird" Ex. 2

Parker's quick mind and keen aural skills are heard at work during his second solo on "The Bird" when he comes upon a simple phrase, probably through improvisation (3:32). Parker seizes upon this fragment and repeats it, varying it slightly as he touches on it for the next minute or so. Even though "The Bird" has no set theme statement (or "head"), this phrase becomes a quasi-head that unifies the latter moments of the performance as the musicians seek to release tension and end the piece. (Parker occasionally used this ad hoc head device on studio performances that had no set theme statement; see "Kim," below) If this device qualifies for the term "thematic improvisation" it is certainly not on the order of creativity found in take A of "Embraceable You" (chapter 4). Still, it is another example of an underused melodic and structural resource available to Parker.

When "The Bird" was completed, Manne was called away to the other Granz recording session on the main Carnegie Hall stage; a version of "Cherokee" was attempted by the remaining trio but was rejected. After the combo date, Parker stopped by the other session within the building. There he found arranger-composer Neal Hefti conducting a jazz big band augmented with Latin percussion, violins, viola, and cello. Hefti had composed a hypnotic ensemble piece called "Repetition" for the *Jazz Scene* album. Hefti recalls Norman Granz spontaneously asking him if Parker could be used for the piece at hand. Although "Repetition" had no improvisational section built in, Hefti readily agreed to have Parker solo on the latter part of the piece. In an interview with Parker scholar Phil Schaap, the violinist and concertmaster for the string section, Gene Orloff recalled:

> It was the most phenomenal thing I ever saw. The lead sheet for him or whatever he had to blow changes on was spread out, a sheet of about ten pages and he had it strewn out over the piano. He was like bending down then lifting his head up as the music passed by, reading it once or twice until he memorized those changes and then proceeded to become godly.[31]

Despite his unfamiliarity with the piece, Parker sounds at home and shows his tremendous ear and quick reflexes. At 1:35, Hefti includes a melody that may derive from Stravinsky's *Rite of Spring*. When Parker enters at 1:49, he manages to work the phrase in, transposing it up a minor third to adjust to the now-prevailing harmony. Being an avid Stravinsky listener, Parker likely appreciated the similarity between Stravinky's and Hefti's melodies (or knew that Hefti was consciously quoting Stravinsky).

Neither Parker nor Granz knew that these two sides were the beginning of a recording partnership that would last until Parker's death. The selections that Granz recorded at that first studio session predict the eclectic approach that Granz would take with Parker in the future: one was a small combo, the other a large orchestra; both were one-time-only ensembles. The resumption of the recording partnership, however, would have to wait until the end of the musicians' strike.

New Interests

Like many jazz musicians of his and earlier generations, Parker in his youth and early adulthood had learned his craft and had expanded his musical abilities through firsthand encounters with more experienced musicians and through the study of recordings. Unlike Dizzy Gillespie, however, Parker did not have a rich experience at the piano with which to organize his discoveries into larger concepts of music theory.

Cobbling together a sense of the fundamentals of music theory and improvisation from many individuals can lead to some unique musical concepts. In 1954, Parker gave a music lesson to a novice player who tape-recorded the session. On the tape, Parker is heard urging the saxophonist to learn all of the major and minor scales. Interestingly, Parker says: "Thirteen scales. *Major* scales. Thirteen minor scales." After Parker states the names of the scales, the following exchange occurs between Dick Meldonian and Charlie Parker:

DM: That'd be twelve.
CP: Twelve?
DM: Uh huh.
CP: Twelve?
DM: Yeah.
CP: All right.[32]

Of course, there are only twelve tones to a chromatic scale, hence twelve major or minor scales. Why Parker specified thirteen is unknown.

Trumpeter Red Rodney recalled asking Parker's help in identifying the chord changes to particular songs:

Many times I asked him, "Bird, where's the bridge [B section] go?" And he'd say, "B-flat." And it would [actually] be F$\sharp$ minor or B, one of those kind of things. And I'd ask him again, for another tune, similar type, difficult bridge. And I'd say "Where's the bridge?" "B-flat." And he'd give me that sheepish little smile and say, "Well that's what I play."[33]

The musical knowledge Parker had attained up to this point derived much more from experience and the imperatives of application than from concepts of music theory. This orientation toward application is consistent with the great immediacy and authority of Parker's improvisational art. At this time, however, he may have needed more theoretical knowledge, whether from a process of self-guided discovery at the piano keyboard (like Dizzy Gillespie) or from formal study.

In the late 1940s, Parker was interviewed for three articles that are notable in part for his references to love of classical music. The first was

Leonard Feather's "Yardbird Flies Home" in the August, 1947, issue of *Metronome* magazine.

> Have you heard that album of music by Schönberg with just five instruments playing while an actress recites some poetry, in German? It's a wonderful thing—I think it's called *Protée*.[34] . . . have you heard *The Children's Corner* by Debussy? Oh, that's so much music! . . . Debussy and Stravinsky are my favorites; but I like Shostakovich . . . Beethoven too . . .[35]

For an article that was published in the August, 1948, issue of *Metronome*, Feather played Parker part of Stravinsky's *The Song of the Nightingale* (*Chant du rossignol*) as part of Feather's "Blindfold Test": "Is it by Stravinsky? That's music at its best. I like all of Stravinsky—and Prokofiev, Hindemith, Ravel, Debussy . . . and, of course, Wagner and Bach. Give that all the stars you've got!" (ellipses in original text) In a section of "afterthoughts," Parker's high esteem for Western classical music may be inferred in this comment: "Of everything you played, I think I enjoyed Stan's [Kenton] record best—the second one, featuring the alto. Kenton is the closest thing to classical music in the jazz field, if you want to call it jazz."[36]

In 1949, Parker gave a wide-ranging interview that became the basis of a *Down Beat* magazine article. He touched upon many subjects including his first exposure to classical music:

> Around this time, the middle of 1939, he heard some Bach and Beethoven for the first time. He was impressed with Bach's patterns. "I found out that what the [jazz] guys were jamming then had already been put down, and in most cases, a lot better.". . . It was on this visit to New York, in late 1942 after he had worked out his basic approach to complex harmony, that Charlie heard Stravinsky for the first time when Ziggy Kelly played *Firebird* for him.[37]

In a 1953 article, he filled in the picture:

> I first began listening [to classical music] seven or eight years ago. First I heard Stravinsky's *Firebird Suite*. In the vernacular of the streets, I flipped. I guess Bartók has become my favorite. I dig all the moderns. And all the classical men, Bach, Beethoven, etc.[38]

In the 1949 article, Parker also was paraphrased as to the future of jazz vis-à-vis classical music:

> He admits the music may eventually be atonal. Parker himself is a devout admirer of Paul Hindemith, the German neo-classicist, raves about his [*Kleine*] *Kammermusik* and *Sonata for Viola and Cello* [probably the *Duet for Viola and Cello*]. He insists, however, that bop is not moving in the same direction as modern classical. He feels it will be more flexible, more emotional, more colorful.[39]

While in Paris in 1949, Parker met and socialized with French jazz fans, artists, and intellectuals. Parker met the "classical" saxophonist Marcel Mule, an encounter that instilled in Parker the possibility of studying "classical" saxophone. Parker was by this time aware of the European classical music approach to the saxophone, as Savoy record producer Teddy Reig recalled: "I'm still cursing him out for taking all my Marcel Mule records. I had three copies of the Concertina de [*da*] Camera [by Jacques Ibert] for saxophone and orchestra and Bird got every one."[40]

It was in contact with jazz critic Charles Delaunay that Parker reportedly formulated a plan to study musical composition with Nadia Boulanger in France (see chapter 1). In the 1949 Levin and Wilson article, Parker revealed a new sense of the possibilities of residence and study in Europe. Also evident is Parker's changing view of the value of *composing* music (as distinct from *improvising* it).

> For the future, he'd like to go to the Academy of Music in Paris [possibly the *Conservatoire Nationale de Musique de Paris* where Mule taught] for a couple of years, then relax for a while and then write. The things he writes all will be concentrated toward one point: warmth. . . . Ideally, he'd like to spend six months a year in France and six months here. "You've got to do it that way," he explains. "You've go to be here for the commercial things and in France for relaxing facilities."[41]

Charlie Parker had accomplished much since his release from Camarillo State Hospital. He had formed, recorded with, and toured with his quintet, the ensemble that in general best showcased his talents. In response to the recording needs of the quintet, Parker wrote the greatest number of his compositions during this period. His best studio and live recordings of the period document a level of creativity in which any separation between conception and execution seems erased. Parker's virtuosity, swing, inventiveness, and poetic qualities all reached new heights, as did his creative command of melody, harmony, and rhythm while improvising.

Although his work from early in the period was characterized by great freshness and spontaneity, his later work showed sign of an artistic plateau. As with all jazz musicians, Parker had a repertoire of pet phrases that came into play as melodic connecting devices and for use when inspiration flagged. Parker's vast inventory of these licks was played with such authority and vitality that only he, as the source of the vocabulary, could muster. But as the decade ended, he increasingly strung these phrases together in lieu of fresh melodic invention and found himself on an artistic plateau.

Parker's statements of dissatisfaction with his art, taken with his desire to study music composition and saxophone technique in the European tradition, signal both a wider musical worldview for him and the beginnings of a change in his aesthetics and goals. This evolution would be a source of both great potential and great frustration for Parker. Dissatisfied with his music as it stood, Parker began to thirst for new musical concepts and instrumental settings. Clearly, he had the talent and vision to begin such an exploration. His brilliance was not in question, but discipline and sobriety were.

Chapter 5

1950–55

The beginning of 1950 found Parker's personal and artistic life in flux. His marriage to Doris was breaking up and a rekindled relationship with Chan Richardson was about to turn into a common-law marriage that would offer him stability and a family life. His quintet was in its final and perhaps technically finest form, but Red Rodney's arrest and other factors would soon hasten the group's demise. Touring as a "single" and appearing and recording with onetime all-star groups became much more common for him in the 1950s. Critical and popular acclaim was at a peak as he entered the new decade; he continued to win the *Esquire* readers' poll as best alto saxophonist and he finally reached the same level in the *Down Beat* poll beginning in 1950.

At the same time that the jazz audience was catching up with his music, Parker's art was reaching a crossroads. His improvisations, although usually energetic and always personal, were becoming routine and in danger of being reduced to a string of stylized signature gestures. Becoming lost was Parker's spontaneous approach to spinning forth fresh melody. In a 1949 interview, Parker warned that Dizzy Gillespie was in danger of becoming stagnant: "He isn't repeating notes yet, but he is repeating patterns."[1] As the new decade began, Parker found himself in the same position he had predicted regarding Gillespie. Judging from his own statements, Parker was aware of his own stagnancy and was feeling frustrated with the forms of jazz. He longed to advance his art to a new stage and was becoming increasingly interested in the European "classical" music tradition as way to expand his musical horizons. At a time when society in the United States as a whole still viewed jazz as entertainment and not art, Parker may have viewed the European tradition as containing a solution to his stagnancy while underestimating his own African-American heritage as a resource for innovation. In part because of his addiction related lack of discipline, Charlie Parker found it difficult to develop the improvisational concepts and techniques he had encountered. A sustained effort to study, assimilate, and adapt the European classical music tradition to his artistic vision would have been at least as difficult.

Earlier in his career, Parker had gone through artistic stages of development such as technical training, copying his predecessors, assimilating and transcending his influences, experimentation with materials, and eventual reaching of artistic maturity and creation of masterpieces, by using an individual musical vocabulary. By 1950, he had reached a stage of summing up all that he had so far discovered. Many artists experience the plateau that Parker was facing; one way to deal with such a plateau is to use the summing-up stage as a springboard into a new stage of artistic experimentation and growth. Another alternative is to simply consolidate what one has learned and be content to repeat one's gestures in a masterful way. Much of the sense of authority found in Parker's music up to that point came from the fact that his musical knowledge derived from experience rather than theory and was always attained in a context of application. A disadvantage to his lack of theoretical knowledge, however, is seen in Parker's difficulties in gathering together the musical resources needed to effect aesthetic change in his art. Charlie Parker yearned to enter a new phase of discovery, but probably because of his lack of discipline and study, he settled for an early artistic consolidation.

Reflecting in large part his artistic stagnation, none of Parker's studio recordings of the 1950s can consistently rival his best work of 1945–49. With regard to *sustained* creativity, no studio performance on the order of "Ko Ko," "Embraceable You," or "Parker's Mood" was recorded in the 1950s. Certainly, all of his studio recordings of the 1950s have moments of characteristic Parker beauty, but a survey of books and articles on Parker's music shows that writers discuss Parker's 1945–49 work much more often than they do his later work. Listeners who are not musicians also seem to return somewhat more often to Parker's earlier work. Although Parker's live recordings of the period also show a decline in freshness and show an inconsistency of inspiration when compared to those of 1945–49, a significant few have possible signs of new directions, although none of those directions was decisively pursued.

Creative matters aside, Parker's music of this final period is largely consistent with the preceding two periods with regard to the more technical qualities (such as timbre, vibrato, and accentuation) first outlined in the criteria found in the "Introduction to the Musical Chapters." His nightclub repertoire continued to be usually chosen by him (although his record producer, Norman Granz, sometimes had influence upon the pieces that Parker recorded) and consisted largely of twelve-bar blues and thirty-two-bar pop song forms. As before, Parker's "compositions" usually involved preexisting chord progressions and a minimum of written material from Parker.

Parker's range of tempos continued to be quite wide. If there is a significant distinction between this and the previous two periods, it might be that he was recorded less often playing at extremely fast tempos than previously (significant exceptions include the versions of "Lester Leaps In" and "Kim," discussed below). This change is partly attributable to the fact that Parker was recording and touring with a string ensemble that was emphasizing slower tempo material. Understandably, his *range* of note values remained wide, largely due to his double-timing and quadruple-timing on ballads. At his best, Parker's control of these rapid passages was, if anything, more sure than before (see the 1953 "Embraceable You," below). At those times, his ability to creatively place accents continued to be unsurpassed.

Parker's approach to the melodic line remained consistent in that he continued to build his solos largely from the same small-scale building blocks associated with him. His medium-scale building blocks were actually *too* consistent with his earlier work; as the 1950s began, his art was in the process of consolidating into a lick-based approach. A few glimmerings of new melodic/harmonic tools do appear in the 1950s and interestingly presage the work of John Coltrane of the late 1950s and early 1960s (see below).

As mentioned in chapter 4, Parker had reestablished ties with Norman Granz in the late 1940s. When the musicians' union strike ended in 1948, Charlie Parker signed with Granz, thus cementing a professional association between the two that would last until Parker's death in 1955. Granz not only recorded Parker with near exclusivity, he also presented Parker on tour with Jazz at the Philharmonic and subsidized Parker financially. Because most of the Granz studio sides were recorded in the 1950s, the bulk of them will be discussed in this chapter (the only exceptions being the two 1949 sessions based around Parker's working quintet and the 1947 *The Jazz Scene* sessions that have been discussed in the previous chapter).

Granz's early agreement with the Mercury label (Granz's Parker recordings at various times appeared on the Mercury, Clef, Norgran, and Verve labels) guaranteed that his recordings would receive better distribution than Dial and Savoy could muster. Granz recorded Parker frequently in settings that varied widely in accordance with Granz's philosophy. Granz felt that recording the live jam-session atmosphere brought out the essence of the excitement of jazz; in the studio, he advocated putting the artist in a variety of settings that might include one-time-only studio combinations and special "theme" albums (now often called "concept" albums): "I think these shifting combinations bring out fresh dimensions in an established artist."[2] These approaches left little room for Parker's working groups; in the more than five years Parker recorded for him, Granz recorded Parker's regular combo only once (the quintet session with Kenny Dorham, discussed in the last chapter) without including additional and sometimes questionable musicians (to be fair, although Granz usually chose the additional musicians, Parker also occasionally chose the extras). Granz's recording philosophy would play a tremendous role in Parker's later career, determining which aspects of Parker's artistry would and would not reach the phonograph record marketplace.

The Granz/Parker studio groups included a string ensemble, an Afro-Cuban big band, a jazz big band, a big band plus strings, a woodwind quintet with vocal group, an all-star reunion with Dizzy Gillespie and Thelonious Monk, several one-time small-group combinations, and (on two occasions) Parker's working quintet with and without guests. The theme albums included a misguided "South of the Border" concept and a somewhat more appropriate album of Cole Porter songs. Partly because Granz seldom recorded Parker in unified groups of compatible players, and partly because of Parker's declining health and lack of practice, the Granz recordings of the 1950s as a body of work do not rival Parker's masterpieces of 1945 to 1949.

Charlie Parker and Strings

On November 30, 1949, Parker entered the Mercury Recording Company studios in New York City to record his first session with an ensemble made up of violins, viola, cello, harp, oboe (and possibly English horn), and jazz rhythm section. Although not as consistently inspired or influential as the Parker-Gillespie sides or the classic quintet sides, this session would have a tremendous impact upon Parker's career.

Parker's encounters with French critics and intellectuals during his May, 1949, trip to Paris may have accelerated his desire to place his saxophone into new musical settings influenced by classical music. Certainly in Norman Granz, Parker had finally met a record label owner who was able and willing to finance some of Parker's more expensive projects. (Herman Lubinsky, the owner of Savoy, would not have been sympathetic to such music; Ross Russell, the owner of Dial, probably would have been sympathetic but had a limited budget.) At any rate, Granz gave a green light to the project, songs were chosen, and Jimmy Carroll was hired to make six arrangements for the ensemble, usually referred to as Charlie Parker and Strings.

Several sessions were required to attain releasable takes on the six chosen pieces. The ensemble's pianist, Stan Freeman, recalled the multiple dates:

> There were three or four where nothing happened. Whether he was high or loaded or what, he had to come back and do it again. He was kind of spaced out on a lot of dates and wasn't talking to anybody much. Mitch Miller, being head of A&R [Artists and Repertoire] at Mercury at the time, probably convinced them that we should do it again on another day.[3]

Parker scholar Phil Schaap paraphrases Mitch Miller on the subject: "One time he [Miller] observed Parker leaving before recording and called Granz on this point. Norman told Mitch Miller that Parker was so overwhelmed by the beautiful sound of the ensemble that he couldn't do it."[4] Schaap takes Granz's statement at face value, but it's just as likely that Granz was placating Miller and covering for Parker's intoxication.

The Granz Parker and Strings sessions have several parallels to Parker's Dial recordings of American popular song. Norman Granz, like Ross Russell, was certainly a supportive in-studio producer. The strings repertoire of songs by George Gershwin, Vernon Duke, Richard Rodgers, Cole Porter, Arthur Schwartz, and others is high quality, as the Dial ballad repertoire had been. On the Granz sides in question, Parker is again given the opportunity to state and decorate memorable melodies and improvise on good pop-song chord changes.

One distinction between the two bodies of work is in the tempos; the Dial American popular song recordings tended to be slow and reflective with all titles slower than quarter note = 120; the Verve string recordings vary more widely in tempo, providing more variety of mood. The most significant differences, however, lie in the arrangements. For the Dial sides, the arrangements were constructed in the studio and not written out. Due to the flexibility of the Dial ballad arrangements, Parker in each case had full freedom with regard to the opening theme statement. He could state a song's melody in a recognizable way, embellishing it, departing from it and returning to it ("My Old Flame," the A take of "Bird of Paradise"), or he could ignore the original theme completely and simply improvise upon the song's harmonies ("Embraceable You" and takes B and C of "Bird of Paradise").

With a string ensemble, the arrangements had to be carefully planned in every aspect and largely written out, right down to the placement and length (but not the content) of Parker's ad-lib sections. Out of eighteen titles recorded in the studio by Parker and Strings (including the session combining strings with big band), ten are comparable to the Dial ballads in tempo (quarter note = 120 or slower). In only *one* of these ten did Parker have a full unbroken chorus to himself to do whatever he wanted, whether to state the theme or to depart from it (the exception to the above is "Summertime;" Parker is allowed to state all of the song's unusually short sixteen-measure melody). Generally, he's locked into sticking close to the original melody for the bars he's assigned it and then ceding the melody to other instruments (the violin section, oboe, French horn, and such) as specified by the arrangement. Of course, it's sound arranging practice to distribute the melody among several different instruments; one would not expect Parker to be in the foreground all the time given the possibilities that this expanded instrumentation offers. But given only three minutes on a 78 RPM record, the result is that on these slow pieces, Parker never gets enough unbroken space to be truly spontaneous in stating the theme (or for that matter, in soloing—amazingly, he never gets a chance to solo for a full chorus).

In this author's opinion, these ballads with strings do not add any new masterpieces to Parker's discography. A significant factor in their not rivaling the Dial ballads is the lack of unbroken time for Parker to create. Another factor in why these sides don't live up to their potential is that the arrangements, while competent, are not very inspiring. The commissioned arrangements of popular songs resembled common Hollywood movie music more than the twentieth-century concert music Parker admired and longed to emulate. In addition, by 1949, Parker's playing was losing some of its freshness. He gradually stopped practicing the saxophone, and his health, at its best in the year of the Dial sides, was again showing the effects of heroin and alcohol addiction.

Just Friends

That Parker could still produce a masterpiece in 1949 is superbly illustrated by the first selection that Charlie Parker recorded with the strings, the thirty-two-bar popular song "Just Friends" (11-30-49; Granz). This stunning Parker performance with strings is taken faster (quarter note = ca. 136) than the Granz ballads discussed above. That small tempo difference allows for three full choruses, plus introduction, interlude, and coda within the time limit of the 78 RPM record. As usual in the string arrangements, Parker makes an initial statement of the theme, which, typically, is broken up by a passage by the strings. More unusually in these string arrangements, however, he also enjoys a full chorus of improvisation in a new key during which he is not required to refer to the melody. In addition, Parker also has three other improvisational sections in the arrangement: an introduction, a final half chorus, and a coda. These factors give Parker the perfect balance between written arrangement and ad-lib opportunities. A complete transcription of this solo is found in Appendix B.

Readers will notice that the featured solo in this chapter, "Just Friends," was recorded a month *before* the chapter's time frame begins. The placing of this recording session within this chapter is for two reasons. As mentioned at the beginning of this chapter, most of Parker's studio recordings for Granz were made in the 1950s, and it makes sense to discuss most of them (e.g., "Just Friends") in chapter 5. In addition, in the author's opinion, Parker's brilliant work on "Just Friends" provides more creative material for discussion than any Parker performance of the 1950s.

The range of note values employed by Parker in "Just Friends" is wide, ranging from thirty-second notes to a dotted half note or longer. Although Parker implies double time (passages in sixteenth notes) for most of the performance, he does occasionally ease back into swing eighth notes. After a rather clichéd opening featuring swelling strings and harp, Parker enters with a thrilling four-bar introduction in double time that retains its freshness over repeated listenings. Part of its appeal comes from the rhythmic snap of Parker's customary accenting of melodic high points. Parker seamlessly blends into the melody statement of "Just Friends," touching on its melody just enough to let the listener get her or his bearings (the circled notes indicate the original melody of "Just Friends").

"Just Friends" Ex. 1

Parker then uses the first chorus to state, embellish, and depart from the song's melody with great freedom and spontaneity, qualities that are too often lacking in other studio performances with strings. His timbre is rich and in control, with just a touch of edge.[5] Around this time, Parker had settled on a King saxophone with a metal mouthpiece and employed that combination almost exclusively until his death.[6] Quite possibly, having a more regular equipment setup lent Parker a new consistency of timbre and control. As expected, Parker uses vibrato sparingly, and only on the longest notes.

A four-bar modulation into a new key leads into Parker's full-chorus solo. Most of Parker's phrases are short, and a few one- and three-measure phrases lend occasional asymmetry. Most common, however, are two-measure phrases that reinforce rather than cut across the song's underlying formal building blocks. Parker also observes the song's larger form by not constructing phrases over the song's larger structural divisions.

An important part of the success of "Just Friends" lies in the melodic freshness of Parker's improvisation. Although he breaks no new melodic ground, Parker uses his characteristic vocabulary in a spontaneous and inventive manner. Not in evidence is his growing tendency to arrange that vocabulary into licks he could employ while on automatic pilot. Instead, Parker is alert and aware as he spins forth gem after surprising gem of melodic invention.

As previously noted, Parker only sparingly quoted other songs while recording in the studio. During Parker's second solo (a sixteen-bar half chorus following a fine half chorus from pianist Stan Freeman), he smoothly slips in a reference to "My Man," a song associated with Fanny Brice and Billie Holiday (Holiday had recorded the song nearly a year before this Parker recording). In context, the quotation does not stick out or seem forced; rather it seems to flow naturally from what preceded it.

"Just Friends" Ex. 2

Given the lyric nature of the arrangement, Parker fittingly sticks fairly close to the basic chord changes without exploring extensive chord alteration, chromatic sequencing, or side-slipping. A good example of Parker's creative use of the song's harmonies comes at the beginning of his thirty-two-bar solo (the second chorus). Parker plays two brief phrases that inventively outline the piece's first two harmonic stations (as marked by numbers in the example). The first phrase goes as high as the major seventh of the chord; the second phrase ascends to the ninth, building intensity. It is a deceptively simple yet very effective gesture.

"Just Friends" Ex. 3

At the end of that solo, Parker's last phrase contains a few notes that would not normally be played on the tonic chord (creating an unlikely "♭6" and "♭7" on the B♭ chord). A quick glance shows that these notes belong to the previous dominant chord (representing a "♭9" and "♯9" on the F7 chord); in spinning out his phrase, Parker just took an extra beat to express an idea, thus displacing that idea slightly. In fact, the last two phrases of that solo could be said to be displaced by one beat. In the following example, the upper part shows how Parker played the phrases and how they lined up with the song's harmonies; the lower part shows how the phrases theoretically (but perhaps less creatively) "should have" lined up with the harmonies. (This example of displaced notes seems to more strongly follow a melodic imperative than the one-bar displacement of the Coleman Hawkins lick as discussed regarding "Body and Soul" in chapter 2.)

"Just Friends" Ex. 4

After his final sixteen-bar solo spot, Parker has a final improvised tag or coda. As in the introduction, Parker responds brilliantly with flurries of driving sixteenth notes, effectively accented. Again, his work shows great spontaneity and avoidance of cliché.

The tag brings to a close a well-integrated arrangement and performance that features Parker extensively in introduction, loose theme statement, full-chorus solo, half-chorus solo and coda. Parker had thrived on this piece for several reasons. "Just Friends" was new material (no earlier Parker recordings of it have surfaced), and therefore a fresh challenge to him. As mentioned above, the arrangement allowed him improvisational flexibility, and allowed him to do what he did best. Further, the chart

"Just Friends" Ex. 5

presented the song's chord progression in two successive keys, keeping Parker on his toes. Finally, the introduction and coda, chord progressions that did not derive from any familiar pop song, encouraged Parker away from his own well-worn improvisational licks. "Just Friends" illustrates what the other Parker and strings recordings could have been if the arrangements had allowed Parker more flexibility in ensemble role and in improvising.

Parker went on to record eight titles with a string section in 1950. All of these titles feature Parker creatively embellishing the songs' melodies, a skill at which Parker excelled. Although none of these recordings equal "Just Friends" in allotted solo space, all include briefer moments of fine improvisation. Supporting the idea that Parker thrived on new challenges, the newly composed coda (not based on the song's chord progression) to "Dancing in the Dark" (3:01; summer, 1950; Granz) inspires him to some of his freshest work on these sides, much as the coda to "Just Friends" had.

In the 1950s, Parker took his string ensemble with jazz rhythm section to nightclubs, concerts halls, and at least one dance hall. Parker and the group needed a bit more variety in the strings repertoire, especially some up-tempo pieces. Three new arrangements were documented when Granz recorded Parker and Strings live at Carnegie Hall in 1950. One was an adaptation for the string ensemble of Neal Hefti's "Repetition" (chapter 4), the only Latin-tinged song in the book. Cole Porter's "What Is This Thing Called Love?" received an up-tempo arrangement that gave Parker latitude in stating the theme and in soloing. Also, saxophonist-composer Gerry Mulligan contributed the fleet original composition

"Rocker" (originally called "Rock Salt") and that also showed off Parker's improvisational skill to advantage. None of these arrangements was ever documented in studio recordings. In addition, at Parker's request, Gerry Mulligan wrote and arranged a swing piece called "Gold Rush" for the full group and composed a hypnotic waltz theme, possibly never titled,[7] for the string ensemble to play (without Parker) at the beginnings or ends of sets. These two were never recorded by Granz at all but survive in live recordings made by private individuals.

When Parker and Strings played in nightclubs, they sometimes modified the arrangements to allow Parker multiple choruses of unbroken improvisation (reportedly as long as fifteen minutes[8]) on the song's basic chord progression. The dual purposes of this technique were to give Parker more solo space and to stretch out the strings' small repertoire. Most of the live recordings of Parker and strings derive from concert or radio broadcast situations in which Parker's song lengths and set lengths were restricted, but one live dance/concert recording from September 26, 1952, does show a limited opening up of the arrangements (several pieces recorded the same night, but without the string section, are discussed later in this chapter).

From that session, Gerry Mulligan's "Rocker" (one of two versions recorded that night[9]) is a good example of how the loosening of the string arrangements freed up Parker's creativity. Parker's official recording of the arrangement for Norman Granz lasts just over three minutes; the expanded version runs a full two minutes longer. Parker responds to the loosening up of the arrangement's structure by doing some of his most melodically and harmonically advanced work of the 1950s

On the live recording of "The Street Beat" discussed in chapter 4, Parker briefly played a striking chromatic idea that he revisits and extends on "Rocker." In "The Street Beat," the four-note pattern in question began on C (concert), leapt up by a minor third, then descended twice by successive major thirds as marked below (in the following example, each note in brackets is an "enharmonic" equivalent of the note immediately preceding; the alternate notations of the pitches are intended to make the various intervals more easy to recognize). Parker then repeated ("sequenced") the pattern down a whole step (beginning on B♭) and was in the process of presenting it down another whole step (from A♭) when he abruptly stopped. Sequencing of the pattern also set up descending augmented triads and ascending diminished triads, as marked below. The pattern's intervallic architecture of thirds and triads may be easily seen in this excerpt:

"Intervallic Pattern"

In the fourth chorus of the 1952 "Rocker," Parker returns to the "Street Beat" pattern, beginning it again on C, and then presenting the pattern *seven* more times, each time a whole step lower. Here is the pattern as played in "The Street Beat" (upper staff) and as played in "Rocker" (lower staff):

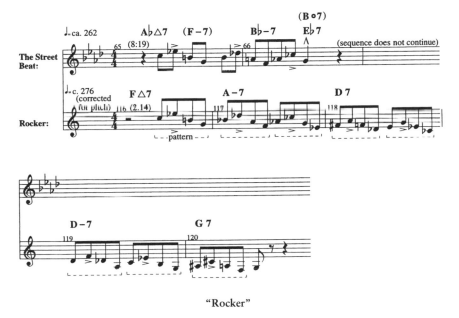

"Rocker"

As may be seen above, "The Street Beat" and "Rocker" are in two different keys; however, the pattern's harmonically ambiguous intervallic structure allows Parker to present the same pattern in the context of any key and obtain chromaticism. By sequencing this simple pattern, which in itself is harmonically ambiguous, Parker attains varying degrees of desirable clash against the accompanimental harmonies. Parker had shown interest in sequenced patterns as early as his first recording, "Honey & Body," but in that case the pattern implied a chain of tonal ii-7–V7–I progressions. In "The Street Beat" and "Rocker," Parker is not trying to imply a chord progression or derive chromaticism from functional harmony-based chord alterations, but is instead trying to chromatically cut across tonality through a form of interval-based architecture. This is a significant advance in Parker's knowledge of ways to obtain chromaticism.

The result is strikingly like the work of saxophonist John Coltrane in the 1960s, when he was deriving patterns for sequencing from Nicolas Slonimsky's *Thesaurus of Scales and Melodic Patterns* (of course, Coltrane often superimposed his patterns over more harmonically static accompaniment). Slonimsky's *Thesaurus* had already been published in 1947, making it possible that Parker may have encountered the book. Because each occurrence of the pattern is presented two half steps lower (as in whole-tone scale; see the circled notes above), a likely place to search for the pattern would be Slonimsky's section titled "Whole-Tone Progression." Because of the way that three notes are inserted between each of those circled notes, the subsection "Infra-Inter-Ultrapolation" (the term refers to the three inserted notes) is a likely place to look. Indeed, on page 81 of Slonimsky's book, the pattern is found.[10]

Slonimsky Pattern #629

Slonimsky calls it pattern number 629; Parker's version matches the descending part of the pattern (above). Significantly, not only are the patterns identical in intervallic construction (in the two examples, a few notes are "spelled" differently but sound identically), but also in both cases Parker begins the pattern *on the same note* (C-concert) as it is presented by Slonimsky. Certainly Parker could have come upon this pattern on his own, but given the book's availability, the pattern's unusual construction, and the identical starting notes, it is quite possible that Charlie Parker anticipated Coltrane and a generation of jazz musicians in using Slonimsky's *Thesaurus* as a resource for chromatic patterns for improvisation. However, as happened too often in the 1950s, Parker did not actively explore this advanced technique that was available to him. Perhaps it was not central to his style, or perhaps he did not pursue this direction because he had already entered into a period of artistic consolidation.

As pointed out by Lewis Porter, Parker plays some other particularly striking ideas in the fourth chorus of "Rocker."[11] One is a series of augmented triads (based on a whole-tone scale) that cut across a C tonality, immediately following the Slonimsky-like pattern (essentially the same augmented triad pattern cited in the 1949–50 "Dizzy Atmosphere" in chapter 4).[12] Another involves Parker quoting Tadd Dameron's "The Chase" in the home key of C and then transposing it to E♭ while the rest of the group stays in C, creating a bitonal effect. Parker's best solos on this live recording equal any of his improvisational work of the 1950s.

Although the arrangements for the string group did not resemble the modern classical music Parker most admired, he never stated for the record whether the eventual arrangements were consistent with his original vision for the project. Parker loved American popular song and was proud of his recordings with strings: "When I recorded with strings, some of my friends said, 'Oh, Bird is getting commercial.' That wasn't it at all. I was looking for new ways of saying things musically. New sound combinations. Why, I asked for strings as far back as 1941 and then, years later, when I went with Norman, he okayed it. I like Joe Lippman's fine arrangements on the second session and I think they didn't turn out too badly."[13] Today, it would not be unusual for a jazz artist to record with a string ensemble, but at the time, only a few jazz artists (most of these more commercially popular than Parker) had recorded with such a group. Another significant achievement is that Parker actually toured with his string ensemble, a difficult feat for a jazz artist in any era.

In 1950, Dizzy Gillespie broke up his big band and was casting about for a new ensemble that would have a wider popular appeal than straight bebop. Inspired both by some Johnny Richards–arranged records that Gillespie himself had made in 1946 and by Parker's more recent success with his string ensemble, Gillespie envisioned a new touring group concept that would unite Bird and Diz.

I'd use five woodwind men, all doubling, and a rhythm section. I want to have Johnny Richards do about 16 arrangements for the group—half standards and half originals. Richards understands what I want and he understands the mechanism of the various instruments. . . . It would be a good thing for us to be together. All we'd need is Charlie and me and a rhythm section. We could play concerts and clubs, picking up the woodwind and string men wherever we go. There wouldn't be any trouble about that. They'd all be longhairs and they wouldn't have to swing. All they'd have to do is read what's in front of them. They could pick it up in one rehearsal. The way I see it, Charlie would play a set with his strings, then I'd play a set with the woodwinds, and then we'd wind up all together. . . . And we'd stress entertainment. Every time we went on a stage, it would be just like a show. We'd make people think we like what we're doing.[14]

Gillespie did go on to sit in with Parker's strings, but nothing came of this idea of truly combining forces.

Large Ensemble and Big Band Recordings

Although Parker was proud of his string group, its arrangements and its repertoire, he soon tried to assert a more challenging direction for any new chamber music recordings. Max Roach remembered: "Bird had all sorts of musical combinations in mind. He wanted to make a record with Yehudi Menuhin and, at least, a forty-piece orchestra."[15] By the 1950s, Norman Granz was financially in a position to commission classical music works for Parker. The idea that contemporary classical composers could be asked to write new works for instrumentalists from the jazz world had precedent in Benny Goodman's commissioning Bartók (1938), Aaron Copland (1947), and Paul Hindemith (1947). In 1953, Parker told critic Nat Hentoff, "Now, I'd like to do a session with five or six woodwinds, a harp, a choral group, and full rhythm section. Something on the line of Hindemith's *Kleine Kammermusik* [Opus 24, No. 2; scored for woodwind quintet]. Not a copy or anything like that. I don't want ever to copy. But that sort of thing."[16]

Although Parker was hoping for a challenging synthesis of twentieth-century classical music composition and modern jazz along the lines of what became known as Third Stream music, he soon settled for something much simpler and potentially more commercial for Granz and his company. Max Roach recalled, "He [Parker] mapped out things for woodwinds and voices, and Norman Granz would holler, 'What's this? You can't make money with this crazy combination. You can't sell this stuff!'"[17] Although Roach later said he had known nothing specific about the organization of this particular recording project, his recollection has parallels to the Hindemith-like concept Parker was proposing and supports the idea that Granz sometimes vetoed Parker's most ambitious concepts and generally pushed for more commercial recording projects.[18]

The eventual ensemble that was recorded included the woodwind quintet (flute, oboe, clarinet, French horn, and bassoon), choral group (mixed chorus of twelve voices), and jazz rhythm section that Parker had wanted but did not resemble the Hindemith piece in style or complexity at all. As with the earlier sessions with strings, the repertoire once again consisted of American popular songs, and not original compositions commissioned for the recording as Parker had evidently hoped.

For the date, Gil Evans was charged with the instrumental part of the arrangements and Dave Lambert was assigned the vocal parts. Evans had written for Claude Thornhill's dance band in the 1940s and had contributed arrangements to Miles Davis's groundbreaking nine-piece ensemble of 1949–50. Although Evans was by far the more experienced arranger, Lambert's voices are in the foreground more often than the winds. This is unfortunate for several reasons. Not only are the vocal arrangements only competently written, they are also sung with inconsistent intonation and poor rhythmic precision. Their rhythmic drag on the two up-tempo pieces and their tuning problems on the ballad selection caused so many retakes (seven on one piece, four on another, and nine on a third piece) that the fourth arrangement prepared for the session was never recorded.[19] Although Parker was a master at stating and embellishing popular song melodies, the voices were given most of the melody statements, thereby minimizing Parker's overall contribution to the sides. With Parker rather hamstrung, the sides had to sink or swim on the basis of their weakest component, the vocal arrangements and the performance of them.

That Parker's creativity was not dulled by the numerous retakes is heard in his work on "Old Folks." Six of the eight takes last at least long enough to complete the four-bar introduction over which Parker ad-libs. Each one of Parker's introductions is different, sometimes markedly so, as the first phrase from each of the final four takes shows. Although the intro as played by the ensemble does not suggest the blues at all, Parker manages to infuse each take with the bluesy essence that was at the core of his style. Again, the fact that Parker does some of his best work over newly composed introductory or concluding material not based on well-worn pop song forms suggests that he was inspired by new material in general, even something as simple as the introduction to "Old Folks."

"Old Folks"

A few weeks after the date, Parker was asked by Boston disk jockey John Fitch (McLellan) about the session. Parker's conspicuous pause reveals his lack of enthusiasm for the way a once-promising concept had turned out.

JF: —I understand that you have something new in the offing.

CP: Yes, we—the other day, two weeks ago Monday, with twelve voices, clarinet, flute, oboe, bassoon, French horn and three rhythm. I have hopes that they might sound [pause] okay.[20]

Parker's first post-recording ban session for Granz placed Parker in the midst of Frank "Machito" Grillo's Afro-Cuban big band with Latin percussion. Parker had not recorded with a big band in the studio since his last session with Jay McShann in 1942, and Parker's saxophone timbre sounds strong in the midst of such a rich and complex musical texture. Like many "Latin" bands, Machito's often featured soloists improvising for indefinite periods over two-chord or one-chord harmonic/rhythmic cycles (often called vamps or *montunos*). The one- and two-chord vamps of bands such as Machito's were much more harmonically static than any pieces Parker had written or was then featuring in his repertoire. These vamps could often be boiled down to just one or two scales, making it potentially easy for the improviser to react and create. The very simplicity of the vamps' harmonies, however, can make it harder for the improviser to create the patterns of tension-and-release that are so associated with modern jazz. By contrast, most bebop pieces featured frequent harmonic deadlines whose shifting key centers required quick reflexes on the part of the improviser. Despite the greater difficulties these harmonies presented the improviser, their variety and movement intrinsically provided a soloist certain possibilities for tension-and-release.

As discussed at the end of the last chapter, Charlie Parker was looking at this time for new sounds. He had confided to friends that he felt constrained with the pop-song and blues forms and chord progressions of jazz. Given this, one wonders how Parker would respond to the open-duration solo sections and harmonically simple two- and one-chord vamps of Machito's "No Noise Part 2." One possible response would have been to improvise more chromatically over the static harmonic accompaniment. Parker, of course, had by the mid-1940s mastered bop's harmonic devices to an extent that his followers would not attain until well into the next decade, perhaps until the full flowering of saxophonist John Coltrane post-1956. In the late-1950s, musicians such as Miles Davis would eventually turn away from the rapid harmonic rhythm and numerous chord substitutions of bop and organize their music with simpler (often called "modal") harmonic concepts. Coltrane, in particular, would combine the bop-derived and modal approaches by erecting chromatic melodic structures through such practices as side-slipping and chromatic sequencing over comparatively static accompaniments that were similar to Latin vamps.

Parker had already explored both side-slipping and chromatic sequencing ("Honeysuckle Rose" and "Honey & Body" respectively; chapter 2) by 1940. The latter technique surfaced in a more highly developed form in the 1950s ("The Street Beat" and "Rocker," above, and and "Sly Mongoose," below). On "No Noise," however, Parker very conservatively observes the scales without taking advantage of his simplified harmonic surroundings to build units of chromatic tension and release. Certainly, staying within the key was more traditional in this music; perhaps Parker merely wished to be appropriate to the style, or perhaps this is another example from the 1950s of Parker having the tools at his disposal and not using them. In the following example, note how in the bracketed area, only three notes lie outside the prevailing A-major tonality (the three, which are circled, are all chromatic passing-tones and do not supply harmonic information).

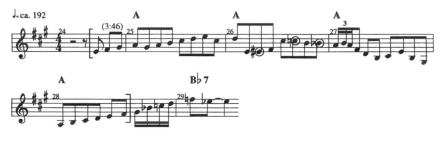

"No Noise Pt. 2"

In 1952, Granz recorded Parker twice with a big band arranged by Joe Lippman. The first date, which also included a string section, has many of the same features as the Parker With Strings dates; Parker is brilliant at decorating melodies, but only occasionally is he allowed the freedom to be really spontaneous. The second date fares a little better; the rhythm section swings more and Parker responds well to the slightly looser arrangements. Parker was also recorded live in the 1950s with at least three other big bands: The Orchestra directed by Joe Timer (originally Theimer), Woody Herman's, and Stan Kenton's. The first two in particular offer good examples of Parker's phenomenal ear as he convincingly navigates big band arrangements without benefit of a rehearsal. The Kenton recording was made during a brief tour that featured Parker and Dizzy Gillespie in front of the Kenton band. Parker plays energetically and sounds all the better for having played the arrangements more than once.

Small Group Recordings of the 1950s

As mentioned in the last chapter, the breakup of Parker's working quintet began early in 1950. Many factors were involved. By summer of 1950, Parker began occasional live appearances with his string ensemble. Although he initially used the piano-bass-drum team from his quintet on these dates, any appearances or tours with the strings took away work from the quintet as a whole. Red Rodney was arrested twice and sentenced for narcotics possession, depriving Parker of an ideal combo front-line partner. Plus, in the 1950s, Parker found that he could make more money touring, as a "single," that is to say traveling alone to each city on his tour and picking up local musicians to accompany him. Some of this touring away from New York was necessitated by Parker's cabaret card being revoked due to an arrest (as discussed in chapter 1). Although Parker sometimes returned to a quartet lineup of Walter Bishop, Jr. (piano), Teddy Kotick (bass), and Roy Haynes (drums), the artistic continuity that the quintet offered was no more.

During November, 1950, Parker toured Sweden (with a stop in Denmark) as a single. On the same tour was trumpeter Roy Eldridge who was temporarily living in Europe. Parker's pick-up rhythm section was quite sympathetic, and Parker was clearly inspired by the fine trumpeter Rolf Erikson. Two of the most remarkable moments of the live recordings made on the tour come on a jam session version of "Body and Soul," during which Parker twice (at 0:09 in the first part and at 2:17 in the second) quotes the Roy Eldridge phrase that Parker had used in his informally recorded 1940–42 versions of the song (chapter 2). Evidently, the encounter with Eldridge had brought the phrase back into Parker's consciousness and Parker used it in a surprising tribute to the trumpeter.

The one advantage to the breakup of the quintet and Parker's increasing work as a single was that, in the 1950s, Parker was more available to appear with outstanding peers, such as Dizzy Gillespie, Bud Powell, Thelonious Monk, and Miles Davis, who were not in Parker's working group of the time. Indeed, Parker did some of his best work of the period in the company of these players who challenged him.

In January, 1951, for a relaxed Granz combo session, Parker was reunited with Miles Davis and Max Roach, who joined Walter Bishop, Jr., and Teddy Kotick. On "K.C. Blues," Parker revisits his favorite passage from the Klosé exercise book (2:46; see also chapter 4). When the performance was released, the quotation caught saxophonist Paul Desmond's ear, and he asked Parker about it:

> PD: I heard a record of yours a couple of months ago that somehow I had missed up to date, and I heard a little 'bout a two-bar quote from the Klosé book that was like an echo from home.
>
> CP: Oh.
>
> PD: [Desmond sings the opening bars of Klosé Exercise 23.]
>
> CP: Yeah, yeah. Well, that was all done with books, you know. Naturally, it wasn't done with mirrors this time, it was done with books.
>
> PD: Now that's, that's very reassuring to hear, because somehow I got the idea that you were just sort of born with that technique, and you never had to worry too much about, 'bout keeping it working.[21]

As noted elsewhere in this book, Parker's 1950s studio combo recordings for Norman Granz were not usually representative of Parker's working groups and produced few or no recordings to rival Parker's 1945–48 sides. A potentially stimulating session on June 6, 1950, reunited Parker, Dizzy Gillespie, and Thelonious Monk. The downside of Norman Granz's habitual tinkering with personnel is seen in the inappropriate inclusion of drummer Buddy Rich. The session's bassist, Curly Russell, diplomatically called the choice of personnel "one of Norman's brainstorms."[22] Roy Haynes, Parker's first-call drummer of this period, was upset about being frequently being overlooked by Granz:

> Bird was under contract to Norman [Granz]. Before a session he'd show Norman the list of musicians he'd like to use. Everything would be all right until he got to my name. "You mean you'd like to use Roy instead of Buddy Rich?" Norman would ask. The answer was on the paper, but Buddy always wound up on the date . . .[23]

Not only was Rich's sense of swing derived from an earlier generation, he was evidently not ready to deliver the rhythmic precision required in modern jazz. His solo on the 12-bar "Blues (Fast)" finds Rich rushing his way through an 11 1/2-bar solo; Parker brings the band back together with a pickup phrase. On the 12-bar "Bloomdido," Rich takes a 23 3/4-bar solo, seemingly because he "turns the beat around." Rich's 4-bar exchanges with Parker and Gillespie come off better, partly because Rich keeps his bass drum going on all four beats; nevertheless, the other musicians seem to be making small rhythmic adjustments. After take 4 of "Leap Frog" breaks down (eleven takes were required), Parker can be heard to emphatically ask, "What in the *world* is wrong here?" Parker and Gillespie were recorded during several other reunions of the 1950s, including an engagement at Birdland with Bud Powell (3-31-51) and an all-star Toronto concert with Powell, bassist Charles Mingus, and drummer Max Roach (5-15-53). On both recordings, Parker and Gillespie inspire one another to fiery and energetic playing.

One notably successful Granz session of the period found Parker in an all-star jam session that included alto saxophonists Johnny Hodges and Benny Carter from the generation immediately preceding Parker's. In a testament to Charlie Parker's pervasive effect on jazz, Carter seems to show a slight Parker influence on "Funky Blues." A potentially historic session that unfortunately never took place would have teamed Parker with one of *his* probable early influences, Art Tatum (see chapter 1). Norman Granz recalls: "A session was set up for Art Tatum and Charlie Parker. Parker showed up but Art didn't. I rented Carnegie hall for the date, which was to have been a duet with no rhythm section."[24] Tatum of course possessed stunning technique and was a master of harmonic and melodic asides, qualities that Parker had also developed. No live recording has surface of the two playing together, but it would be revealing to hear how these two virtuosos from different generations adapted to each other.

At the 1952 dance/concert referred to earlier in this chapter, Parker played some selections without the string section. One such piece that might even show an Art Tatum influence is the West Indian–inflected "Sly Mongoose." During one version played that night,[25] Parker briefly departs from the prevailing F tonality[26] by sequencing up by half steps a simple four-note pattern that is most simply described as the first, second, third, and fifth steps of a major scale. Because his accompanists remain in the prevailing tonality, Parker's chromatically ascending figure has the effect of implying moments of bitonality.

"Sly Mongoose"

Readers may recognize this "1-2-3-5" pattern as one most associated with John Coltrane during his "Giant Steps" period (circa 1959). It is not known whether Coltrane might have learned the pattern through contact with Parker, but it is known that Parker was not the first to employ the pattern in jazz. Art Tatum, a likely influence upon the young Charlie Parker, incorporated the pattern into his 1934 composition "The Shout," and Parker could have first heard the pattern from a Tatum recording, live Tatum appearance, or some other source.

Another piece without strings recorded at the same dance/concert should be mentioned here. It's "Lester Leaps In," based on Rhythm changes and first recorded by Lester Young in 1939. This, along with "Bird Gets the Worm" (quarter note = ca. 356; discussed in the previous chapter), is one of the fastest tempos that Parker sustained (corrected for pitch, it reaches approximately quarter note = 336). Aside from its rapidity of tempo and stunning drive, the solo is notable for a moment at the beginning of the sixth solo chorus when Parker states the "Lester Leaps In" melody in its normal key of B♭ (2:09, corrected for pitch) and then immediately (2:15) restates the melody a major third higher (a device used in "Rocker," above), in effect superimposing the key of D♭ upon the song's B♭ tonality, creating another moment of bitonality.

As noted in chapter 4, the first take of the 1947 "Embraceable You" was unusual because Parker improvised thematically, stating and developing a six-note motive to unify the opening measures of his solo. In late 1952 (or early 1953), Parker recorded another improvisation that could also be said to use a unifying motive, although not as creatively as in "Embraceable You." The piece in question is the second take[27] of "Kim," a rapid "I Got Rhythm"–derived improvisation recorded for Granz that has no set melody statement.[28]

In the second take's first A section, Parker concludes his second phrase with the following figure:

"Kim" (Take 2) Ex. 1

Readers will recognize it as the voiceleading figure noted first in "Honeysuckle Rose" (chapter 2) and later in "Billie's Bounce" (chapter 3) and "Klact-oveeseds-tene" (chapter 4). As before, the final pitch is the goal or "target" of the voiceleading. In this second take of "Kim," Parker plays the figure seventeen times in various forms, usually targeting D as circled above. Parker proves the figure's versatility by placing it in a variety of harmonic settings: for example, the D target tone might be a component of a G7, B♭Δ7, D7, D-7, or C9 chord. Although the figure is most easy to spot at the ends of phrases when Parker uses it to end A sections (as above), it also appears in the middle of phrases in both the A and B sections. Following is an example of Parker employing the figure in the middle of a phrase and targeting the circled F instead of the usual D:

"Kim" (Take 2) Ex. 2

Given the frequent occurrences of the voiceleading figure, one might wonder whether this take of "Kim" qualifies as an example of motivic development to rival Parker's solo on the first take of "Embraceable You" or the various takes of "Parker's Mood" (chapter 4). Several factors keep "Kim" from approaching in quality the earlier example. One such factor is that, in this solo, Parker didn't significantly develop the figure in its subsequent presentations. Too much verbatim repetition of any one figure tends to weaken the unifying potential of that figure. As mentioned above, Parker does vary the placement of the figure within his melodic line, but the actual figure is usually played the same note-for-note (the most significant exceptions being the two times that the figure targets F instead of D). In fairness to Parker, just being able to solo and swing at this fast tempo was an achievement, but there are a number of ways (such as simple rhythmic augmentation) that Parker could have developed the motive even at this speed (techniques of motivic development are discussed in chapter 4 with regard to "Embraceable You"). Although it is a composition and not an improvised solo, Parker's "Moose the Mooche" (chapter 3) is a good example of how a simple motive can be creatively developed. In that piece, Parker presents his motive with many different starting- and ending-notes, and with a variety of melodic contours.

Another factor that weakens the effect of the "Kim" figure is that, unlike the unusual motive employed in "Embraceable You," the "Kim" figure is very common in Parker solos, especially during this period.[29] As the listener becomes more conversant with Parker's musical vocabulary, verbatim repetition of a common figure begins to lose its power to creatively unify a solo. Although spontaneous improvisation is the ideal of jazz, every jazz musician of course has on tap at the reflex level many such small-scale building blocks to be used as aids in navigating the sometimes difficult chord progressions of jazz. Parker, in his brilliance, had a huge repertoire of these motives, many of which he had minted, ready to plug in when needed. At his best, his deft usage of the motives contributed to the flow and drive of his solos as intended. By 1950, however, his usage of these characteristic motives had become increasingly routine; whether because of lack of practice and study or because of intoxication or other factors, he increasingly played on a sort of automatic pilot, mixing and matching his motives more mechanically than before (although, it must be said, on a level of skill that was the envy of most jazz musicians).

These small-scale building blocks may be used creatively or may lapse into mere cliché. In "Kim," Parker has a chance to take this favorite motive and transform it into an element that creatively unifies the solo, but by presenting the motive so many times with little variation, Parker veers away from creative motivic use and toward automatic cliché. In an important respect, Parker's solo on "Kim" symbolizes the crux of Parker's art in his last period. On one hand, although it breaks no new ground, the solo is thrillingly played with an abundance of energy and authority. On the other hand, "Kim" does not live up to its potential in that Parker has in his hands the raw materials and tools to make this improvisation fresh and unified, yet too often he fails to use them.

Much of what was said of Parker's short figures with regard to "Kim" may be said of Parker's general use of larger-scale building blocks that musicians tend to call "licks." Examples already discussed in this book include the rapid sixteenth-note run found in "Billie's Bounce" and the blues lick noted in "Now's the Time" (chapter 3). These slightly longer phrases tend to help improvisers when inspiration flags for a moment. When used deftly by an improviser, most listeners recognize and even look forward to these signature gestures, but when used too repetitively, or without creativity, these licks can sap a solo of its freshness. In the 1950s, these licks became more prevalent in Parker's work and tended to substitute for moments of real invention.

Despite his gradually declining health, 1953 was a generally good year for Parker's music. His studio recordings for Granz that year were few, but his live appearances were documented extensively by amateur tape recordists. Parker was reunited with Bud Powell and Dizzy Gillespie (their concert at Toronto's Massey Hall found them, plus Charles Mingus and Max Roach, in good form), and Parker toured America from east to west. Although he was coasting artistically and not actively pursuing his own goals, he often performed powerfully using the musical vocabulary that he had created. A good example of his continuing ability to stun the listener with powerful drive and whiplike accentuation comes in this quadruple-time passage on a 1953 Montréal version of "Embraceable You." Musical notation does not do this passage justice; it must be heard to be appreciated.

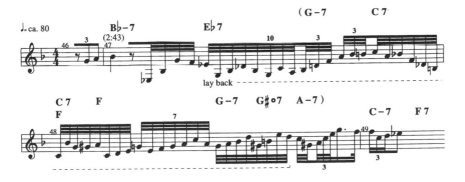

"Embraceable You" (1953)

Charlie Parker's last studio recording session (and, as of this writing, his last available recording of any kind) took place on December 10, 1954, for Norman Granz. Granz was gradually formulating his concept of "songbook" albums that would later become one of his label's signatures. In this case, he had in mind a Charlie Parker plays Cole Porter theme and in March had already recorded four Porter songs played by Parker. For the December session, two more Porter pieces were recorded, and possibly more had been planned; Phil Schaap paraphrases the date's guitarist, Billy Bauer, as saying that Parker and Granz got into an intense argument over what songs would be recorded.[30] Possibly, Parker did not appreciate Granz's Cole Porter theme or choice of individual songs or just did not like being told what to record. Because this book's study of Charlie Parker begins with his first-known recording session, it's appropriate to include some music from this, his last-known session.

Although the titles are from the era of the LP record and both sides run over five minutes each, Parker does not get too much solo space on either "Love For Sale" (64 bars) or "I Love Paris" (32 bars). Despite the argument with Granz, Parker sounds relaxed if not particularly challenged by the job at hand. Some of his best moments come in the alternate take of "I Love Paris."[31] At four points in his solo (1:55, 2:03, 2:17, and 2:41), he indulges in stating an idea (or motive) and then repeating it with a rhythmic, registeral, or melodic variation. Below is a simple yet effective example in which, for each statement, the motive is slightly shifted in time, and is occasionally altered melodically:

"I Love Paris" (Take 2)

This example is rhythmically easier to play by ear than to accurately notate and then read, a tribute to the subtle abilities of Charlie Parker in the last minutes of his recording career (one more take of the piece was completed). Although he was not breaking new ground, he was communicating with vitality in a vocabulary of his own making.

New Goals

Parker's statements of the late 1940s regarding new artistic goals continued and even increased in number during the early 1950s. To his fellow musicians, Parker continued to express dissatisfaction with the common musical forms of jazz in general and with his art in specific. According to Red Rodney,

> He did feel stagnant with the thirty-two bar forms. He wanted more. . . . Well, he wanted more now, more than the bebop forms, more than the thirty-two bar form, more than the twelve-bar blues form. He wanted things that Miles came along with. . . . Now, he thought about other things, and he did describe this to me, this feeling that he had, but he just thought about it, he could never come up with any of those things. . . . Well, in certain conversations, he says, "Jazz has to go on from here, we just can't stop with this," you know. And I agreed, I said, "Who's gonna show us the way?" He says, "I'd like to be the one to do that." He says, "I've done this up to now," you know, which was very unusual for him to say; he was very modest.[32]

The fact that Parker had generally stopped practicing saxophone could not help him in the pursuit of his goals. It is well known that some working jazz musicians gradually stop practicing when they reach a certain level of mastery, preferring to develop their art on the bandstand. Parker, however, seemed unable to realize his new musical goals without study and practice (and sobriety).

In 1954, Parker expressed his desire for continued artistic growth in an interview with saxophonist Paul Desmond:

> CP: (And) lots of other fellows (have) come along, you know, since that era, that particular era [the early days of bebop], that (really?) makes you feel that everything you did wasn't for naught, you know, that you really tried to prove something and—
>
> PD: Well, man, you really proved it.
>
> CP: Well—[chuckles]
>
> PD: I think you did more than anybody in the last ten years to leave a decisive mark on the history of jazz.

CP: Well, not yet, Paul, but I intend to. I'd like to study some more; I'm not quite through yet. I'm not quite—I don't consider myself too old to learn.[33]

Parker of course was most conversant with the jazz idiom, but study of the classical music idiom and classical saxophone technique increasingly held a promise of new horizons for him. Indeed, the majority of his public statements of artistic aspirations from the late 1940s until his death in 1955 mention classical music. His desire to study in Europe, first publicly outlined in 1949 (chapter 4), was revisited in the interview with Paul Desmond:

PD: No, I know many people are watching you at the moment with the greatest of interest to see what you're going to come up with next in the next few years, myself among the—the front row of them, and, well, what have you got in mind? (What) are you going to be doing?

CP: Well, seriously speaking, I mean, I'm going to try to go to Europe to study. I had the pleasure to meet one Edgard Varèse in New York City, he's a classical composer from Europe. He's a Frenchman, a very nice fellow, and he wants to teach me, in fact, he wants to write [radio static] for me some things for me for a—you know, more or less on a serious basis, you know?

PD: Mm hm.

CP: And if he takes me over, I mean, after he finishes with me, I might have a chance to go to Academie de Musicale [possibly the *Conservatoire Nationale de Musique de Paris* where saxophonist Marcel Mule taught] in Paris itself and study, you know. And, well, the principal—the prime—my prime interest still is learning to play music, you know. (unintelligible)

PD: Would you study playing, or composition, or everything?

CP: I would study both. I never want to lose my horn.

PD: Yeah, you never should; that would be (a) catastrophe.

CP: Never want to do that. That wouldn't work.[34]

Although he never acted on his desire to train in Europe, Parker held high hope that study of classical music would provide the knowledge required to advance his art to the next stage. His respect for the European musical tradition tended to be idealized, as can be inferred from Varèse's own account of his meetings with Parker:

> He stopped by my place a couple of times. . . . He'd come in and exclaim, "Take me as you would a baby and teach me music. I only write in one voice. I want to write orchestral scores." . . . He was so dramatic it was funny, and I finally promised myself I would try to find some time to show him some of the things he wanted to know. I left for Europe and told him to call me up after Easter when I would be back. Charlie died before Easter.[35]

In the 1950s, Parker also met composer Stefan Wolpe through clarinetist Tony Scott, as Scott relates: "One afternoon I introduced them when Wolpe was in my loft and Parker made one of his unscheduled visits. . . . 'You know, Mr. Wolpe, I want you to write for as many men as you care to, seventy-five if necessary. Norman Granz will do it if I tell him.'"[36] As discussed earlier in this chapter, Granz was not interested in commissioning contemporary composers of classical music to write for Parker.

In a 1953 radio interview, John Fitch asked Parker to "say a few words" about composer Béla Bartók. Although Parker admired and even idealized classical music, he quite rightly points out that he was not very conversant with it during the development of bebop, and stands up for his and his colleagues' innovations of the 1940s:

> CP: Well, there's—I mean, as far as his history is concerned, I mean, I read that he was Hungarian-born, he died in American exile in Manhattan General Hospital [actually West Side Hospital] in New York in 1945. At that time, I was just becoming introduced to modern classics, contemporary and otherwise, you know? And, to my misfortune, he was deceased before I had the pleasure to meet the man (unintelligible). As far as I'm concerned, he is one—beyond a doubt, one of the most finished and accomplished musicians that ever lived.
>
> JF: Well, now, you made a very interesting point, then, when you said that you heard him in 1945.
>
> CP: Yeah.
>
> JF: Because, this brings up a question that I've—I'd like to ask you,

and if some of these questions sound as though I wrote them out ahead of time, I did. At a certain point in our musical history, prior to 1945, as a matter of fact, you and a group of others evidently became dissatisfied with the stereotyped form in which music had settled. So, you altered the rhythm, the melody and the harmony, rather violently, as a matter of fact. Now, how much of this change, that you were responsible for, you feel was spontaneous experimentation with your own ideas, and how much was the adaptation of the ideas of your classical predecessors, for example, as in Bartók?

CP: Well, it was a hundred-percent spontaneous. A hundred-percent. Nothin'—not a bit of the idiom in which music travels today, known as progressive music, was adapted or even inspired by the—older composers.

JF: Well it—

CP: Our predecessors.[37]

In an interview for a 1953 article by Nat Hentoff, Parker strongly expressed his opinion that jazz is as artistically valid as Western classical music:

> They're different ways of saying things musically, and don't forget, classical music has that long tradition. But in 50 or 75 years, the contributions of present-day jazz will be taken as seriously as classical music. You wait and see.[38]

Over forty years later, one hopes that Parker's prediction is coming to pass.

But despite Parker's belief in the validity of the jazz tradition, it's notable that his public statements of artistic intent from the 1950s did not include African-American musical traditions as sources of materials, concepts, techniques, or inspiration for his continued artistic growth. Certainly, the African-American roots of jazz (such as folk blues, spirituals and gospel music, ragtime, work song, and even Western African–derived musics) were reasonably available to Parker and were being consciously tapped by others during his lifetime (for example, Dizzy Gillespie began collaborating with the Afro-Cuban percussionist Chano Pozo in 1947; Horace Silver recorded his seminal "soul jazz" composition, "The Preacher," in 1954).

It is not known *why* Parker chose not to further explore those roots. Perhaps his limited understanding of earlier jazz forms (see chapter 3) prevented him from appreciating his own musical heritage; perhaps he was unconsciously influenced by the prevailing white American senti-ment that jazz had little lasting artistic value. Historically, jazz in the United States has not been accorded the same high respect as Western classical music and has too often been viewed as merely an entertainment form created by a minority class. In a society that did not accept jazz as art music, Parker may have sought a measure of musical legitimacy by embracing classical music, may have underevaluated the rich possibilities for innovation rooted in his African-American musical heritage, and may have oversimplified the process in which classical music study could help advance his own art.

None of this is intended to fault Parker for looking to the European tradition. There were many aspects of the Western classical musical tra-dition that Parker had every reason to admire, including a well-developed and formal system of training and mastery. However, looking back over a half century of jazz since the advent of bebop, it's clear that the inno-vations that have become integrated into the fabric of jazz are the ones that either sprang from the African-American tradition (such as Afro-Cuban–derived polyrhythmic concepts, or the gospel, blues, and work song influences of the "soul jazz" movement) or those from other musi-cal traditions that were thoroughly assimilated by jazz artists who had an organic need for the new techniques (e.g., John Coltrane's use of melodic patterns derived from Nicolas Slonimsky's *Thesaurus* or pianists' use of Hindemith-derived fourth intervals in accompaniment). In order for Parker to have successfully integrated twentieth-century classical music techniques with the jazz tradition, he would have had to steep himself in modern classical music with a depth approaching that of his knowledge of jazz. To this date, no jazz or classical music artist has succeeded in the thorough integration of the two idioms (or "streams") in a way that has established a new entity (a "third stream") that is as vital as its jazz and classical music sources (of course, interesting and worthwhile "third stream" music has been created, but I do not feel that a new idiom as vital as its sources has been attained). Or on a more modest scale, the third stream works that have been created have not returned highly significant nourishment to one or both of the idioms that inspired them.

Parker's goals of formal classical study and a subsequent emphasis on composition may not have been realistic for him. It's unlikely (though not impossible, given his brilliance) that Parker, who only wrote out music when absolutely necessary, could be transformed into a composer of larger forms merely through study of European-derived classical music. Parker was above all a virtuoso soloist and not as concerned with overall structure as were his peers Dizzy Gillespie, Thelonious Monk, Miles Davis, and Tadd Dameron. The likely effect of Parker's addictions to heroin and alcohol on his ability to set and meet long-range goals such as formal study should also be considered.

New Directions

Setting aside discussion of whether either the European or the African-American tradition might have been more fruitful for Parker to draw upon, it is also insightful to examine some of the more specific musical techniques that Parker could have drawn upon, some of which cut across the jazz and classical music idioms. This is not an exercise in conjecture; not only did Parker expressly state his desire to seek new musical horizons, but most of the techniques and approaches discussed below were touched upon by Parker but left undeveloped by him. In addition, more speculative discussions of other musical directions that Parker could have explored will be found in footnotes.

Harmony

In the area of harmony, Parker had many possibilities in front of him. He could have further explored chromaticism in the context of the functional harmonies of jazz. He had shown interest in side-slipping (defined in the "Introduction to the Musical Chapters") as early as his 1940 recording of "Honeysuckle Rose" (chapter 2), but the technique never became an prominent tool of his art. Chromatic sequencing (see the "Introduction to the Musical Chapters") likewise appeared in Parker's work in 1940 ("Honey & Body," chapter 2) and was an occasional feature of his work of the 1950s ("Rocker," "The Street Beat," and "Sly Mongoose," above) but again was not actively pursued.

Parker did occasionally play with pianists whose harmonic conceptions might have spontaneously led him in new harmonic directions, but recordings with pianists Thelonious Monk (1950) and Lennie Tristano (1951) do not show Parker markedly responding to pungent voicings or reharmonizations.[39] Interestingly, Parker specifically expressed to pianist

Walter Bishop, Jr., his interest and enthusiasm for just such piano accompaniment:

> I got a chance to play with Bird, and a curious thing happened. We were playing this tune called [Stomping at the] "Savoy." Coming out of the bridge, I had—my hand slipped and hit a wrong chord. And Bird was sitting, uh, front stage, he whipped around, you know. And of course, I tensed up, you know, (I) thought he was going to chide me for hitting a wrong chord. And Charlie Parker smiled this incredible smile, from ear to ear, like the sun was shining on me, and he said "Ooh! What was that?"[40]

Another harmonic area Parker could have explored was being practiced by pianist and band leader Lennie Tristano. On his 1949 recordings "Intuition" and "Digression," Tristano and group improvised without (among other things) preset key centers or chord progressions. In Parker's 1953 radio interview, John Fitch expresses his lack of comprehension of that improvisational process, and Parker does not seem to grasp it either when he suggests that there must be a chord structure to create a melody (Parker's words, however, are far from clear):

> JF: There [in Tristano's approach] we have, uh, what they try to do occasionally, complete, uh, collective improvisation with no theme, no chorus, uh, no, no chord changes on which to work. Just six men, or whatever it may be, improvising together. Is that, uh—it's always struck me as being extremely difficult to understand how it's possible in the first place.
>
> CP: Oh, no, see [?], those are just like you said, mostly improvisations, you know, and, uh, if you listen close enough, you can find the melody traveling along with any chord str—any series of chord structures, you know? And, uh, rather than to make the melody predominant in, in the style of music that Lennie and them present, it's more or less heard or felt.
>
> JF: Well, I refer more particularly to uh—they made one record called "Intuition," and I've heard them do it in concert, uh, in which they start off with no key, no, uh, basic set of chord changes or anything.
>
> CP: Uh huh. There must be a build-up to—to the r—to the—to the, um, both the key signature and the, uh, the chord structure that tends to create the melody.

JF: As they go along.
CP: Yes.[41]

Through his experience with Afro-Cuban bands, Parker was exposed to improvisation over static chord progressions known as vamps or *montunos* (discussed in connection with "No Noise," above) that tended to "horizontalize" improvisation (in effect, to move improvisation from a "vertical" chord-by-chord approach to a "horizontal," scalar conception). Bud Powell, among others, was occasionally interested in applying pedal points under moving harmonies, which also tended to horizontalize. These, although "in the air," were evidently not an important part of Parker's conception.

When looking for new techniques, Parker could have turned to the classical music composers that he admired. Bartók, for example, could have inspired Parker to further explore bitonality. Although he was not prepared to compose new music using the technique, Parker occasionally touched upon bitonality as a soloist (see "Rocker" and "Lester Leaps In," above). Used in this manner, bitonality did not require any prior organization and was thus a technique that he could easily put into effect on the spur of the moment while improvising. However, Parker only occasionally explored the technique.[42]

Melody

From a melodic standpoint, Parker demonstrated that he was familiar with melodic patterns derived from intervallic architecture (which have both melodic and harmonic qualities; again, see "Rocker," "The Street Beat," and "Sly Mongoose," above) although that approach constituted just a tiny part of Parker's melodic palette. One reason Parker might not have pursued this direction was the fact that, at his most creative, he excelled in the spontaneous creation of melody; to improvise from a standpoint of unusual intervallic relationships requires considerable practice and absorption before it becomes spontaneous. However, it must be pointed out that, beginning with Parker's circa 1950 artistic consolidation, his melodic approach became increasingly lick-based, itself not a very spontaneous approach. Study, practice, and reflection were likely to be part of any new directions open to Parker, and the sobriety and discipline required for these activities were hard to come by for Parker in the 1950s.

Thematic improvisation, already discussed with regard to "Embraceable You," "Parker's Mood," "The Bird," and "Kim," presented a highly accessible melodic (and structurally unifying) resource available to Parker. This technique required no new theoretical concepts to implement, and Parker had certainly shown a keen aural memory in being able to recall and manipulate phrases discovered through improvisation. Even though he was ideally suited to the creative usage of thematic improvisation, this is another technique that Parker did not actively pursue.[43]

Rhythm

Although Charlie Parker had an unsurpassed command of rhythm (and could play the drums—see chapter 3), he did not take a very active role in shaping the rhythmic aspect of his performing or recording groups. Certainly, he hired creative drummers who could swing and who had good "time," but primarily he set a rhythmic standard by his own exemplary time and swing. By contrast, Dizzy Gillespie actively sought out Afro-Cuban percussionist Chano Pozo, studied Pozo's rhythmic conception and used it to add to his group's rhythmic complexity. Parker showed only occasional interest in expanding his working groups' polyrhythmic possibilities through added percussion instruments (for example, he occasionally had conga drummers sit in with his combos, but they were never integral to his group sound.). In the recording studio during the 1950s, Parker was both a featured soloist with Afro-Cuban ensembles and also was the leader of two record dates that featured one or two Latin percussionists. It's not clear whether Charlie Parker or Norman Granz played a larger role in the planning and execution of the Parker-led dates, but the fact that only one of these Latin-tinged songs ("My Little Suede Shoes"[44]) entered Parker's regular nightclub repertoire supports the idea that Parker was most interested in the swing rhythmic concept with which he came of musical age.

One rhythmic technique that Parker reportedly used in some live performances involved the rhythmic displacement of his melodic lines one beat away from the rest of his group, as Miles Davis experienced in the 1940s:

I remember how at times he used to turn the rhythm section around. Like we'd be playing the blues, and Bird would start on the eleventh bar, and as the rhythm section stayed where they were and Bird played where he was it sounded like the rhythm section was on one and three instead of two and four. Every time that would happen, Max Roach used to scream at Duke Jordan not to follow Bird, but to stay where he was. Then, eventually, it came round as Bird had planned and we were together again.[45]

The complex rhythmic and formal push-pull created by this type of displacement seems not only ripe for further development by Parker, but was also a technique that Parker could have readily implemented as a soloist. Nevertheless, this was another approach that he touched upon occasionally but did not actively pursue even during the 1950s when he was seeking a broader musical palette.[46]

Compositional Forms

As already discussed, Charlie Parker was interested in studying classical music composition with a goal of writing new pieces of his own. He was also interested in commissioning one or more classical music composers to write new music for him, but his record producer was not interested in such a project. What sort of musical settings did Parker have in mind? Aside from the Hindemith-like piece previously mentioned, Parker evidently had some interest in combining classical music composition with jazz improvisation, as Charles Mingus wrote:

> For instance, Bird called me on the phone one day and said, "How does this sound?" and he was playing—ad-libbing—to the Berceuse, or Lullaby, section of Stravinsky's *Firebird Suite*! I imagine he had been doing it all through the record, but he just happened to call me at that time and that was the section he was playing his ad-lib solo on, and it sounded beautiful.[47]

Turning to formal possibilities within the jazz idiom, Charlie Parker specifically stated, as noted earlier, that he was dissatisfied with the common forms of jazz. In a 1953 radio interview, John Fitch had the insight (or naiveté or audacity) to ask Parker a direct question that addressed part of Parker's artistic stagnancy, his lack of new repertoire.

> JF: Well, what about your, your own group, the people you work
>   with, the other musicians who started with you? I've noticed

that, for example, you play "Anthropology" and "52nd Street Theme," perhaps, but they were written a long time ago. What is to take their place and be the basis for your future?

CP: Hm. That's hard to tell, too, John. See, like, your ideas change as you grow older. Most people fail to realize that most of the things that they hear, either coming out of a man's horn ad-lib, or else things that are written, you know, say, original things, I mean, they're just experiences. The way you feel, the beauty of the weather, the nice look of a mountain, maybe a nice fresh cool breath of air. I mean, all those things you can never tell what you'll be thinking tomorrow, but I definitely can say that music won't stop. It'll be—keep going forward.

JF: And you feel that you, yourself, change continuously.

CP: I do feel that way, yes.

JF: And, in listening to your earlier recordings, you become dissatisfied with them? Do you feel that—

CP: Well, I still think that the best record is yet to be made, if that's what you mean.[48]

Parker, of course, was expressing a truth; as an artist, he drew inspiration from many sources, and, when he was healthy, those factors lent a tremendous freshness and vitality to his already well-explored art. However, he was also sidestepping Fitch's question, which was related to the issue raised by Red Rodney in chapter 4 about the lack of rehearsal of new material to be played on the job. In the last four years of his life, Parker wrote and recorded thirteen new pieces (not counting five performances with no set melody). Of these, only one song, "My Little Suede Shoes," definitely was added to his nightclub repertoire, as documented in known live recordings. Otherwise, Parker and his groups for the most part played the same jazz originals and popular songs over and over again (he was more likely to add to his pop song repertoire than his jazz original repertoire).

Given Parker's stated interest in studying music composition, there were many form-related alternatives available to him that would have been relevant to his musical search. Most easily, he could have written newly composed forms in the popular song tradition. Dizzy Gillespie, Thelonious Monk, Tadd Dameron, and Bud Powell often did just that when they wrote compositions with original chord progressions and melodies that were nonetheless consistent with Tin Pan Alley traditions in form. As has been noted many times in this book, Parker much preferred to write new melodies over preexisting chord progressions. Even given that preference, he never took the time in the 1950s to write a truly unified melodic composition on the order of his own previous "Moose the Mooche" (based on Rhythm changes; chapter 3). Instead, Parker often quickly composed just eight measures of a thirty-two-bar piece immediately before a record date.[49]

Instrumentation

Due to Norman Granz's desire to record Charlie Parker in a variety of settings, Parker's discography of the 1950s does show a significant variety of instrumentation. Of the more unusual (noncombo) recording ensembles, Parker stated or implied that he was the impetus for the dates with strings and the session featuring an expanded ensemble that produced "Old Folks" (above). As mentioned earlier, the latter instrumentation was evidently an adaptation of Parker's Hindemith-inspired wind quintet concept. Parker approached at least one classical music composer (Stefan Wolpe, see below) to write music for him, saying that Granz would pay for the work. Unfortunately, Granz was evidently not sympathetic to commissioning works that he thought would not sell many records. Parker of course intended to study composition and write his own music but was unable to follow up on the idea of formal study.

One instrumentation alternative available to Parker was closer to his African-American heritage, namely the integration of Afro-Cuban percussionists into his performing and/or working groups. Again, Parker never took the same initiative as Dizzy Gillespie in this sphere, and Granz may have conceived of and planned Parker's Afro-Cuban recordings.

Music as Conversation

One of the most powerful aspects of Parker's art was his unusual rapport with his listeners, as Dizzy Gillespie recalled:

> I saw something remarkable one time. He didn't show up for a dance he was supposed to play in Detroit. I was in town, and they asked me to play instead. I went up there, and we started playing. Then I heard this big roar, and Charlie Parker had come in and started playing. He'd play a phrase, and people might never have heard it before. But he'd start it, and the people would finish it with him, humming.[50]

This rapport was the basis for an interesting aspect of Parker's art that he wanted to develop in his last years, namely his desire and ability to transmit musical messages that would be apprehended by listeners. In an interview with the author of this book, his last wife, Chan, recalled:

> CP: . . . a couple months before he died, he thought—he said to me, "I'm hearing music differently. I'm hearing it as conversation." And I think that he was moving in a different direction, and it had nothing to do with imitators or nightclubs or quintets which I'm sure was boring to him by that point, you know. I think he was just hearing these different things in his head.
>
> CW: What do you think he meant by "music as conversation?"
>
> CP: Well, to play like he would speak. One example he gave me, he said, you know, "Chan, did I tell you how pretty you look tonight?" That way. Conversation. To play out of his horn the conversation he had in his head.
>
> CW: And, so, through a conversational approach, the listener would understand his meaning?
>
> CP: Oh, I always did! [laughs][51]

Bassist Charles Mingus also reported Parker's intent to make music communicate specific ideas (a concept that Mingus later explored with wind player Eric Dolphy): "We [Parker and Mingus] used to get into long, involved discussions between sets about every subject from God to man, and, before we realized it, we would be due back on the stage. He used to say, 'Mingus, let's finish this discussion on the bandstand. Let's get our horns and talk about this.'" In 1954, Parker emphasized the storytelling and descriptive aspects of music:

> There's definitely—there's stories and stories and stories that can be told in the musical idiom, you know? . . . it's so hard to describe music other than the basic way to describe it: music is basically melody, harmony and rhythm. But I mean, people can do much more with music than that—it can be very descriptive in all kinds of ways, you know?[52]

This concept of music conveying specific ideas in listeners seems to be complementary to Parker's creative use of musical quotations to send text-based messages (consisting of the words to songs) as discussed in chapter 4. In the 1950s, Parker seems to have been interested in a more abstract and wide-ranging cause-and-effect relationship between himself and the listener, in which he could convey ideas or thoughts that were not dependent on song lyrics. Discerning listeners could detect a similar effect in his playing as early as his days with Jay McShann, as McShann bassist Gene Ramey related:

> He got into his music all the sounds around him—the swish of a car speeding down a highway, the hum of wind as it goes through the leaves . . . Bird kept everybody on the stand happy, because he was a wizard at transmitting musical messages to us, which made us fall out laughing. . . . Everything had a musical meaning for him. If he heard a dog bark, he would say the dog was speaking. If he was in the act of blowing his sax, he would find something to express and would want you to guess his thoughts. . . . I don't remember exactly what Bird was telling us in his "Jumpin' Blues" solo [chapter 2 of this book], but I do remember that we all used to start joking from the very first bars. It was, I remember, a simple phrase that we already had occasion to use before, but which later became a sort of leitmotiv like "Ornithology."[53]

The use of the term *leitmotiv* (or *leitmotif*) is interesting and fitting. It refers to composer Richard Wagner's use in his music dramas of recurring musical themes (motives) that become associated in the listener with a character, idea, or emotion. This is certainly a concept compatible with Parker's stated goal.

In an area related to communicating ideas (in this case, more general ones) through music, Parker also had a desire to translate painterly images into sound, as reported by painter Harvey Cropper: "In art he liked Picasso and Rembrandt very much. Toulouse-Lautrec delighted him, and he was going to make a musical album of impressions of them."[54] It's not known whether this was a casual comment of Parker's or whether he intended to actively pursue such a project, nor is it known from a compositional or improvisational standpoint what form such a project would have taken.

Sadly, Charlie Parker's story of the 1950s concludes without the realization of so many of goals and potential directions: the further elaboration of "music as conversation," the development of thematic improvisation, the pursuit of Slonimsky-like resources, study with Varèse, Mule, or

Boulanger, a commission of Wolpe, the album of Toulouse-Lautrec impressions. How should we evaluate Parker's later work? Even though it became repetitive in the 1950s, isn't it enough that he generally played forcefully and authoritatively until his death? After all, the musical ideas that he was repeating were based on the distinct jazz vocabulary that he was instrumental in developing during the 1940s. Career-long aesthetic evolution (Pablo Picasso and John Coltrane come to mind) is the exception, not the rule in art. Parker made many articulate statements pertaining to new artistic objectives during the second half of his professional career. To evaluate his work of the 1950s, we must consider Parker's recorded work of the period both on its own and in context of his statements of artistic aims and changing aesthetic values. Parker's most creative recordings of the 1950s do support the idea of new musical horizons for Parker, but not necessarily in the directions his public statements would suggest.

During this period, Parker maintained most of the nontechnical and technical values associated with his music. When in good physical shape, Parker was still fully capable of the virtuosic aspects of his style such as mastery of rapid tempos, fleet double timing, and creative accenting. However, for several reasons, these qualities were displayed less often than they had been in his previous two periods. Parker's string ensemble for the most part played slow to medium tempos; the ensemble did not lend itself to bravura up-tempo performances. Many of Parker's recordings for Norman Granz were more highly organized than Parker's previous Savoy and Dial sessions; these particular ensembles did not foster uninhibited playing from Parker. During this period, Parker toured the country more often as a "single" with local rhythm sections; the level of ability of these musicians varied considerably, and the unavoidable limitations of ever-changing accompanists made the fastest performances harder to bring off successfully.

Along with the effects of heroin and alcohol on Parker's reflexes, he had at least one heart attack during this period and was in frequent pain from stomach ulcers. These factors sapped some of the personal energy and awareness required for not only high-energy improvisation but also for spontaneous invention and thoughtful, poetic improvisation. Parker in the 1950s made fewer additions to his melodic and harmonic vocabularies than he had in the 1940s, and he consolidated what he had previously learned into a stylized, lick-based approach to soloing that served him well when he was not physically and spiritually well.

Although the 1950s were not his most musically innovative period, Charlie Parker did attain some significant career advancements during the time. Parker recorded regularly for the labels of Norman Granz, who presented Parker respectfully and promoted him eagerly. Parker's combination string ensemble/jazz rhythm section not only recorded extensively, but also went on tour on several occasions, a rare event in jazz then or now.

As noted above, most of Parker's statements of artistic goals during the late 1940s and 1950s mention classical music. Because Parker did not succeed in having new works commissioned for him, and because he did not follow up on his desires to study composition and then compose his own new works, the influence of the classical music tradition on his recorded music was slight. Given Parker's primary strength as an improvising soloist, it makes sense to look beyond his statements of intent to be a composer, however provocative, and search his *improvisational* work of the period for traces of vital developments in his art. Indeed, it is in his best improvisational work of the 1950s (for example "Rocker" and "Sly Mongoose") that such developments are found. The techniques of chromatic sequencing and bitonality found in those performances could be readily implemented by Parker and were decidedly useful to him as an *improviser*. Charlie Parker's best soloistic work of the 1950s suggests that he had much more to say to us.

Some Final Thoughts

Charlie Parker accomplished much in his thirty-four years. Springing from Kansas City, one of jazz's most vital centers, Charlie proved himself to be one of the greatest students of jazz, carefully studying jazz musicians of the previous generation both in person and via the phonograph record. Of course, Parker was not just a composite of his influences; he absorbed, grasped, and transformed musical concepts in a way that only the most brilliant artists can. Parker proceeded to transcend his influences and develop a unique and recognizable melodic, harmonic, and rhythmic musical vocabulary. Just as importantly, Charlie Parker developed into one of the most emotionally, spiritually, and poetically compelling artists of his century. His brilliant powers of conception were wedded with his stunning resources of execution in the pursuit of artistic expression. More than fifty years after his reaching musical maturity, the music of Charlie Parker continues to move and challenge listeners and musicians alike.

Parker's pre-1944 apprenticeship period, previously poorly documented on commercial recordings, is now well represented on a variety of recordings, especially those made noncommercially. By the time of his first recordings at age twenty (in 1940), Charlie Parker was already equal or superior to his older band mates in many respects. His great dexterity on the saxophone and his internal sense of "time" allowed him to improvise and swing over a broad range of tempos. During this period, Parker gradually increased the tempo at which he could double-time and he developed his ability to creatively accent important notes in his melodic lines. His harmonic knowledge, while still developmental, was thorough enough in the early 1940s to allow him to record several convincing

performances without any harmonic accompaniment, an accomplishment that placed him among the best saxophonists in the entire United
States. Parker's best noncommercial recordings of the time (such as the
Charles White discs, the Bob Redcross discs, and "Honey & Body") contain some of his freshest and most spontaneous work of any period.

Parker's 1945 recordings with Dizzy Gillespie signaled the flowering
of Parker's explorations into a coherent approach to music. Parker's brilliant artistic imagination was wedded with a virtuosic command of the
saxophone to produce jazz of new peaks of sophistication and complexity. Even as Parker had reached a striking level of virtuosity and ability to
swing at furious velocity, he also demonstrated convincingly the continued relevance (and even necessity) of the blues in the increasingly complex and sophisticated musical style known as bebop or modern jazz.
Parker's first recordings under his own name exhibit the wide range of his
mature artistic expression, including as they do an up-tempo virtuoso
test-piece, a reflective ballad, and two modern interpretations of the
blues. The year 1945 also marked the first time that Charlie Parker's
compositions were recorded. Many of these early pieces, such as "Billie's
Bounce" and "Anthropology," are still being performed by jazz musicians today.

Beginning in 1947, Parker formed, recorded with, and toured with
his classic quintet, the ensemble that in general best showcased his talents. Every studio recording by the classic quintet is an important statement in the then-new modern jazz style, and many touch artistic high
points to equal the best recorded jazz of any era. His best studio and live
recordings of that period document a level of creativity in which any separation between conception and execution seems erased. Parker's recordings of the period demonstrate how he had increased the tempo at which
he could creatively improvise and swing, and how he had perfected his
ability to accent points of melodic change of direction to give his lines a
snap. His improvisational ability to spin forth asymmetrical melodic lines
that cut across a song's structural divisions reached a new height. The
maturation of the reflective side of Parker's art was expressed in a
1947–48 series of slower tempo studio recordings of American popular
songs and a blues. On these, he attained an extremely wide range of emotional expression from gentle lyricism to headlong flights of double- and
quadruple-time.

Parker's commercial recordings of the late 1940s and the 1950s are
extremely varied, and present Parker in many different instrumental set-

tings. At the end of 1949, Parker recorded with an ensemble that combined a jazz rhythm section with stringed instruments associated with Western classical music. This expanded group was popular enough for Parker to occasionally take it on tour in the 1950s, a tribute to Parker's growing mainstream appeal. The melodic content of Parker's improvisations of the 1950s, however, raises complex issues for the discerning listener. During that period, Parker seldom added new components to the musical vocabulary he had created, and too often he reduced that vocabulary to a thesaurus of licks that could be strung together, albeit brilliantly. Beginning around 1949, Parker expressed to colleagues his feelings of artistic stagnation, and until his death he made numerous public statements about new goals he was setting for his music. In many of these statements, he mentioned the study of Western classical music composition and classical saxophone technique as resources he wished to explore. He never undertook such study, nor did he consistently pursue many other possible artistic directions that he had touched upon. The distinctions between his stated musical goals and his actual path of the 1950s form an unfulfilled aspect to Parker's artistic story.

The unfulfilled aspects of Charlie Parker's last years should not detract from his many accomplishments. His innovations were far-reaching and influenced musicians on all instruments. His communicative gifts moved audiences on the deepest artistic levels, and Charlie Parker's music continues to speak to listeners today. In 1954, Parker told a novice saxophonist, "You see, once you stop wantin' to learn things, you're not alive anymore. And it's the truth, I mean, as vast as music is, you'll *never* learn it all."[1]

Appendixes

Appendix A

A Selected
Charlie Parker Discography

From 1940 to 1954, Charlie Parker recorded so much creative, stimulating, and interesting music that it cannot all be listed and discussed in this limited space. Instead, this selective Parker discography is organized with respect to the musical examples included in this book and is intended as an aid to the reader in search of those recordings. Readers who would like to more fully explore Parker's recorded legacy may wish to refer to *The Charlie Parker Discography* (Bregman, Bukowski, and Saks 1993).

Chapter 2

Title of Example	CD Code (see below)
Honey & Body (complete version)	1
Honey & Body (shortened version)	2
Body and Soul (Wichita version)	3
Honeysuckle Rose (Wichita version)	3
Oh, Lady Be Good! (Wichita version)	3
Cherokee (Jerry Newman version)	3
My Heart Tells Me	2
I've Found a New Baby (Charles White version)	2
Swingmatism	4
The Jumpin' Blues	4
I'm Forever Blowing Bubbles	3
Sweet Georgia Brown	2

Body and Soul (Bob Redcross version)	2
Boogie Woogie	2
Three Guesses	2

Chapter 3

Title of Example	CD Code (see below)
Red Cross (take 1)	12, 27
Dizzy Atmosphere	5
Billie's Bounce (take 5)	9, 27
Now's the Time (take 3)	9, 27
Now's the Time (take 4)	9, 27
Ko Ko (take 2)	9, 27
Oh, Lady Be Good! (Jazz at the Philharmonic version)	28
Ornithology (Finale Club version)	25
Moose the Mooche	7, 26
Ornithology (Dial version)	7, 26
Famous Alto Break (A Night in Tunisia, take 1)	8, 26
Lover Man	7, 26

Chapter 4

Title of Example	CD Code (see below)
Relaxin' at Camarillo	7, 26
Klosé Exercise (Wee)	6
Bird Gets the Worm (take 1)	10, 27
Constellation (take 5)	11, 27
Klact-oveeseds-tene (take A)	26
Little Willie Leaps	12, 27
Dexterity (take B)	7, 26
Donna Lee (take 2)	12, 27
Out of Nowhere (take A)	8, 26
Embraceable You (take A)	26
Parker's Mood (take 2)	10, 27
Parker's Mood (take 4)	11, 27
Parker's Mood (take 5)	11, 27
Salt Peanuts	23
Cheryl	16

The Street Beat   17
The Bird   14, 28

Chapter 5

Title of Example	CD Code (see below)
Just Friends	13, 14, 28
Rocker	18
Old Folks (takes 6, 7, 8 and 9)	28
Old Folks (take 9)	13
No Noise	15, 28
Sly Mongoose	18
Kim (take 2)	28
Embraceable You (1953 Canadian version)	19
I Love Paris (take 2)	28

Interviews

Charlie Parker, Marshall Stearns, John Maher interview   20
Charlie Parker, Leonard Feather interview (1951)   22
Charlie Parker, John Fitch (McLellan) interview   25
Charlie Parker, John Fitch, Paul Desmond interview   21
Charlie Parker, Dick Meldonian sax lesson   24

CDs Cited Above

Unless stated otherwise, the compact discs listed here were all in print or readily obtainable in the United States when this list was compiled in early 1996. All CDs are released under Charlie Parker's name unless stated otherwise.

CD Code   CD Title and Catalog Number

1 *Young Bird, Volumes One and Two*, Masters of Jazz (Média 7) MJCD 78/79 (French import)
2 *The Complete Birth of the Bebop*, Stash ST-CD-535
3 *Early Bird*, Stash ST-CD-542
4 *Blues from Kansas City*, Decca GRD-614 (released under Jay McShann's name)

5 *Shaw 'Nuff,* Musicraft MVSCD-53 (released under Dizzy Gillespie's name)
6 *The Complete Dean Benedetti Recordings of Charlie Parker,* Mosaic MD7-129
7 *The Legendary Dial Masters, Volume One,* Stash ST-CD 23
8 *The Legendary Dial Masters, Volume Two,* ST-CD 25
9 *The Charlie Parker Story,* Savoy Jazz SV 0105
10 *Charlie Parker Memorial, Volume One,* Savoy Jazz SV 0101. (*Note:* Take 2 of "Parker's Mood" is incorrectly labeled as take 1.)
11 *Charlie Parker Memorial, Volume Two,* Savoy Jazz SV 0103. (*Note:* Take 5 of "Constellation" is incorrectly labeled as take 4, and takes 4 and 5 of "Parker's Mood" are incorrectly labeled as takes 2 and 3, respectively.)
12 *The Immortal Charlie Parker,* Savoy Jazz SV 102
13 *Confirmation: Best of the Verve Years,* Verve 314 527 815-2
14 *Bird: The Original Recordings of Charlie Parker,* Verve 837 176-2
15 *South of the Border,* Verve 314 527 779-2
16 *Charlie Parker and the Stars of Modern Jazz at Carnegie Hall, Christmas 1949,* Jass J-CD-16
17 *Bebop & Bird Volume One,* Hipsville/Rhino R2 70197
18 *Bebop & Bird Volume Two,* Hipsville/Rhino R2 70198
19 *Charlie Parker, Montréal, 1953,* Uptown UPCD 27.36
20 *Bird's Eyes, Volume Seven,* Philology W 80.2
21 *Bird's Eyes, Volume Eight,* Philology W 80.2
22 *Bird's Eyes, Volume Nine,* Philology W 120.2
23 *Bird's Eyes, Volume Ten,* Philology W 220.2
24 *Bird's Eyes, Volume Sixteen,* Philology W 846.2
25 *Bird's Eyes, Volume Eighteen,* Philology W 848.2
26 *The Complete Dial Sessions,* Stash ST-CD 567-68-69-70 (four CDs)
27 *The Complete Savoy Studio Sessions,* Savoy ZDS 5500 (three CDs; out of print)
28 *Bird: The Complete Charlie Parker on Verve,* Verve 837 141-2 (ten CDs)

Appendix B

Four Complete
Solo Transcriptions

Honey & Body

(1) **part one: Honey**

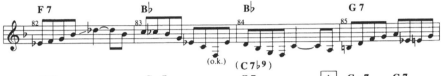

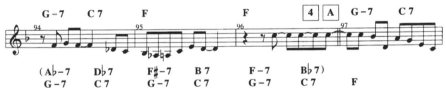

Oh, Lady Be Good! (1946)

Parker's Mood (Take 5)

Just Friends (32-Measure Chorus)

Notes

Preface

Epigraphs from Michael Levin and John S. Wilson, "No Bop Roots in Jazz: Parker," *Down Beat,* September 9, 1949, 19 and 12, and Robert George Reisner, *Bird: The Legend of Charlie Parker* (New York: Citadel Press, 1962), 21, respectively.

1. Charlie Parker, interview by John Fitch [radio name: John McLellan], WHDH, Boston, June, 1953.

2. Aaron Chaifetz, broadcast interview, WQED, Pittsburgh.

3. Reisner, *Bird,* 190. Parker went on to say, "Let's celebrate. We have Bartók and gin—what else do we need?"

4. Levin and Wilson, "No Bop Roots in Jazz," 12.

5. Charles Parker, broadcast interview with Paul Desmond and John Fitch, WHDH, Boston, January 1954.

6. Levin and Wilson, "No Bop Roots in Jazz," 1.

7. Charlie Parker and Dick Meldonian, audiotape of music lesson 1954.

8. Parker, 1954 interview.

9. Ibid.

Chapter 1

1. His mother referred to the day as the 28th (Reisner, *Bird,* 167). In a magazine article, Parker was paraphrased as saying that he was born in 1921 (Levin and Wilson, "No Bop Roots in Jazz," 12), although in an earlier article (Leonard Feather, "Yardbird Flies Home," *Metronome,* August, 1947, 14), he was directly quoted giving the August, 29, 1920, birthdate. Writers have often referred to him as Charles *Christopher* Parker, but his mother clearly stated that he had no middle name (Reisner, *Bird,* 167).

2. There is a question as to his mother's maiden name; it may have been Bailey, Bayley, Boyley, or Boxley (Gary Giddins, *Celebrating Bird: The Triumph of Charlie Parker* [New York: Beech Tree Books, 1987], 26). Official documents list "Bailey," "Bayley," or "Boyley."

3. Charlie Parker, interview by Marshall Stearns and John Maher, May, 1950.

4. Levin and Wilson, "No Bop Roots in Jazz," 12.

5. Giddins, *Celebrating Bird,* 26.

6. Reisner, *Bird,* 158.

7. Giddins, *Celebrating Bird,* 26.

8. Reisner, *Bird,* 158, 162.

9. Ibid., 129–30.

10. Levin and Wilson, "No Bop Roots in Jazz," 12.

11. Parker, 1950 interview.

12. Rebecca Parker was often mentioned in Parker literature but was never traced until the remarkable and persistent jazz critic Stanley Crouch located her and interviewed her. Some of the fruits of Crouch's research are found in Giddins, *Celebrating Bird.*

13. Reproduced in Giddins, *Celebrating Bird,* 43. Of course, teenagers often lie about their ages in order to get married.

14. Parker, 1950 interview.

15. Reisner, *Bird,* 129.

16. Parker, 1950 interview.

17. Levin and Wilson, "No Bop Roots in Jazz," 12.

18. Reisner, *Bird,* 185.

19. Parker, 1954 interview.

20. Parker, 1950 interview.

21. Nat Shapiro and Nat Hentoff, *Hear Me Talkin' to Ya* (New York: Rinehart, 1955; reprint, New York: Dover, 1966), 288.

22. Feather, "Yardbird Flies Home," 14.

23. Ibid., 43.

24. Reisner, *Bird,* 172.

25. Chan Parker and Francis Paudras, *To Bird with Love* (Poitiers: Éditions Wizlov, 1981), 72.

26. Reisner, *Bird,* 124.

27. Giddins, *Celebrating Bird,* 40.

28. Reisner, *Bird,* 129.

29. Ibid., 41.

30. Ibid., 185–86.

31. Gene Ramey, broadcast interview, National Public Radio.

32. Parker, 1950 interview. As this audiotape opens, one of the interview-

ers paraphrases Parker to the effect that the above incident took place when he was *seventeen*.

33. Ross Russell Collection. Harry Ransom Humanities Research Center, University of Texas, Austin. The clipping does not identify which newspaper it is from.

34. Gary Giddins and Kendrick Simmons, *Celebrating Bird,* videotape (New York: Sony Video Software Company, 1987).

35. Telephone interview, November 1, 1994. If one calculates Charlie's addiction from 1937 as Rebecca does, Charlie died in the eighteenth year. During the appointment, the doctor also advised Rebecca to have Charlie eat "greasy" foods to help him in some way that she did not understand. This anecdote suggests that, even though heroin had been illegal in the United States since 1924, the doctor's medical knowledge of opiate addiction was limited.

36. Reisner, *Bird,* 67.

37. Ibid.

38. Charlie Parker and Dick Meldonian, audiotape.

39. Reisner, *Bird,* 185.

40. Ibid.

41. Gene Ramey, interview by Stanley Dance, September 1978, Institute of Jazz Studies, Jazz Oral History Project, 6.

42. Jay McShann, "Interview," *Cadence,* October, 1979, 13.

43. Reisner, *Bird,* 214.

44. Ibid.

45. Giddins, *Celebrating Bird,* 49.

46. Telephone interview, November 1, 1994.

47. Reisner, *Bird,* 67.

48. Ibid., 163.

49. Levin and Wilson, "No Bop Roots in Jazz," 12.

50. Buster Smith, "Interview," *Cadence,* June, 1978, 17, and Reisner, *Bird,* 215.

51. Smith, 17.

52. Russell Collection. Paraphrased in a summary of an interview with Harlan Leonard: "'A genius.' But would not hire him for a good reed section. Tone too cutting. . . . Had check made out to Parker for 2.00, endorsed back by Parker, Jan 10 1939 dated, pinning down tenure w band." Leonard estimated that Parker was in the band one to two weeks.

53. Gene Ramey, interview by Jay Trachtenberg, KUT, Austin, Texas, June, 1983.

54. Reisner, *Bird,* 84.

55. Ibid., 215.

56. Smith, p. 17.

57. Levin and Wilson, "No Bop Roots in Jazz," 12.

58. Telephone interview, March 25, 1989.

59. Reisner, *Bird,* 138.

60. Ira Gitler, *Swing to Bop* (New York: Oxford University Press, 1985), 68.

61. Telephone interview, March 25, 1989.

62. Ibid.

63. Leonard Feather, *Inside Jazz* (New York: Da Capo, 1977), 12. It's not clear what Parker means by "a relative major . . . against a seventh chord."

64. Levin and Wilson, 12.

65. Shapiro and Hentoff, *Hear Me Talkin' to Ya,* 354.

66. Telephone interview, August 28, 1994. Hentoff believed that Shapiro edited the Parker section in question, but he felt it was unlikely that Shapiro would have simply altered the *Down Beat* text to make it read better. Hentoff could not recall if perhaps Shapiro worked from notes supplied by Levin or Wilson. Attempts to pursue this point with John S. Wilson, coauthor of the original article, have thus far failed.

67. Telephone interview, March 25, 1989.

68. Levin and Wilson, 12.

69. Telephone interview, November 1, 1994.

70. Levin and Wilson, 12.

71. Bob Locke, "Jitbugs Fade in Kaycee," *Down Beat,* February 15, 1940, 21.

72. Jay McShann, interview by Helen Oakley Dance, December, 1978, Institute of Jazz Studies, Jazz Oral History Project, 26; and Reisner, *Bird,* 147.

73. Leonard Feather, Untitled essay (liner notes), *Harlan Leonard and His Rockets,* RCA Victor, 1966.

74. McShann, interview, 27.

75. Reisner, *Bird,* 149.

76. Buster Smith in Reisner, *Bird,* 215. Smith, however, was not present in Kansas City at the time.

77. Reisner, *Bird,* 186.

78. Phil Schaap, Untitled essay (liner notes), *Bird at the Roost, Volume One,* Savoy Records, 1985.

79. Parker and Paudras, *To Bird with Love,* 72.

80. Chan Parker declined to clarify this statement in a telephone interview, August 2, 1991.

81. Reisner, *Bird,* 186.

82. Parker, 1954 interview.

83. Reisner, *Bird,* 186–87.

84. Levin and Wilson, "No Bop Roots in Jazz," 12.

85. Reisner, *Bird,* 150.

86. Parker, 1954 interview.

87. Schaap, Untitled essay, 1985.

88. Reisner, *Bird*, 143.

89. Ramey, interview with Stanley Dance, 47–48.

90. Parker, 1953 interview.

91. Russell Collection. Interview with Al Hibbler.

92. Feather, *Inside Jazz*, 13.

93. Reisner, *Bird*, 150.

94. Feather, *Inside Jazz*, 15.

95. Leonard Feather, "A Bird's-Ear View of Music," *Metronome*, August, 1948, 21.

96. Gunther Schuller, *The History of Jazz*, vol. 2, *The Swing Era* (New York: Oxford University Press, 1989), 290.

97. Giddins and Simmons, *Celebrating Bird*.

98. Reisner, *Bird*, 111.

99. Maitland Edey, "An Interview," *Paris Review*, no. 35 (1965): 141.

100. Dizzy Gillespie with Al Fraser, *to BE, or not . . . to BOP* (Garden City, N.Y.: Doubleday, 1979), 151.

101. Shapiro and Hentoff, *Hear Me Talkin' to Ya*, 356.

102. Billy Eckstine in Ibid., 356.

103. Giddins, *Celebrating Bird*, 71.

104. Telephone interview, January 1, 1995. Rebecca's statement contradicts Gary Giddins's understanding that she and Charlie did divorce (Giddins, *Celebrating Bird*).

105. Telephone interview, January 1, 1995.

106. Reisner, *Bird*, 25.

107. Ibid., 108.

108. Levin and Wilson, "No Bop Roots in Jazz," 13.

109. Frank Driggs, "The Story of Buddy Anderson, *Jazz Journal*, February, 1962, 12. Other members of this group included Leonard "Lucky" Enois (guitar), Winston Williams (bass), Sleepy Hickox (piano), and Edward "Little Phil" Phillips (drums).

110. In Gillespie with Fraser, *to BE*, the Onyx Club job is presented as taking place after he and Parker toured with Billy Eckstine when in fact, Gillespie worked the Onyx Club job first, then he and Parker went with Eckstine.

111. Gillespie with Fraser, *to BE*, 189.

112. Ibid., 199.

113. Brian Lanker, *I Dream a World* (New York: Stewart, Tabori and Chang, 1989), 134. This incident could have occurred during a different period; Vaughan was not specific. Jimmy Heath remembers seeing Parker with a score for "The Firebird" in 1948 (telephone interview, April 4, 1995).

114. Lucky Thompson, "Interview," *Cadence*, June, 1978, 12.

115. Parker, 1950 interview.

116. Gillespie with Fraser, *to BE,* 231.

117. Reisner, *Bird,* 79.

118. Telephone interview, August 15, 1994.

119. Gillespie and Fraser, *to BE,* 243.

120. Harry "The Hipster" Gibson, "Bird Lives" (unpublished manuscript), Harry Ransom Humanities Research Center, University of Texas, Austin.

121. Gillespie and Fraser, *to BE,* 250.

122. Most sources say that only Parker stayed behind; however, drummer Roy Porter reports that Milt Jackson and Ray Brown also remained in Los Angeles for a while (Porter, Roy, p. 56).

123. Parker and Paudras, *To Bird with Love,* 72.

124. Gitler, "Portrait of a Legend," 173.

125. Levin and Wilson, "No Bop Roots in Jazz," 13.

126. Eliott Grennard, "Sparrow's Last Jump," *Harper's,* May, 1947.

127. Howard McGhee, Institute of Jazz Studies Jazz Oral History Project, 31.

128. Lewis Porter, *A Lester Young Reader* (Washington, D.C.: Smithsonian Institution Press, 1991), 59.

129. Gitler, *Swing to Bop,* 175.

130. Telephone interview, August 15, 1994.

131. Ibid.

132. Doris Parker, interview, WKCR, New York, August, 1973.

133. Russell Collection.

134. Feather, "Yardbird Flies Home," 43.

135. Levin and Wilson, "No Bop Roots in Jazz," 13.

136. Charlie Parker, interview by Leonard Feather, Voice of America, Spring, 1951.

137. Telephone interview, August 15, 1994.

138. Not 1945, as has been occasionally reported. (Telephone interview, August 15, 1994.)

139. Miles Davis with Quincy Troupe, *Miles, the Autobiography* (New York: Simon and Schuster, 1989), 100.

140. Levin and Wilson, "No Bop Roots in Jazz," 19.

141. Davis with Troupe, *Miles,* 99–100.

142. Davis was eventually replaced by McKinley "Kenny" Dorham who was in turn replaced by Red Rodney. The piano chair was primarily occupied by Duke Jordan and Al Haig. Max Roach was later succeeded by Roy Haynes.

143. Spoken during a broadcast from Boston's Hi-Hat Club, probably January 1954.

144. Spoken during a broadcast from New York's Band Box Club, March 30, 1953.

145. Davis with Troupe, *Miles,* 107–8.

146. Russell, *Bird Lives!* (New York: Charterhouse, 1973), 267.

147. Davis with Troupe, *Miles,* 107–8.

148. Russell, *Bird Lives!* (p. 271) recounts Parker's meeting with Sartre; Chan Parker reports the encounter with Mule in *Ma Vie en Mi Bémol* (Paris: Plon, 1993), 67.

149. Francis Paudras, in a conversation with the author on July 28, 1991, stated that Parker had written French jazz critic Charles Delaunay, inquiring about renting an apartment in Paris with the purpose of studying with Boulanger.

150. Unsigned (December 1950), pp. 1, 11.

151. Ibid.

152. The earlier *Melody Maker* statement that Parker "must return to seek shelter under the wing of his agent from a pending brush with the law" seems to refer to the New York police and Parker's arrest, although it could refer to French police and some completely different incident.

153. Chan Parker, *Ma Vie,* 76 (translated from the French).

154. James Patrick, "Charlie Parker," in *The New Grove Dictionary of Jazz,* 2 vols. (New York: Grove's Dictionaries of Music, 1988), 287.

155. Cab Calloway, "Is Dope Killing Our Musicians?" *Ebony,* February, 1951, 22–24, 26–28. The musicians pictured are John Simmons, Miles Davis, Eddie Heywood, Gene Krupa, Billie Holiday, Howard McGhee, Art Blakey, Dexter Gordon, and Fats Navarro.

156. Parker, Spring, 1951 interview. Feather is probably referring to "Yardbird Flies Home" (Feather, 1947): "He declares (and every great musician admits it sooner or later) that he plays best when he is under the influence of nothing at all." Parker's mentioning of "an investigation" could refer to the *Ebony* article or, considering his arrest that same year, to a police investigation.

157. Telephone interview, August 2, 1991.

158. Mark Miller, *Cool Blues: Charlie Parker in Canada 1953* (London, Ont.: Nightwood, 1989), 32.

159. Parker, *Ma Vie,* 103–4.

160. Telephone interview, August 17, 1991.

161. Harvey Cropper in Reisner, *Bird,* 71.

162. Nat Hentoff, "Counterpoint," *Down Beat,* January 28, 1953, 15.

163. Telephone interview, August 12, 1994.

164. Ibid.

165. Parker, *Ma Vie,* 75 (translated from the French).

166. Chan Parker, in Russell Collection.

167. Maxwell T. Cohen (ellipses in original article). "With Care and Love," *Down Beat,* March 11, 1965, 20.

168. Perhaps his ally, the Baroness Pannonica "Nica" de Koenigswarter had an influence in the return of the cabaret card.

169. Re-created in Parker and Paudras, *To Bird with Love,* 337–38.

170. Julie MacDonald in Reisner, 141 (ellipsis in original).

171. Parker, *Ma Vie,* 94 (translation from the French).

172. Ahmed Basheer in Reisner, *Bird,* 38.

173. Reisner, *Bird,* 152 (Mingus), 81 (Dorham).

174. Leonard Feather, "Parker Finally Finds Peace," *Down Beat,* April 20, 1955, 6. (The Gillespie quote is part of an unsigned section and may not have been transcribed by Feather.)

175. Russell, *Bird Lives!* 163.

Introduction to the Musical Chapters

1. This book was originally planned to have a separate chapter devoted to the compositions of Charlie Parker. Due to copyright restrictions, however, the number and length of Parker compositional excerpts had to be limited.

2. Thomas Owens, "Charlie Parker: Techniques of Improvisation" (Ph.D. diss., UCLA, 1974).

3. Owens, "Charlie Parker," 2:1–10. Owens identifies sixty-four primary "motives" (plus variants). His approach, applied in an additive process, can also shed light on Parker's medium-scale melodic language. Owens analyzes four complete Parker solos with regard to these motives. One of these solos includes a ten-and-one-half measure section that is made up entirely of Owens's cataloged motives (vol. 1, 30–35). Note: in his later book "Bebop: The Music and Its Players," Thomas Owens more appropriately calls these melodic building-blocks "figures," not "motives."

Chapter 2

1. Because Parker was recorded at few sessions during the four-year period that this chapter examines, and because his work was rapidly evolving during that period, a comparatively high percentage of those 1940–43 sessions will be discussed in this chapter.

2. Parker did write at least one original song, "What Price Love?" while he was with McShann, but it was not recorded until 1946 when it was retitled "Yardbird Suite." See chapter 3.

3. The disc's label also appears to read "pt 1," raising the possibility of another disc recorded at the same time.

4. Parker and Paudras, *To Bird with Love,* 21.

5. Because the disc-cutter that Clarence Davis used evidently did not turn at a perfectly constant rate, transcription of "Honey & Body" requires a variable-speed tape deck, a normal tool for transcribing amateur recordings of this period. The speed of the recording drifted from beginning to end of the disc, and a gen-

eral sharpening trend must be offset by a gradual slowing of the tape in order to keep the playback in tune. The opening eight or so bars of "Honey" drift so radically, however, that a brief but extreme retuning is required to bring the opening measures into agreement with later passages (thereby reconciling the repeated-note motive found in measures 16, 49, and 112). In addition, the first seven notes (measures 14–15; a very common Parker motive) of "Honey" are virtually the same as the corresponding ones in measures 1 and 2 of Parker's July 2, 1942, solo on "The Jumpin' Blues" (also in the key of "F"); this retuning of the first measures brings the opening notes in "Honey" to the same pitch level.

6. There is in Parker's discography one other performance of length without harmonic accompaniment (bass, piano, or guitar). That is "Boogie Woogie," recorded by Bob Redcross on February 28, 1943, on which Parker is accompanied only by percussion (brushes).

7. Although Parker quotes Waller's melody at one point (m. 97–100), identifying the song "Honeysuckle Rose" as the harmonic basis for "Honey" is made somewhat difficult due to the fact that all available versions of the performance begin in the middle of the first chorus, specifically at m. 14 of the 32-bar AABA form (pointed out by Lawrence O. Koch in written communication [July 20, 1991] and also found in Tony Williams, "Stop Press," *Discographical Forum*). Repeated listenings help to relate the improvisation to the AABA form of "Honeysuckle Rose." The second part, "Body" (performed at approximately half the tempo of "Honey"), however, is easier to identify as an improvisation based on the form of Johnny Green's composition "Body and Soul" because Parker states and embellishes the song's melody from its beginning.

8. The tempo marking depends somewhat on the speed adjustment made on one's tape deck; also, Parker gradually slows his tempo over the course of "Honey."

9. Owens, "Charlie Parker," 2:1.

10. Harmonic analysis suggested by Larry Koch in written communication, July 20, 1991.

11. The exact release date of the recording is not known; Commodore owner/producer Milt Gabler kept no record of the record's release date. According to Gabler (telephone interview, March 13, 1993), Commodore records generally took six to eight weeks to reach the market. Gabler imagined that the Berry disc was released by Christmas 1938, although he had no specific recollection. The idea of an early 1939 release of this record is supported by the fact that *Down Beat* first reviewed the disc in their April, 1939, issue.

12. Clarence Davis, from an unpublished interview by Stanley Crouch as paraphrased by Crouch in a telephone conversation, April 27, 1988. Chu Berry was an early favorite of Parker.

13. During a live recording of "The Song Is You" from September 25, 1954, Parker again plays this phrase (a whole step higher). The fact that he then

extends it through the point where the words "I thought about you" occur makes this later quotation certain.

14. As covered in chapter 1, a notice in the February 15, 1940, issue of *Down Beat* magazine may support an early-1940 arrival in K.C. for Parker. If January, 1940, is the earliest that "Honey & Body" seems to have been recorded (upon Parker's return to Kansas City), there still remains the question of how *late* it could have been made. McShann and his band recorded in Chicago during November, 1941, and the band reportedly did not return to Kansas City before their New York debut in February, 1942. Parker's 1942 New York playing is clearly more confident and mature than "Honey & Body," making it certain that the disc was recorded before the band left for Chicago and the East Coast. The period during which "Honey & Body" could have been recorded, then, would be from the beginning of 1940 through late 1941. Further narrowing the time period is tricky. Comparing Parker's timbre, sense of swing, and confidence on "Honey & Body," with his April, 1941, Decca recordings very tentatively suggest that "Honey & Body" was recorded earlier. "Honey & Body" and Parker's November, 1940, Wichita recordings are more similar, however, cautiously supporting (but certainly not establishing) 1940 as the most likely year of recording of "Honey & Body." Jazz critic Gary Giddins (written communication, March 6, 1987) has pointed out that Parker's November, 1940, solo with Jay McShann on "Body and Soul" contains a quote from Coleman Hawkins's famous October, 1939, recording of "Body and Soul" (see below); this quote is not present in "Body." Giddins conjectures that the absence of the Hawkins quote in "Body" suggests that the Clarence Davis disc was recorded before Parker had learned and absorbed the Hawkins solo. This hypothesis, then, also estimates the date of recording of "Honey & Body" as being between Parker's return to Kansas City at the beginning of 1940 and the November, 1940, Wichita session.

15. Bebop players were especially known for playing the tritone substitution as an altered seventh chord with a *diminished fifth* [in jazz terminology a "flat fifth"], but Parker more conventionally begins each D7 arpeggio on an "A" pitch, in other words on the *perfect fifth*.

16. Bob Davis, "The Golden Bird," *Down Beat,* December, 1990, 18.

17. Ibid.

18. This quotation was pointed out by jazz scholar Kent Engelhardt. The Basie recording was made on January 21, 1937.

19. Thomas Owens labels this component Motive 5B (Owens, "Charlie Parker," 1:28.)

20. Thomas Owens, *Bebop: The Music and Its Players* (New York: Oxford University Press, 1995), 32. Ellington first recorded the piece on March 15, 1940, for the Victor label.

21. Ramey, interview with Stanley Dance, 10; brackets in original. This account is found in a very similar but not identical quotation in Reisner, 188.

22. Discographies sometimes list Trumbauer as only playing the C-melody saxophone on some of his most famous recordings, but he often recorded on the alto in the 1920s and was often pictured with an alto sax in his hands (better discographies list Trumbauer as playing both saxophones but do not delineate track by track). Lester Young specifically cited as a favorite Trumbauer's February 4, 1927, recording of "Singin' the Blues" (Porter, *A Lester Young Reader*, 256), evidently an alto sax performance (Trumbauer's high concert Fs aurally match high Ds on an alto and not the top palm key of a C-melody sax, plus his two shifts across the sax's register break around 0:18 sound correct when played on an alto). One of many other famous Trumbauer alto performances of the same period is the May 9, 1927, "Riverboat Shuffle" (listen to his smooth high concert A♭ [the highest note of the alto but above the range of the C-melody] at 2:36).

23. It should be noted that Hodges and Carter were not the only two African-American models for alto saxophonists in the 1930s. To name two others, Charlie Holmes and Otto Hardwick[e] employed clear, singing, and more compact tone qualities.

24. Levin and Wilson, "No Bop Roots in Jazz," 12.

25. Ibid.

26. Giddins and Simmons, *Celebrating Bird*.

27. Recorded for the Decca label, November 11, 1940.

28. Owens, "Charlie Parker," 1:39–40.

29. Examination of six LPs of material recorded by Newman at Minton's or Monroe's found that all such released material is listed as being recorded in 1941, leaving open the possibility of a late 1941 date for "Cherokee."

30. Reisner, *Bird,* 188.

31. Interestingly, Parker may not have been the source of the "Tea for Two" pattern that he taught to the McShann bandmembers. Speaking of the pattern and Parker's usage of it, Pianist Allen Tinney (with whom Parker played at Monroe's in 1939) claims ". . . I did bring it to Monroe's . . ." although Tinney acknowledged that he, too, might have picked the lick from someone else even earlier (Patrick, "Charlie Parker," 160).

32. For this effect, one fingers the saxophone's low C♯ (concert E) and manipulates the air column to produce a middle C♯ with a slightly veiled timbre.

33. White has stated to the author that he entered the Armed Forces sometime in 1943 and was discharged in 1944 (he could not recall the exact dates). He believed that he had recorded the discs before his wartime service, but, given the song's copyright date, and the fall of 1943 motion picture and recording release dates, he felt that the discs may have been recorded after his return to civilian life.

34. Frank Driggs, "The Story of Buddy Anderson," *Jazz Journal,* February, 1962, 12.

35. Robert Bregman, Leonard Bukowski, and Norman Saks say August 9, 1940 (*The Charlie Parker Discography* [Redwood, N.Y.: Cadence Jazz Books, 1993], 1).

36. Louis Gottlieb, "Why So Sad, Pres?" *Jazz: A Quarterly of American Music,* no. 3 (Summer 1959), 190. The passage occurs at measures 59–60 of Young's solo (1:35).

37. Cited in Gottlieb, Ibid., 190. Original source is Dave Brubeck and Lee Konitz, "A Conversation with Two Jazz Musicians," *Northwest Review* 1, no. 3 (Spring 1958).

38. Nathan Pearson, *Goin' to Kansas City* (Urbana: University of Illinois Press, 1987), 209.

39. Paraphrased by Feather, *Inside Jazz,* 12.

40. It is interesting to compare the Decca version of "Lonely Boy Blues" with the McShann's 1944 "live" Armed Forces Radio Service "Jubilee" version, as session that includes John Jackson but not Parker. Again, there are two solo spots for alto sax, but both sound like the *same* saxophonist, and indeed sound like the first saxophonist (thought to be John Jackson) on the Decca recording.

41. In the fourth chorus of the second solo (assuming the opening, incomplete chorus is the first; between measures 97 and 111), the form is lost, resulting in six beats being omitted (by measure 112, they are back on track). This discrepancy could be due to a flaw in the actual disc; John R.T. Davies, who made the "transfers" in preparation for LP mastering, however, stated that no splicing had been by done by him to correct for any skips [phone conversation, April 3, 1989]. Aural evidence, specifically the unbroken clapping on beats two and four during this chorus [possibly by Gillespie] suggest that Parker and Pettiford truly got lost and made a rhythmic adjustment.

42. In his book *How to Play Bebop,* vol. 1, David Baker has codified the ways that Parker and others tended to use chromatic tones into two basic "bebop scales." Usage of these scales helps the improviser maximize the number of chord tones that fall on the beat.

43. Charlie Parker, 1950 interview.

Chapter 3

1. Hennessey, p. 45.

2. Charlie Parker, 1953 interview.

3. Charlie Parker, 1954 interview.

4. Levin and Wilson, "No Bop Roots in Jazz," 1 (could Parker have said "bastard" instead of "love-child"?).

5. Ibid.

6. Gillespie, "Bird Wrong; Bop Must Get a Beat: Diz," *Down Beat,* October 7, 1949, 1. The bulk of this article details Gillespie's attempts to regain the dancing audience through simplifying his big band's beat. Gillespie is paraphrased as saying that the two most important characteristics of bop are its harmonies and its phrasing, and that rhythmic variety isn't essential. The last idea is surprising considering that one of Gillespie's most important contributions to jazz came in his integration of bop with Afro-Cuban rhythmic concepts.

7. Feather, "A Bird's-Ear View of Music," 14.

8. Charlie Parker, 1953 interview.

9. Ibid.

10. The Ware solo is found in the introduction to Harlan Leonard's "Rockin' with the Rockets" recorded January 11, 1940. In a soon to be published research paper, Kent Engelhardt discusses this passage with regard to a practice he calls "side-slipping."

11. Feather, "A Bird's-Ear View of Music," 21.

12. Levin and Wilson, "No Bop Roots in Jazz," 1.

13. Curly Russell, interview by Phil Schaap, WKCR, New York, September, 1983.

14. Max Roach, interview on "Horizons," National Public Radio.

15. To add to the complications of the session, another pianist, Argonne Thornton (later known as Sadik Hakim), played piano part of the time.

16. Not to be confused with Duke Ellington's 1940 "Ko-Ko." This Parker piece has been referred to in print as "Koko," "Ko Ko," and "Ko-Ko." The original handwritten Savoy ledger reads "KoKo" or "Ko Ko," but this is perhaps not a significant point because the title was evidently supplied by the producer, Teddy Reig, not by Parker. The original Savoy label reads "KO KO."

17. Bob Porter, "Talking with Teddy," *The Complete Savoy Charlie Parker Studio Sessions.*

18. Ibid.

19. Thomas Owens labels the first three or so beats of this run Motive 5C (Owens, "Charlie Parker," 28).

20. Although "Body and Soul" was performed slowly with a quadruple-time implication, in order to better compare it with "Billie's Bounce," the former is presented here as if it were performed twice as fast but with only a *double-time* implication (in either case, the notes are played with the same velocity; only the notation has changed). In addition, because the alto and tenor saxophones are "transposing" instruments, this lick, while fingered identically on both saxes, sounds in different concert keys (C for the tenor and F for the alto). Presenting both examples in their saxophone keys makes clear their equivalency to the saxophonist.

21. This bluesy lick appears even earlier (and in the same key) during Parker's solo on Clyde Bernhardt's "Triflin' Woman Blues" recorded in January, 1945.

22. See Owens, "Charlie Parker," 2:207 for a full-score transcription.

23. Max Roach, interview by Terry Gross, National Public Radio.

24. Barry Ulanov, George Simon, and Leonard Feather, review of "Ko Ko," *Metronome,* May, 1946, 24. The negative comment is unusual because Ulanov and Feather were quite sympathetic to the new music. Far from being "beatless," the solo was 32 bars long (one-half of a chorus), and therefore clearly related to the song's form.

25. Gillespie stated that drummers Kenny Clarke and Max Roach were unavailable for the California trip because both were working better-paying jobs with other leaders (Gillespie and Fraser, *to BE,* 243).

26. Gillespie and Fraser, *To BE,* 250.

27. Phil Schaap, "The Sessions," liner notes for *The Complete Charlie Parker on Verve,* Verve Records, 1988, 15.

28. Leonard Feather, *From Satchmo to Miles* (New York: Stein and Day, 1972), 119.

29. Schaap, "The Sessions," 15.

30. Ibid.

31. Gitler, "Portrait of a Legend: Joe Albany," *Down Beat,* October 24, 1963, 21 (the evident expletive is omitted in the original article).

32. Russell, *Bird Lives!* 209.

33. Roy Porter, *There and Back* (Baton Rouge: Louisiana State University Press, 1991), 56.

34. The chord progression of "Yardbird Suite" resembles in part those of several earlier songs, but it is not clear that Parker based his progression on that of any previous song.

35. As recorded by Earl Coleman, November 11, 1948, for Dial Records.

36. Lee Konitz and Lennie Tristano, interview by John Fitch, WHDH, Boston, March, 1956.

37. Russell, *Bird Lives!* 212.

38. Levin and Wilson, "No Bop Roots in Jazz," 13.

Chapter 4

1. Feather, *Inside Jazz,* 15.

2. Schuller, *History of Jazz,* 55.

3. Phil Schaap, "Charlier Parker Time Line," liner notes for *The Complete Dean Benedetti Recordings of Charlie Parker,* Mosaic Records, 1990, 26. Schaap stated in a telephone conversation with the author that at least one musician who remembered the Kirby theme sang it to Schaap in a way similar, but not identical to, Parker's version. Schaap has also determined that Parker's original title for "Cool Blues" was "Blues Up and Down."

4. Russell, *Bird Lives!* 240.

5. Feather, "Yardbird Flies Home," 44.

6. Ibid., 43.

7. Schaap, "Charlie Parker Time Line," 13. According to Schaap, McGhee had returned to California upon learning that Parker had become re-addicted to heroin.

8. Perhaps Navarro had already developed his heroin habit, and Parker did not want another addict in the band (the members of Parker's quintet were generally "clean" when he hired them). Perhaps Navarro was already exhibiting signs of tuberculosis, from which he died in 1950; Charles Mingus recalled Navarro being sick with the disease in 1948 (Charles Mingus, *Beneath the Underdog* [New York: Penguin Books, 1980], 139).

9. "Dexterity," "Bird of Paradise," and "Embraceable You" were recorded on October 28, 1947. "Bongo Beep" was recorded December 17, 1947.

10. August 14, 1947.

11. Pointed out by jazz scholar William E. Anderson in personal communication.

12. David Baker has pointed out that boppish lines using chromatic passing tones (his "bebop scales") often descend (David Baker, *How to Play Bebop*, vol. 1 (Van Nuys, Calif.: Alfred, 1985), 2, 12. Thomas Owens has more specifically written about Parker's melodic lines' tendency to descend, a characteristic he calls a "scalar descent." Of particular interest is his analysis in those terms of Parker's solo on the September 18, 1949, recording of "The Closer" (Owens, *Bebop*, 35–36).

13. James Patrick analyzed this solo through measure 8, saying "This passage is constructed almost entirely of three very short ideas, developed and combined (bars 4 and 8), with silences of subtly varied length throughout" (Patrick, "Charlie Parker" 2:288). Scott Sandvik analyzed the entire solo from melodic, harmonic and metric standpoints (Scott Sandvik, "Polyharmony, Polymeter, and Motivic Development in Charlie Parker's *Klact-Oveeseds-Tene* (Take 1) Solo," *Jazzforschung*, 1992, 83–97.

14. Levin and Wilson, "No Bop Roots in Jazz," 12.

15. On the first take (not originally issued) of "Bird of Paradise," the one ballad performance that they *did* retitle, Parker extensively features Kern's original melody; had they decided to issue that take, it would have been issued under its original title ("All The Things You Are") like the others.

16. Gunther Schuller, "Sonny Rollins and the Challenge of Thematic Improvisation," *Jazz Review*, November, 1958, 6.

17. Bregman, Bukowski, and Saks, *The Charlie Parker Discography*.

18. Max Roach, interview by Phil Schaap, WKCR, New York, September, 1989.

19. The authorship of "Donna Lee" has been debated. It was copyrighted under Charlie Parker's name, but many have thought that it did not sound like a

Parker composition; in fact, it resembles Miles Davis's "Little Willie Leaps" of the same period more than any other Parker piece. James Patrick has pointed out that several phrases resembling "Donna Lee" were played and recorded at the Hi-Hat Club (see earlier in this chapter) in solos by Parker months before the actual composition was recorded, possibly suggesting that Parker was indeed the writer (Patrick, "Charlie Parker," 20). Of course, Davis may have picked up some Parker phrases when they worked together in 1946, or Davis could have been working on "Donna Lee" when last they played together. Eventually, however, Miles Davis stated specifically that "Donna Lee" indeed was his composition (Davis with Troupe, *Miles,* 103–4).

20. Telephone interview, August 17, 1991.

21. Chan Parker recorded Charlie at Manhattan's Open Door nightclub on July 26, 1953. He quotes "Over There" during "The Song is You" and "My Old Flame."

22. Owens, "Charlie Parker," vol. 2.

23. This version is listed first in Bregman, Bukowski, and Saks, *Charlie Parker Discography.*

24. Interview, April 24, 1992.

25. Ibid.

26. Reisner, *Bird,* 224.

27. The usual date given for this recording is May 17, 1950. It has been suggested many times that the recording must have been made at an earlier date because Fats Navarro was unlikely to have played this strongly so soon before his death from tuberculosis and heroin addiction on July 7, 1950. Supporting this notion, Ira Gitler reported seeing a very ill Navarro playing weakly at Birdland in 1950, and Gitler doubted that Navarro could have played this well in May, 1950 (Ira Gitler, *Jazz Masters of the Forties* [New York: Macmillan, 1966], 101). (An undated photo of an emaciated "100 pound" Navarro playing soon before his death is found in Calloway, "Is Dope Killing Our Musicians?" 27). Birdland opened on December 15, 1949, so if the recording was in fact made at that night-club, it must have been made during the last weeks of 1949 or the first half of 1950. The possibility exists that this recording was made earlier in 1949 at a different nightclub.

28. Older discographies list the drummer as Art Blakey and the bassist as Curly Russell.

29. Parker and Navarro were recorded commercially only once (the Metronome All-Stars date of January 3, 1949). Other live Parker/Navarro recordings include the "Bands for Bonds" broadcast of November 8, 1947, and a thus far unreleased Jazz at the Philharmonic concert of February 11, 1949.

30. Russell Collection.

31. Schaap, "The Sessions," 16.

32. Parker and Meldonian, audiotape, 1954. One might guess that Parker

was counting both the F♯ and G♭ scales which, although they sound exactly the same, are notated differently, but this explanation is contradicted by the fact that Parker does not mention both F♯ and G♭ in his list; on the tape, he clearly says ". . . F, G♭, G . . ." and so forth.

33. Gene Lees, *Cats of Any Color: Jazz Black and White* (New York: Oxford University Press, 1994), 98–99.

34. Parker was probably referring to Schoenberg's *Pierrot Lunaire; Protée* (*Suite Symphonique No. 2*) was composed by Darius Milhaud.

35. Feather, "Yardbird Flies Home," 43 (ellipses in original text).

36. Ibid., 21–22 (ellipses in original text).

37. Levin and Wilson, "No Bop Roots in Jazz," 12 and 13.

38. Hentoff, "Counterpoint," *Down Beat,* January 28, 1953, 15.

39. Levin and Wilson, "No Bop Roots in Jazz," 1.

40. Bob Porter, "Talking with Teddy."

41. Levin and Wilson, "No Bop Roots in Jazz," 19.

Chapter 5

1. Levin and Wilson, "No Bop Roots in Jazz," 12.

2. John McDonough, "Pablo Patriarch Part 2," *Down Beat,* February 15, 1940, 76.

3. Schaap, "The Sessions," 21.

4. Ibid.

5. A *Down Beat* review of Parker and strings in performance referred to his tone as "a flat, monotonous, squawking thing" and said Parker had "allowed his playing to degenerate into a tasteless and raucous hullabaloo" (unsigned [August, 1950]).

6. A photo from this recording session indeed shows him using that horn and mouthpiece. It can be seen in the photo section of this book.

7. Mulligan, in a telephone interview, August 16, 1994.

8. Chaifetz, interview.

9. This version was the only one issued on the LP *Bird is Free* (Charlie Parker Records PLP-401). It was titled "Rocker #2" on the LP "Charlie Parker Live at Rockland Palace" (Charlie Parker Records CP [2] 502).

10. Nicolas Slonimsky, *Thesaurus of Scales and Melodic Patterns* (New York: Scribner, ca. 1947), 81.

11. Lewis Porter and Michael Ullman, *Jazz from Its Origins to the Present* (Englewood Cliffs, N.J.: Prentice-Hall, 1993), 231. The authors include a highly recommended transcription of Parker's fourth chorus.

12. It's not clear whether Parker was actively adding to his repertoire of intervallically conceived patterns; both the Slonimsky-like pattern and the augmented triad pattern noted in "Rocker" are found in the 1949–1950 version of

"Dizzy Atmosphere" discussed in chapter 4. As pointed out by saxophonist Lee Konitz (telephone interview, June 2, 1995), Parker later played the Slonimsky-like pattern on the sixth take of his July 30, 1953, recording of "Chi Chi" (1:34).

13. Hentoff, "Counterpoint," 15. The reference to "1941" is unclear; at that time he was with McShann, an unlikely band to be augmented by strings. Possibly, he was referring to the Earl Hines band; in another interview of the time, Parker stated he joined Hines's band in 1941 (reportedly December, 1942); Hines was sympathetic to strings and employed a string section around 1943, after the time that Parker left.

14. John S. Wilson, "Bop at End of Road, Says Dizzy," *Down Beat,* September 8, 1950, 1. It's amusing that Gillespie says "We'd make people think we like what we're doing," as if the concept would be a bit of a chore for him and Parker.

15. Reisner, *Bird,* 194.

16. Hentoff, p. 15. Parker reportedly used the opening phrase(s) of *Kleine Kammermusik* to call his musicians back to the bandstand (Gitler [1974], p. 48).

17. Reisner, *Bird,* 194–95.

18. Telephone interview, August 18, 1994.

19. The three pieces that were recorded were "In the Still of the Night," "Old Folks," and "If I Love Again." "Yesterdays" was prepared by Evans and Lambert but was not recorded. All four arrangements are photographed in Unsigned (1994), p. 29.

20. Charlie Parker, 1953 interview.

21. Charlie Parker, 1954 interview.

22. Curly Russell, interview.

23. Nat Hentoff, "Granz Wouldn't Let Me Record With Parker, Says Roy Haynes," *Down Beat,* April 4, 1952, 7.

24. McDonough, "Pablo Patriarch," 35. The session might have been inspired by a nightclub engagement that featured the two players: "In 1950 he [Parker] played Café Society Downtown. Art Tatum was the other attraction, and they alternated on the stand. When Bird's trick was through, Tatum took over. One night Bird stepped down, and Art started to play. Charlie listened a few minutes and was so moved by what he heard that he stepped back on the stand and played right through to his next set" (Ray Turner in Reisner, *Bird,* 227). Pianist John Lewis placed the engagement around 1951 and called it "priceless" (Ross Russell Collection).

25. Parker played the song twice that night; one version was released on Charlie Parker Records PLP-401, another version has been heard in its entirety only on a tape circulated among collectors. Charlie Parker Records CP (2) 502 contains parts of both versions, poorly spliced together (the tempo and tuning changes at the splice). Although the following example was played at approxi-

mately 3:45 on the privately circulated version (speed corrected for pitch), it is most easily found on the spliced issue occurring at approximately 4:19 into the LP cut (uncorrected for pitch).

26. Although the LP versions are pitched in the vicinity of G♭, comparisons with other pieces recorded that night clearly show that the correct pitch for this song is about one half-step lower. Indeed, the privately circulated version (which derives directly from Chan Parker, who recorded the concert) is pitched in the vicinity of F.

27. Sometimes incorrectly called the first take.

28. The two issued takes of "Kim" begin with very different improvisational statements, making it clear that the song has no set melody. Unusually, however, Parker in each take revisits his opening improvisational idea when he returns for one last solo chorus. This has a unifying effect on each take, almost as if there were a set melody to "Kim." See also "The Bird," in this chapter.

29. Owens, "Charlie Parker" 1:101. Owens calls this figure Motive 5B and reports hundreds of examples of it in recorded Parker solos. He writes that although it is rare in Parker of the 1940s, the motive "becomes prominent in the 1950s." Owens includes a motivic analysis of the first forty measures of Parker's solo on this take of "Kim" (1:31).

30. Schaap, "The Sessions," 31.

31. The earlier, alternate take is called take 2 on Verve CDs and take 1 in *The Charlie Parker Discography.*

32. Red Rodney, interview, April 4, 1992.

33. Charlie Parker, 1954 interview.

34. Ibid.

35. Reisner, *Bird,* 229–30.

36. Ibid., 211.

37. Charlie Parker, 1953 interview. "Progressive" jazz was a term sometimes used as an alternative to "bebop" or "modern jazz."

38. Hentoff, "Counterpoint," 15. One hopes that Parker's prediction comes to pass.

39. Tristano, however, reported another time when Parker *did* avidly respond to Tristano's harmonically challenging accompaniment: ". . . I was sitting at the piano, playing something. He started playing with me, and he played his ass off. He wasn't used to the chords I played. I play sort of my own chords. In a lot of ways, they were different. I don't remember the tune, but whatever I did, he was right on top of the chords, like we had rehearsed" (Reisner, *Bird,* 224).

40. Walter Bishop, Jr., interview on "Horizons," National Public Radio.

41. Charlie Parker, 1953 interview. Fitch's and Parker's words have been left unedited in this exchange.

42. As noted earlier in this chapter, Parker expressed interest in composer Paul Hindemith. Some of Hindemith's work included harmony based on the interval of the fourth instead of the third as found in most Western music. These pieces could have inspired Parker to explore the jazz application of such "quartal" harmonic concepts. In addition, freely-arrived-at "atonal" improvisation was also a possible direction for Parker but was far from his known interests. The brilliant Parker certainly grasped and appreciated the work of twentieth-century composers, but greater discipline was required to carefully study and implement their concepts.

43. Pentatonic scales were another melodic resource that could have required less study to master than Slonimsky-like architectures. Parker might have been exposed to pentatonic scales through many sources ranging from the work of Bartók, to various world musics to the blues. Although numerous jazz players of the 1960s and 1970s found pentatonic scales to be useful tools, outside of the blues usage of the pentatonic scale, they were not important in Parker's conception of melody.

Taking a different tack, Parker could have deemphasized the role of melody and focused on the creation of musical textures. Either the classical music tradition (for example, a technique like *klangfarbenmelodie,* or "tone-color melody") or the African-American tradition (speechlike timbres and inflection) could have provided stimulus in this regard for Parker. As with so many of the possibilities open to Parker, he touched on the latter practice but did not develop it. Author Lewis Porter points out that a passage in Parker's 1952 recording of "Rocker" (discussed earlier in this chapter) resembles the 1960s approach of reed player Eric Dophy in its speech-like "squawking" (Porter and Ullman, *Jazz from Its Origins,* 231).

44. Unlike the Parker classic quintet pieces (chapter 4) that featured a Latin rhythm during the melody statement but then switched to swing for the solos, studio and live recordings of "My Little Suede Shoes" find Parker maintaining the Latin accompaniment throughout the performances.

45. Quoted in Nat Hentoff, "Miles Davis—Last Trump," *Esquire,* March, 1959, 90.

46. One of many other sources that Parker could have tapped for rhythmic inspiration was the music of Igor Stravinsky, which he admired, actively listened to, and even studied (chapter 1). In addition, the multiple and simultaneous tempos found in the free-form improvisations of Lennie Tristano could have provided Parker with yet another alternative, had Parker been familiar with them (discussed earlier in this chapter).

47. Charles Mingus, liner notes for *Let My Children Hear Music,* Columbia Records, 1972, unpaginated.

48. Charlie Parker, 1953 interview.

49. As noted earlier, Parker had expressed dissatisfaction with the blues and song forms common in jazz. In response, he could have written pieces with new structures not derived from song forms (structures that quite possibly would involve a different balance between written and improvisational material than Parker's usual combo material). Certainly Duke Ellington's "extended" works could have been an inspiration to Parker, although it's not clear that Parker held much interest in Ellingtonia in general (under his own name, Parker never recorded any Ellington pieces in the studio, and Parker seldom played Ellingtonia in public). Closer to Parker's world would have been the example of the Dizzy Gillespie–George Russell–Chano Pozo composition "Cubana Be-Cubana Bop," an extended composition not based on preexisting forms. Parker hoped that study of classical music composition would give him the tools to write new music, but to a great degree his lack of discipline that held him back in this area.

Aside from the formal possibilities presented by more extensive writing, Parker also could have explored freely-arrived-at improvisational forms as exemplified by Lennie Tristano's recordings "Intuition" and "Digression." As noted earlier in this chapter, Parker showed no real familiarity with such an approach when asked about it in 1953.

50. Dizzy Gillespie with Gene Lees, "The Years with Yard," *Down Beat,* May 25, 1961, 23.

51. Telephone interview, August 17, 1991.

52. Charlie Parker, 1954 interview.

53. Reisner, *Bird,* 186, 186–87, and 188.

54. Reisner, *Bird,* 72.

Some Final Thoughts

1. Parker and Meldonian, audiotape, 1954.

References

Books

Baker, David. *How to Play Bebop.* Vol. 1. Van Nuys, Calif.: Alfred, 1985.

Bregman, Robert M.; Bukowski, Leonard; and Saks, Norman. *The Charlie Parker Discography.* Redwood, N.Y.: Cadence Jazz Books, 1993.

Davis, Miles, with Troupe, Quincy. *Miles, the Autobiography.* New York: Simon and Schuster, 1989.

Feather, Leonard. *From Satchmo to Miles.* New York: Stein and Day, 1972.

———. *Inside Jazz.* New York: Da Capo, 1977. (Reprint of *Inside Be-Bop,* J. J. Robbins and Sons, 1949.)

Giddins, Gary. *Celebrating Bird: The Triumph of Charlie Parker.* New York: Beech Tree Books, 1987.

Gillespie, Dizzy, with Fraser, Al. *to BE, or not . . . to BOP.* Garden City, N.Y.: Doubleday and Company, 1979.

Gitler, Ira. *Jazz Masters of the Forties.* New York: Macmillan, 1966; reprint, New York: Collier Books, 1974.

———. *Swing to Bop.* New York: Oxford University Press, 1985.

Hennessey, Mike. *Klook: The Story of Kenny Clarke.* London: Quartet Books, 1990.

Koch, Lawrence O. *Yardbird Suite: A Compendium of the Music and Life of Charlie Parker.* Bowling Green, Ohio: Bowling Green University Popular Press, 1988.

Lanker, Brian. *I Dream a World.* New York: Stewart, Tabori and Chang, 1989.

Lees, Gene. *Cats of Any Color: Jazz Black and White.* New York: Oxford University Press, 1994.

Miller, Mark. *Cool Blues: Charlie Parker in Canada 1953.* London, Ont.: Nightwood Editions, 1989.

Mingus, Charles. *Beneath the Underdog.* New York: Penguin Books, 1980.

Owens, Thomas. "Charlie Parker: Techniques of Improvisation." Ph.D. diss. UCLA.

———. *Bebop: The Music and Its Players*. New York: Oxford University Press, 1995.

Parker, Chan. *Ma Vie en Mi Bémol*. Paris: Plon, 1993.

Parker, Chan, and Paudras, Francis. *To Bird with Love*. Poitiers: Éditions Wizlov, 1981.

Patrick, James. "Charlie Parker." In *The New Grove Dictionary of Jazz*. 2 vols. New York: Grove's Dictionaries of Music, Inc., 1988.

Pearson, Nathan. *Goin' to Kansas City*. Urbana: University of Illinois Press, 1987.

Pop, Including Bird—The Chan Parker Collection. London: Christie's, 1994.

Porter, Lewis. *A Lester Young Reader*. Washington, D.C.: Smithsonian Institution Press, 1991.

Porter, Lewis, and Ullman, Michael. *Jazz from Its Origins to the Present*. Englewood Cliffs, N.J.: Prentice-Hall, 1993.

Porter, Roy. *There and Back*. Baton Rouge: Louisiana State University Press, 1991.

Reisner, Robert George. *Bird: The Legend of Charlie Parker*. New York: Citadel Press, 1962.

Russell, Ross. *Bird Lives! The High Life and Hard Times of Charlie (Yardbird) Parker*. New York: Charterhouse, 1973.

Schuller, Gunther. *The History of Jazz*. Vol. 2, *The Swing Era*. New York: Oxford University Press, 1989.

Shapiro, Nat, and Hentoff, Nat. *Hear Me Talkin' to Ya*. New York: Rinehart, 1955; reprint, New York: Dover Publications, 1966.

Slonimsky, Nicolas. *Thesaurus of Scales and Melodic Patterns*. New York: Scribner, ca. 1947.

Periodicals

Calloway, Cab. "Is Dope Killing Our Musicians?" *Ebony,* February, 1951.

Cohen, Maxwell T. "With Care and Love." *Down Beat,* March 11, 1965.

Davis, Bob. "The Golden Bird." *Down Beat,* December, 1990.

Driggs, Frank. "The Story of Buddy Anderson." *Jazz Journal,* February, 1962.

Edey, Maitland, Jr. "An Interview." *Paris Review,* no. 35 (1965).

Feather, Leonard. "Yardbird Flies Home." *Metronome,* August, 1947.

———. "A Bird's-Ear View of Music." *Metronome,* August, 1948.

———. "Parker Finally Finds Peace." *Down Beat,* April 20, 1955.

Gillespie, Dizzy. "Bird Wrong; Bop Must Get a Beat: Diz." *Down Beat,* October 7, 1949.

Gillespie, Dizzy, with Lees, Gene. "The Years with Yard." *Down Beat,* May 25, 1961.

Gitler, Ira. "Portrait of a Legend: Joe Albany." *Down Beat,* October 24, 1963.

Gottlieb, Louis. "Why So Sad, Pres?" *Jazz: A Quarterly of American Music,* no. 3 (Summer 1959).

Grennard, Elliott. "Sparrow's Last Jump." *Harper's,* May, 1947.

Hentoff, Nat. "Granz Wouldn't Let Me Record With Parker, Says Roy Haynes," *Down Beat,* April 4, 1952.

———. "Counterpoint," *Down Beat,* January 28, 1953.

———. "Miles Davis—Last Trump." *Esquire,* March, 1959.

Levin, Michael, and Wilson, John S. "No Bop Roots in Jazz: Parker." *Down Beat,* September 9, 1949.

Locke, Bob. "Jitbugs Fade in Kaycee." *Down Beat,* February 15, 1940.

McDonough, John. "Pablo Patriarch Part II." *Down Beat,* November, 1979.

McShann, Jay. "Interview" (part two). *Cadence,* October, 1979.

Parker, Charlie. "My Best on Wax." *Down Beat,* June 29, 1951.

Patrick, James. "Al Tinney, Monroe's Uptown House, and the Emergence of Modern Jazz in Harlem." *Annual Review of Jazz Studies,* 1983.

Ramey, Gene. "My Memories of Bird Parker," *Melody Maker,* May 28, 1955.

Sandvik, Scott. "Polyharmony, Polymeter, and Motivic Development in Charlie Parker's *Klact-Oveeseds-Tene* (Take 1) Solo." *Jazzforschung,* 1992.

Schuller, Gunther. "Sonny Rollins and the Challenge of Thematic Improvisation," *Jazz Review,* November, 1958.

Smith, Buster. "Interview." *Cadence,* June, 1978.

Thompson, Lucky. "Interview." *Cadence,* January, 1982.

Ulanov, Barry; Simon, George; and Feather, Leonard ("The Three Deuces"). Review of "Ko Ko." *Metronome,* May, 1946.

Unsigned. "Bird Wrong; Bop Must Get a Beat: Diz." *Down Beat,* October 7, 1949.

———. "Bird, Backed by Strings, Disappoints at Birdland." *Down Beat,* August 25, 1950.

———. "The Incredible Story of Parker in Paris." *Melody Maker,* December 9, 1950.

Williams, Tony. "Stop Press." *Discographical Forum,* no. 45, unpaginated and undated insert.

Wilson, John S. "Bop at End of Road, Says Dizzy." *Down Beat,* September 8, 1950.

Liner Notes

Feather, Leonard. Untitled essay. *Harlan Leonard and His Rockets.* RCA Victor, 1966.

Mingus, Charles. Untitled essay. *Let My Children Hear Music*. Columbia Records, 1972.

Patrick, James. "The Complete Dean Benedetti Recordings of Charlie Parker." *The Complete Charlie Parker on Verve*. Verve Records, 1988.

Porter, Bob. "Talking with Teddy." *The Complete Savoy Charlie Parker Studio Sessions*. From interviews during July and August 1978.

Schaap, Phil. Untitled essay. *Bird at the Roost Volume One*. Savoy Records, 1985.

———. "The Sessions." *The Complete Charlie Parker on Verve*. Verve Records, 1988.

———. "Charlie Parker Time Line." *The Complete Dean Benedetti Recordings of Charlie Parker*. Mosaic Records, 1990.

Unpublished Manuscripts

Gibson, Harry "the Hipster." "Bird Lives." Unpublished Manuscript. Harry Ransom Humanities Research Center, University of Texas, Austin.

McGhee, Howard. Institute of Jazz Studies Jazz Oral History Project. Interviewer unknown. 1982.

McShann, Jay. Institute of Jazz Studies Jazz Oral History Project. Interviewed by Helen Oakley Dance. December, 1978.

Ramey, Gene. Institute of Jazz Studies Jazz Oral History Project. Interviewed by Stanley Dance. September, 1978.

Russell, Ross. Collection. Harry Ransom Humanities Research Center. University of Texas, Austin.

Interviews on Audio or Video Tapes, and Compact Disc

Bishop, Walter, Jr. Broadcast interview. National Public Radio, "Horizons." Date unknown. Transcribed by the author.

Chaifetz, Aaron. Broadcast interview. WQED. Pittsburgh. Date unknown. Transcribed by the author.

Giddins, Gary, and Simmons, Kendrick. *Celebrating Bird* (videotape). New York: Sony Video Software Company, 1987. Transcribed by the author.

Konitz, Lee, and Tristano, Lennie. Broadcast interview with John Fitch [radio name: John McLellan]. WHDH. Boston. March, 1956. Transcribed by the author.

Parker, Charlie. Audiotape interview with Marshall Stearns and John Maher. May, 1950. Transcribed by the author.

———. Broadcast interview with Leonard Feather. Voice of America. Spring, 1951. Transcribed by the author.

————. Broadcast interview with John Fitch [radio name: John McLellan]. WHDH. Boston. June, 1953. Transcribed by the author.

————. Broadcast interview with Paul Desmond and John Fitch [radio name: John McLellan]. WHDH. Boston. January, 1954. Transcribed by the author.

Parker, Charlie, and Meldonian, Dick. Audiotape of music lesson. 1954. Transcribed by the author.

Parker, Doris. Broadcast interview (interviewer unknown). WKCR. New York City. August, 1973. Transcribed by the author.

Ramey, Gene. Broadcast interview with Jay Trachtenberg. KUT. Austin, Tex. June, 1983. Transcribed by the author.

————. Broadcast interview. National Public Radio. Program and date unknown. Transcribed by the author.

Roach, Max. Broadcast interview with Phil Schaap. WKCR. New York City. September, 1989. Transcribed by the author.

————. Broadcast interview. National Public Radio, "Horizons." Date unknown. Transcribed by the author.

————. Broadcast interview with Terry Gross. National Public Radio. Program and date unknown. Transcribed by the author.

Roach, Max, and Gillespie, Dizzy. *Max Roach + Dizzy Gillespie Paris 1989.* A&M CD 6404, 1989. Transcribed by the author.

Russell, Curly. Broadcast interview with Phil Schaap. WKCR. New York City. September, 1983. Transcribed by the author.

Index